D0419153

WITHDRAWN
MAY 3 1 2017

WITHDRAWN

MAY 3 2001

POLITICAL INSTABILITY AND AMERICAN FOREIGN POLICY

WITHDRAWN
MAY 3 1 2017

Political Instability and American Foreign Policy

THE MIDDLE OPTIONS

John David Orme

Associate Professor of Political Studies
Oglethorpe University
Atlanta, Georgia

St. Martin's Press   New York

© John David Orme 1989

All rights reserved. For information, write:
Scholarly and Reference Division.
St. Martin's Press, Inc., 175 Fifth Avenue, New York, NY 10010

First published in the United States of America in 1989

Printed in Hong Kong

ISBN 0–312–03212–9 cloth
ISBN 0–312–03213–7 paper

Library of Congress Cataloging-in-Publication Data
Orme, John David
    Political instability and American foreign policy: the middle
options / John David Orme.
        p.   cm.
    Includes index.
    ISBN 0–312–03212–9. — ISBN 0–312–03213–7 (pbk.)
    1. United States—Foreign relations—1945–   2. United States–
–Foreign relations—Developing countries.   3. Developing countries–
–Foreign relations—United States.   4. Developing countries–
–Political and government.   5. World politics—1945–   6. Political
stability—Developing countries.   I. Title
E840.076   1989
327.73—dc20   89–31392
                                                              CIP

E
840
· 076
1989

To my parents

Contents

Acknowledgements

The author wishes to thank Stanley Hoffmann and Samuel Huntington for their advice and encouragement when this project was at the dissertation stage; Jorge Dominguez for his very generous commitment of time and many constructive questions and suggestions on the earlier version; and Richard Kraus and Stephen Schwark for their helpful comments on earlier and later drafts. None of them, of course, bears any responsibility for the errors of fact or interpretation which remain.

Chapter 2 is reprinted with permission from *Political Science Quarterly* 103 (Summer 1988) pp. 245–65.

Introduction

The problem posed by the vulnerability of governments friendly to the United States is one of the most persistent and difficult faced by American statesmen in the current era. Beginning with the Chinese and Greek civil wars of the forties and continuing on to El Salvador and Nicaragua in the eighties, every post-war administration has had to contend with these situations. The dilemma is familiar: the government may be venal, reactionary or repressive but is reliably anti-Soviet. It is challenged by a movement that stands a good chance of overthrowing it but which may contain elements unfriendly to the West. Every option available seems to have its drawbacks. Support for the government risks charges of 'intervention' in support of reactionary forces and interference in the domestic affairs of the country; restraint risks seeing allies of the Soviets seize power. How have American officials dealt with these situations in the past? What ought they to do in the future?

According to many of those writing in the aftermath of Vietnam, there is a pattern in the responses of the United States to political instability in the developing world. When confronted with the dangers of change, the United States has tended to intervene to block it. As Richard Barnet declared in 1968:

> From the Truman doctrine on, the suppression of insurgent movements has remained a principal goal of US foreign policy. Where . . . an insurgent group or a revolutionary regime has attempted radical social change, even suggesting a Communist influence, the United States has sooner or later intervened against it on the grounds that the revolutionaries were acting for a foreign power.[1]

Six years later, Melvin Gurtov reached a similar conclusion:

> Anti-nationalism and intervention have been conspicuous in American foreign policy ever since the emergence of the United States in this century as a global military and economic power. American administrations have been no more willing internationally than domestically to condone or accommodate disobedience, violence, civil strife, and insurgency. In both spheres, coercion of one kind or another has been the common response.[2]

1

In the same year, these views were seconded by an eminent Realist thinker, the late Hans Morgenthau:

> With unfailing consistency, we have since the end of the Second World War intervened on behalf of conservative and fascist repression against revolution and radical reform. In an age when societies are in a revolutionary or prerevolutionary stage, we have become the foremost counter-revolutionary status quo power on earth. Such a policy can only lead to moral and political disaster.[3]

According to these critics, if a revolutionary movement does manage to reach power despite American opposition, it will find that 'the reaction of the United States to revolutionary governments is generally hostile, even before it is clear how they will turn out'.[4] Most of the revolutionary governments would respond to gestures of friendship from the United States, but the reflexive hostility of the US drives them to the Soviet Union:

> There is only one reason why a country would want to adopt Marxist socialism today. Unfortunately, it is often a valid reason. Marxism—socialism is often the only way a country can avoid American imperialism. . . . As we have seen in country after country, the US has rarely been tolerant of any sentiments contrary to its own. The first scent of national divergence has quickly evoked repression by covert or overt US military action. The need for protection from US intervention is what has given the Soviet Union the world influence we complain about.[5]

These critics of American policy argue that continued intervention in the internal evolution of third world countries is costly, unnecessary, morally indefensible and ultimately futile because the changes are bound to come in any event. They advocate instead 'non-intervention' in these struggles. Barnet suggested in the late sixties that the United States halt all military assistance to foreign countries and Gurtov went so far as to recommend non-intervention in domestic disputes abroad, even when the Soviets are actively backing the other side.[6]

The non-interventionist critics had the best of the academic debate in the sixties and much of the seventies and were also somewhat successful in reshaping American policy during the Ford and Carter administrations. But in 1979, a forceful response came from the right. Writing in the November issue of *Commentary*, Jeane Kirkpatrick delivered a broadside against the polices of the Carter administration entitled 'Dictatorships and Double Standards'.[7] She too saw a pattern in American policy, but a very different one from that of Barnet and Gurtov.

Typically, she asserted, the United States interprets violence staged by guerrillas armed by Moscow as evidence that a friendly government has 'lost the support of its people' and demands ill-advised concessions from the government that will weaken it without satisfying the opposition. After the prophecies of American liberals about the regime's instability have become self-fulfilling, they will demand that the US try to replace the government with a 'broad-based coalition' or a moderate opponent of the regime. These attempts will only accelerate the erosion of order in the country and eventually bring to power forces that will remain hostile regardless of what the United States does. The implication of the argument seemed to be that the US must stand by its friends faithfully when they face internal opposition. Even if they lose, the steadfastness of the US will increase the confidence of governments elsewhere in its reliability and discourage the anti-Western forces. Such an approach, she concluded, would not only serve American interests more effectively, but would also be a more ethical foreign policy in that it chooses the lesser evil—an authoritarian government—over the greater evil of totalitarianism.

Dr Kirkpatrick's article, though not without its own problems, provided a useful corrective to the distorted description of American policy presented by the non-interventionist critics. I will contend here, along with Jeane Kirkpatrick, that the non-interventionists have ignored a major strand in American policy since 1944, one that involves some aspects of their programme, but is more accurately seen as an intermediate position between their hands-off policy and the right's staunch support of any anti-Communist government.

This middle strand has included four different sorts of policies. First, US officials have in many instances used their influence to prod hesitant governments into changes of policy which, in their view, would increase the regime's stability. These attempts have involved the US to a sometimes surprising degree in the domestic politics of these countries. They are unquestionably a form of 'intervention', but not intervention in support of the status quo; they may or may not be advisable or defensible, but they are not 'reactionary'. This strategy I will call 'reformist intervention', and it will be taken up in chapter 1.

For better or worse, Dr Kirkpatrick is also correct in asserting that the United States has frequently decided not to 'go down with the ship' but has tried instead to impose political solutions to internal conflicts. Political solutions are similar to reformist intervention in that both usually involve a change of personnel in the government. The difference is that the changes are effected under the reformist strategy as a way of modifying the government's policies but are undertaken with the political solution in order to alter the nature of the regime itself. Hence, the latter are usually more drastic policies applied later in the crisis at a point at which changes in policy alone would no longer be enough to assuage the public.

As she notes, political solutions can be of two varieties. In the first, the mediators attempt to draw the moderate opposition into the government; in the second, a coalition between various elements, perhaps including supporters of the existing government, is the aim. If successful, either will limit the influence of the radical opposition; the first by excluding them from power directly, the second by counterbalancing them in the government with the right and centre. This policy is again an intermediate one, offering an alternative for the United States and the public in the country between the old regime and the radical revolutionaries. The political solution will be the focus of chapter 3.

After regimes friendly to the United States have been overthrown, the non-interventionists favour a policy of conciliation with the new government, though they lament that the US usually does not make the effort, preferring instead to try to isolate, punish or 'destabilise' revolutionary regimes. I will argue in chapter 4 that the US has attempted conciliation more often than these critics seem to realise. The examination of these instances will thus be a partial test of the non-interventionists' prescriptions, though not a completely satisfactory one, since they also advocate non-involvement prior to this last stage and that has usually not been practised.

To repeat, one purpose of all these chapters is to set the historical record straight and correct the misleading impressions about American foreign policy created by the non-interventionists. This study has an additional and more difficult aim, and that is to consider the effectiveness of the set of policies described and attempt to explain why they have succeeded or failed. Chapter 2, which covers human rights policies, will do so indirectly. Four efforts by autocratic regimes to liberalise will be analysed there, only one of which involved the United States closely. The rationale for the approach is this: if American human rights policies are to succeed, the leadership in autocratic regimes must be persuaded to undertake liberalisation, and the liberalisation must then proceed without running out of control. A successful human rights policy, in other words, implies a successful liberalisation of (and by) an authoritarian government. Hence, it would be well worth knowing why some repressive governments have been able to do this and others have not. As it happens, some of the clearest successes and most instructive failures of liberalisation have occurred in countries where the United States was not playing an important role, and these cases can tell us a great deal about the difficulties the US will face in promoting human rights in repressive, potentially unstable regimes.

Before turning to these topics, a brief word about the author's own viewpoint may be in order. My own preferences lie somewhere between those of Jeane Kirkpatrick and the non-interventionists, so I would prefer to tell readers that the middle options discussed here have been unambiguously successful and provide a clear alternative to the less agreeable possibilities further to the left and right. Unfortunately, that is not exactly what the historical record shows, at least as I read it. I will face up to this, weigh the consequences and try to draw out the implications for future policy in the concluding chapter.

Notes

1. Richard Barnet, *Intervention and Revolution* (New York: New American Library, 2nd edn, 1972), pp. 20, 67.
2. Melvin Gurtov, *The United States Against the Third World* (New York: Praeger, 1974), pp. 1, 202.
3. Hans Morgenthau, 'Repression's Friend', Letter to the *New York Times*, 10 October 1974, p. 46.
4. William LeoGrande, quoted in 'Can the US Live with Latin Revolution?', *Harpers*, vol. 268, no. 1609 (June 1984), p. 42.
5. Jonathan Kwitny, *Endless Enemies* (New York: Congdon & Weed, 1984), pp. 389–90.
6. Gurtov, *The United States Against the Third World*, p. 214; Barnet, *Intervention and Revolution*, p. 328.
7. The article is reprinted in *Dictatorships and Double Standards* (New York: Simon & Shuster, 1983).

1 Reformist Intervention

How often we have heard critics decry American intervention in the third world. This sort of criticism has usually involved the allegation that the United States, animated by an obsessive urge to arrest the spread of Communism, is meddling in the domestic affairs of other societies to prop up reactionary political forces. One cannot deny that there are instances, such as Guatemala in 1954, where the critics are right. There is another side to American 'intervention', however, which is frequently overlooked—intervention for the purpose of promoting reform. In this chapter, eight American efforts of this kind will be considered: China during the Second World War, Greece and the Philippines in the late forties and early fifties, Vietnam in the mid-fifties and after, Iran, the Dominican Republic and Venezuela during the early sixties, and El Salvador from the late seventies on.

All eight of these societies were either in some sort of crisis or at least potentially unstable. All were underdeveloped countries, beset with serious social problems. Many of them were governed by venal or repressive leaders, and most faced violent opposition. In these circumstances, the aim of American intervention has been to persuade or compel the government to take steps to ameliorate the economic, political or military evils of the status quo with a view to 'winning the hearts and minds of the people' and in so doing to diminish the appeal of the far left.

Three sorts of reform have been prescribed by American officials: (1) land reform, which could mean either a transfer of land from large landholders to poor peasants or regulation of the terms under which land is rented; (2) reform of the armed forces, which usually involves curbing human rights abuses or corruption by the military as well as steps to improve its effectiveness as a fighting force; and (3) other miscellaneous measures, usually with some redistributionist tendency. All of these, of course, are likely to provoke serious opposition.

How successful have been these efforts at 'reformist intervention'? Judged only by the rate of survival of the governments to which the policy has been applied, reformist intervention has produced mixed results. Four of the eight regimes lasted through the immediate crises they faced (Greece, the Philippines, Iran and Venezuela), although the Shah was eventually overthrown and the future of the Philippines is uncertain at present. China and Vietnam fell to Communist insurgents and the reformist government in the Dominican Republic was toppled, setting the stage for civil war two years later. El Salvador, of course, is still being decided. What, then, distinguishes the successes from the failures? Can the rate of success be improved?

If reformist intervention is to succeed, three things must happen. First, the government must adopt a reform programme. This means that the United States must either convince the existing leadership to undertake reform or, failing that, bring to power someone who will. Intervention at this stage may also take the form of support or protection to reformers who have come to power without US assistance but are now in some danger. Any of these approaches can lead the United States into deep and perhaps controversial involvement in the country's domestic politics. Second, once the reformers are in power they must be able to put the changes through against the opposition of the forces who stand to lose from them. Again, considerable US interference may be necessary if resistance to the reform is to be overcome. Finally, when the reforms are implemented they must have the effect intended, that is, they must increase the stability of the government in the long run. If these three conditions are met, the policy can be considered successful.

Let us take up the last point first, and quite briefly. I would contend that most of the advice offered to third world leaders along these lines has been sound.[1] In other words, the changes suggested would have been and will continue to be effective in building support for governments endangered by instability an. improving their chances of survival. Consider first land reform. Roy Prosterman has found that societies in which 40 per cent of the people are landless peasants are in 'critical' danger of revolution. Whether the revolution breaks out or not in the short run depends on a number of factors, but in the long run, favourable conditions for the government only delay the inevitable.[2] Conversely, land reform has had, again in the long run, a profoundly stabilising effect where it has been carried out thoroughly. The experience of countries such as Mexico, Taiwan, South Korea and Japan is ample evidence of this. As Samuel Huntington concluded nearly two decades ago:

> The peasantry may be the bulwark of the status quo or the shock troops of revolution. . . . No social group is more conservative than a land-owning peasantry, and none is more revolutionary than a peasantry which owns too little land or pays too high a rental. The stability of governments in modernizing countries is thus, in some measure, dependent upon its ability to promote reform in the countryside.[3]

Critics will point out that land reform failed to prevent revolutions in Ethiopia, Iran and South Vietnam. That is true, but does not refute its proponents. Haile Selassie did not reduce the number of landless peasants below the 30 per cent level that Prosterman considers the dividing line between stable and unstable situations. In Vietnam, the Land to the Tiller programme nearly eliminated the Vietcong but could not protect the South from an invasion by the North's 22 divisions in 1975. In Iran, as will be explained below, the Shah later undid most of the good he accomplished in the early sixties.

One must not overstate the case, of course. Land reform may not provide a regime with complete security against urban revolts. The revolutions in Iran and Cuba were not primarily peasant revolutions and may be a better guide to the future than China and Vietnam. Even so, Iran's rapid and destabilising urbanisation might have proceeded at a safer pace if the Shah's agricultural policies had been sounder. Further, land reform may not solve all of the problems of a country like El Salvador where the ratio of land to population is extremely unfavourable and the intensive cultivation of small plots may not be feasible. Still, the bulk of the evidence that has accumulated over two decades corroborates Huntington's conclusions and the basic rationale behind much of American reformist intervention. Whatever the wisdom of the other aspects of American reform programmes, land reform does seem to work. That is, it enhances the stability of the governments that enact it and does so because it improves the lot of a great many people.

The rationale for reform of the armed forces is equally convincing. It has been stated best by Douglas Blaufarb. The pattern, as he explains, is for a regime with a weak base of support to purchase the allegiance of the army or other institutions by offering opportunities for graft in exchange for political support. The 'political armies' resulting from these unholy alliances are invariably poor fighting forces because promotion becomes based on political loyalty rather than professional competence and qualities of leadership. Moreover, political armies are not only ineffective, but also oppressive. When officers become corrupt they usually lose interest in the welfare of their troops, who are then forced to prey upon the public in order to fend for themselves.[4] Armies of this sort have failed time and again, as will be evident later, to defeat insurgent forces far smaller and less well-equipped than they. If allies of the United States are to cope with Communist-led insurgencies, reform of political armed forces is essential.

In short, the reforms suggested by American officials, at least along these lines, have been sensible. The difficulty with reformist intervention has not been that American officials have offered bad advice, but rather that the advice has not always been accepted or, more frequently, that the government has not been able to implement a reform programme against the opposition of those who stand to lose from it. Let us then review what happened in these eight cases, dealing first with the question of whether the leaders will undertake reform, and later with the problem of implementation.

I

The first of these attempts, and probably the least successful, occurred in China during the Second World War.[5] A reformist strategy was urged on Washington for two years by General Joseph Stilwell, who had been sent to the Orient in 1942 to serve as Chiang Kai-shek's Chief-of-Staff. In Stilwell's view (which was quite accurate), the Chinese forces were poorly fed and equipped, rotten with corruption and often incompetently led. The Chinese army was, it seems, a prototypical 'political army'. Divisional commanders were allowed to allocate funds as they chose and many of them kept their divisions far below the strength they reported, simply pocketing the difference. Some augmented their take by depriving their men of food and selling the surplus. Discipline was extremely harsh—flogging, ear-cropping and exposure were among the methods employed by the officers—but even the best troops were sometimes guilty of molesting the public, who came to fear their own forces only slightly less than those of the Japanese.[6]

The origin of these wretched conditions was in Chiang Kai-shek's tenuous control over the entire structure. The Generalissimo himself had direct control over only about 30 of the army's 300 divisions.

Japanese intelligence estimated that two-thirds of the forces were in the hands of independent regional commanders, many of whom were former warlords who had rebelled against the central government at one time or another. Chiang had been able to extend his control (and, it must be understood, only to a limited extent), by favouring those loyal to him in the allocation of supplies, appeasing some of the rest by turning a blind eye toward the pervasive graft and, when circumstances permitted, crushing his opposition.[7]

Stilwell wanted to create two well-trained and equipped armies of 30 divisions; one in Yunnan province (the 'Y-force', which was to be used to reopen the land route to China through Burma), and another at Kweilin in east China. The most pressing concern for Chiang, however, was not defeating the Japanese but maintaining his fragile authority over the armed forces, and he feared that Stilwell's reform would endanger it. Specifically, the Yunnan force might escape his control; more generally, allocation of resources and honours on the basis of performance rather than loyalty, as Stilwell proposed, could pose a direct threat to his position. While the Generalissimo's own troops had acquitted themselves fairly well, the performance of his Whampoa associates' armies had frequently been less impressive than that of the regional forces, despite the favouratism shown them in the allocation of supplies. Finally, consolidation was bound to provoke opposition from those generals not loyal to Chiang who stood to lose their commands.[8]

For these reasons, Chiang staunchly resisted Stilwell and was largely successful in stalling his reform plans for two years. Prior to the decision in 1944 to strike at Japan from the Pacific islands, it appeared vital to the US leadership to keep China in the war so that American planes would have access to bases on the Asian mainland. Consequently, President Roosevelt chose to ignore Stilwell and avoid open conflict with Chiang, siding instead with General Claire Chennault, whose advocacy of air power freed Chiang from the necessity of reforming his military. Most of the supplies reaching China by air transport in 1943 were devoted to Chennault's air force, though Stilwell was able to put together 15 divisions in Yunnan despite Chiang's efforts at obstruction.[9]

In the spring of 1944, under heavy US pressure, Chiang sent the Y-force into Burma. Soon after, the Japanese began advancing toward the US airfields in east China. Because the commanders in that region were disloyal, Chiang refused to resupply them, but still seized on the Japanese offensive as a pretext to withdraw the Y-force from Burma. This glaring subordination of strategy to politics finally convinced Roosevelt to employ the pressure tactics Stilwell had long been advocating. On 6 July, he demanded that Stilwell be given command of all Chinese forces, including those of the Communists. Chiang's reply came two days later. The Generalissimo did not reject Roosevelt's proposal openly, but requested a 'preparatory period' before Stilwell assumed command. Alluding to the situation discussed above, Chiang noted that 'Chinese troops and their internal political conditions are not as simple as in other countries'—as frank an admission of his own political problems as one can imagine under the circumstances. He also suggested that the President send a 'personal representative' with 'far-sighted political vision and ability' to 'adjust the relations [with] General Stilwell', which Roosevelt was happy enough to grant, thinking that the issue had been settled at least in principle. General Patrick Hurley, a man with no previous experience of China, was selected for the assignment on the grounds that he would enjoy the confidence of both Stilwell and Roosevelt.[10]

Roosevelt was content to leave the working details of the arrangement till later, but Chiang and Stilwell had entirely different conceptions of the role of the commander. Stilwell wanted complete authority to reward, punish, promote and dismiss, along with the power to disburse lend lease aid, perhaps to the Communists as well as the regional forces. Despite the pressing military circumstances, Chiang was not about to appoint Stilwell until he was confident that the American general would not undermine his control of the armed forces. In August, H.H. Kung called on Roosevelt and asked if divisions with politically unreliable commanders could be excluded from Stilwell's command and thus denied US assistance. Roosevelt and Stilwell later gave way on the issue of the Communists, but would not acquiesce on this point.[11]

After a delay of over two months, Stilwell was growing impatient. On his advice, the President sent Chiang an ultimatum on 19 September threatening to withdraw all American aid unless Stilwell were immediately given 'unrestricted command' of the Chinese forces. But just as Stilwell was beginning to gloat over his long-awaited triumph over the 'Peanut', as he referred to Chiang, Roosevelt's special emissary intervened to thwart him. General Hurley had become convinced, as he told Roosevelt, that 'there is no other issue between you and Chiang Kai-shek' than Stilwell, and advised the President that if he were removed, the other issues could be resolved quickly. After his discussions with Hurley, Chiang informed Roosevelt on the 24th that he would not accept Stilwell and later threatened to fight on alone if the US deserted him. Roosevelt hesitated for several weeks, then, on 18 October, recalled the acerbic general.[12]

To one distinguished scholar, 'what the recall of Stilwell symbolized above all was the defeat of the United States in her tactics of pressure, due to a failure of judgment and will rather than the objective weakness of her political position'.[13] But this was not the end of the episode. Stilwell was replaced in October by General Albert Wedemeyer, a man known and respected by Chiang for his service in the China-Burma-India theatre. The Generalissimo offered Wedemeyer command of the Chinese armies soon after his arrival. He declined, accepting instead Stilwell's original position as Chief-of-Staff. Wedemeyer inherited from his predecessor the plan to train and equip 30 more divisions. In December he told Chiang that in building the force he intended to give preference to 'divisions loyal to the Generalissimo and soldiers who are willing to fight'. After receiving this assurance, Chiang not only gave his enthusiastic support to the plan but also agreed in February to mount an offensive for the first time against the Japanese on Chinese soil. The war concluded before either of these initiatives could be brought to fruition, but Wedemeyer did bring noticeable improvement in the morale and condition of the Chinese forces within a few months, though not enough to alter the outcome of the civil war to come.[14]

Thus, though the effort to reform the Chinese army was a frustrating experience for US officials, especially Stilwell, it cannot be classified as a complete failure. It may also be that better results would have been achieved had Roosevelt adopted different tactics. The 'reformer' the United States was trying to put in place was an American, and an unusually abrasive one at that. Chiang would have suffered some embarrassment in accepting any foreigner as commander of his armed forces, but Stilwell was probably the worst sort of irritant one can imagine to the intensely nationalistic Chinese leader.[15] Perhaps if Roosevelt had offered assurances to Chiang early on regarding the disbursement of aid and found a more tactful representative, the success achieved under Wedemeyer would have come earlier. Tang Tsou, on the other hand, attributes the progress after Stilwell's departure mostly to the increased volume of US assistance. He believes that Roosevelt took Chiang's implicit threat to pursue a separate peace with Japan too seriously and believes much more would have been accomplished if the President had backed Stilwell consistently from the beginning.[16] We need not attempt to settle this matter of interpretation here; the key point is that enough questions can be raised about American tactics in China to suggest that reformist intervention there was not necessarily doomed to failure. In any case, the experience in China proved to be the exception to the rule. After the war American officials were to enjoy greater success in convincing governments to adopt reform, beginning in Greece.

In the famous Truman Doctrine speech of March 1947, the President—a man not known for understatement—admitted that the Greek government was 'not perfect'. The extension of aid to Greece, he continued, 'does not mean that the United States condones everything that the Greek government has done or will do'.[17] The government that Truman had decided to assist was a democracy in form, but in practice a deeply flawed one. The right-wing Populist party had won the 1946 elections through intimidation of the voters, and the bureaucracy was largely staffed by rightist holdovers from the Metaxas dictatorship of the thirties and the German occupation. Not surprisingly, the government was viewed by a large segment of the Greek public with either suspicion or outright hostility. Over the previous three years, rightist gangs had carried out a campaign of terror against members of the Greek left, to which the government had turned a blind eye.[18] The police and gendarmerie were poorly trained and equipped and the army was hampered by poor morale, bickering among the commanders and political interference. By late 1947, according to counter-insurgency expert Edgar O'Ballance, the government of Greece was 'tottering' in the face of the rebellion launched by the Communist-led Democratic Army.[19]

US efforts at reformist intervention began in the fall of 1947 when American representatives encouraged a group of moderate rightist ministers to press for the dismissal of Napoleon Zervas, who was suspected of fomenting the right-wing terror. The Prime Minister refused and the government fell. Rather than permitting Constantine Tsaldaris to form another cabinet, the Americans persuaded the octogenarian Liberal, Themistocles Sophoulis, to head a government still dominated by the Populists. Tsaldaris was told to acquiesce or face the withdrawal of American aid, and he relented. The coalition was threatened at different times by the Populists' attempts to eliminate the Liberals and by Sophoulis's threats to resign, but survived for over a year as a result of American pressure.[20]

Despite the improved political situation, American officials remained greatly concerned about the performance of the Greek
National Army (GNA). To address the problems they began pressing
in the winter of 1948–9 for the appointment of Alexander Papagos
as commander-in-chief. On 4 January 1949, the Greek Ambassador
in Washington was warned that 'unless it can be shown that the
Greeks are doing all in their power to solve their internal problem',
the United States would consider cutting off assistance.[21] A few days
later, King Paul, working without the blessing of the US Ambassador,
gathered leading politicians at the palace and threatened to impose
'another solution' (that is, an authoritarian regime, by means of a
coup) if they were unable to put together a government within 24
hours. The King's threat was effective—perhaps more so than the
Americans'—and the coalition was organised forthwith. Papagos
was granted sweeping powers as commander-in-chief, including the
freedom to replace military commanders and institute martial law
without consulting the civilians. Under his capable command, the
Greek National Army drove their opponents from the field inside of
a year.[22]

The next American effort in Greece came in 1949 and 1950, after
the death of Sophoulis. By this time the civil war was won, and
the thoughts of American officials were turning to the problems of
the Greek economy. In particular, they were interested in seeing the
government's budget deficit eliminated so that American aid would
not be wasted making up the shortfall. They proposed that the budget
be brought under control through a variety of measures, including
cuts in military spending and higher taxation on the rich.

To accomplish this, Ambassador Henry Grady announced that
the United States favoured new elections, assuming that they would
weaken the Populists and make it possible for an alternative coalition
of the centre and centre-left to govern. As Grady had expected, the
Populists sustained a crushing defeat in the elections and afterward, at
least initially, it appeared that three centre parties would coalesce to
form a government under the progressive General Nicholas Plastiras.
But just as things seemed to be falling into place, the leader of
one of the parties, Sophocles Venizelos, broke ranks and joined a
coalition with the Populists. Grady then sent a letter to Venizelos
demanding that Plastiras be included in the cabinet and also hinting
that aid might be reduced if he refused. Venizelos resigned just three
weeks after taking office and Plastiras formed a cabinet the following
day.[23]

The US was just as deeply involved in the Philippines, which faced a crisis of several dimensions in 1950. The Huks, as the Communist-backed insurgents were called, controlled much of central Luzon and were planning to take Manila itself by Christmas. The government's response to the threat had been entirely inadequate. Only 9 per cent of the peasants of central Luzon owned the land they worked, and studies showed a close correlation between the extent of tenancy and the Huks' success. The looting and indiscriminate brutality of the Philippine constabulary, an organisation recruited by the Japanese from the island's prisons, was driving otherwise conservative villagers to the rebels in large numbers. The army was less abusive but its tactics were ineffective and its morale derisory. Faced with these formidable problems, the appointees in President Elpidio Quirino's administration seemed more interested in lining their own pockets than in taking corrective measures. (A Philippine journalist is said to have overheard one of the politicians asking 'What's the use of being the majority party if we can't have a little honest graft?') Finally, imports had exceeded exports by 100 per cent in 1949, creating a serious balance of payments problem. Although that situation was easing somewhat by the next year, the government was still keenly interested in receiving American aid.[24]

In this unpromising set of circumstances, the American Ambassador and the head of the US military advisory group identified Congressman Ramon Magsaysay as the one man who might be capable of leading the Philippines out of the crisis. Under American pressure, Quirino appointed Magsaysay Secretary for National Defence on 1 September 1950, giving him full authority to conduct the campaign against the Huks. Within a year the Huks were all but beaten.[25]

Earlier, in July 1950, a group of 25 American observers headed by Daniel W. Bell had arrived in the islands to study the situation and make recommendations. The Bell Mission suggested that the United States grant $250 million in aid to the Philippines over the next five years, but on the condition that several reforms be adopted, including a minimum wage law, land reform and a change in the tax structure. American officials envisaged an American mission of 150–200 which would 'in effect have to assume direction of most of the Philippine government activities'.[26]

In November, Quirino agreed to submit a legislative programme including several of the reforms suggested by the Bell Mission, though not land reform, and also accepted the legion of American advisors.

The Truman administration then promised to present the $250 million aid package to Congress. Why the Truman officials backed away on the issue of land reform is not entirely clear. According to one account, their view was that it would be difficult enough just to see that honest elections were held in 1953; pressing for much more would be 'futile'. A minimum wage law was passed in 1951, but went largely unenforced. The Philippine economy recovered anyway, benefiting from the rise in commodity prices brought by the Korean war, and the country survived the crisis of the early fifties.[27]

In 1953, Magsaysay defected to the opposition Nacionalista party and challenged Quirino for the Presidency. Although the American Ambassador officially declared his neutrality, there was little doubt in anyone's mind whom the US favoured in the election. One source claims that the CIA channelled covert aid to Magsaysay's campaign. Such support was hardly necessary, as Magsaysay was immensely popular in the islands and won the election in a landslide.[28]

At the first stage, then, reformist intervention by the Truman administration was also successful in the Philippines. Magsaysay rose to prominence through American support and the lackadaisical Quirino administration was prodded into reform efforts by American pressure. On the other shore of the South China Sea, however, progress was not so easily achieved.

At the time of Ngo Dinh Diem's takeover in 1954, just 2500 people owned one-quarter of Vietnam's agricultural land. Land reform programmes had been promulgated under Bao Dai, but never enacted. When American advisors arrived on the scene, they put 'unrelenting' pressure on the government to redistribute land. Initially, Diem was hesitant to provoke the landlords and stalled the Americans for several months. By late 1954, however, the flow of refugees from the north had grown so large that he was in desperate need of US financial help. When General Lawton Collins informed Diem in November that land reform would be a condition of American assistance, he had no choice but to acquiesce.[29]

At about the same time, American officials became concerned that the political rivalry between Diem and the Hoa Hao and Cao Dai religious sects might weaken South Vietnam and recommended that Diem resolve it by bringing representatives of the sects into the government. In April 1955 Ambassador Collins went so far as to advocate the replacement of Diem with someone more acceptable to the sects if he remained adamant. But American objections were soon quieted. Diem broke the sects' resistance in the spring by diverting an estimated $12 million in American aid funds into bribes for some of their leaders, and eventually defeated their armies and took control of most of their territory.[30]

The American Ambassador continued to press for changes through the rest of the Eisenhower administration, but received no strong reinforcement from Washington, and Diem continued along the course he had embarked on earlier. Over the next several years, Diem proceeded to construct a police state in the South. In 1959, he banned meetings of more than seven and set up military tribunals for security cases which recognised no right of defence. By 1962, there were 20,000 political prisoners in South Vietnam. Many of them were Vietcong, of course, but Diem jailed much of the non-Communist opposition as well.[31] In addition, Diem interfered in the affairs of the armed forces in such a way as to shape the Army of the Republic of Vietnam (ARVN) into a 'political army'. Suspicious of the officer corps, especially after an attempted coup in 1960, Diem sought to forestall any sort of threat from the army by promoting on the basis of loyalty rather than ability, and also intervened constantly in the conduct of the war, moving units around in the field from the confines of the palace.[32]

Towards the end of the administration, Eisenhower officials drew up a 'Counterinsurgency Plan for Vietnam', which proposed that the United States finance an expansion of the security forces if Diem would agree to steps to broaden his base of support. These would include bringing members of the opposition into the government and permitting the National Assembly to investigate corruption. President Kennedy adopted the plan; negotiations began in February 1961 and continued for several months. In the end, the US agreed to enlarge the army and Civil Guard and Diem made some ambiguous promises to win over the peasants; the other conditions were dropped. Later in the year, Diem requested additional American support, again to increase the size of the armed forces. General Maxwell Taylor and W. W. Rostow were sent to Vietnam in mid-October to evaluate the request and returned with a long list of suggestions. Among them were recommendations that Diem decentralise administration (including that of the army), cease persecuting the opposition and make major economic changes. In a letter of 15 December 1961, Kennedy advised Diem to implement many of these measures, as well as land reform. Diem's brother Nhu responded by orchestrating a campaign in the press accusing the United States of harbouring 'imperialist designs' on Vietnam, and advocating a reconsideration of Vietnam's relations with the US. The crisis was resolved in January of 1962. The US granted Diem nearly everything he had demanded, but failed to extract a clear commitment from the Vietnamese government to enact any of the proposed reforms.[33]

Kennedy's leverage on both occasions was weakened by the Ngo's belief that, as David Halberstam put it, '[they] had [their] ally in a corner, that [they] could do anything [they] wanted, that continued support would be guaranteed because of the Communist threat, and that after the commitment was made, the US could not suddenly admit that it had made a vast mistake'. Nor were Diem and Nhu wrong to think so. Shipments of military equipment were already on their way to Vietnam in November 1961, and after the anti-American barrages in the press, Washington had instructed the American mission in Saigon to 'get along with President Diem's regime come hell or high water'.[34]

Thereafter, Ambassador Nolting pursued what he referred to as 'money in the bank' tactics. His assumption was that if the embassy went along with Diem most of the time, 'credit' would accrue on which the US could draw when a truly important issue arose. Not coincidentally, American suggestions for reform were largely ignored over the next two years. Nevertheless, the size of the US military mission increased from around 2000 in late 1961 to 15,000 towards the end of 1963.[35] By the late summer of 1963, with opposition from the Buddhists mounting, it was clear that Nolting's patiently accumulated credit was not going to be sufficient to alter the confrontational policy of the government. Kennedy made one last attempt to influence Diem at this point, warning the Vietnamese leadership that 'unless there can be important changes and improvements in the apparent relations between the government and the people, American public and Congressional opinion will make it impossible to continue without change their joint efforts'. As before, the US admonition went unheeded. In the early morning hours of 21 August, Nhu ordered forces personally loyal to him to attack Buddhist pagodas in Saigon, Hue and several other cities, provoking large-scale demonstrations against the government. Three days later, Kennedy sent word to the US embassy in Saigon that American officials were not to protect Diem from the numerous coup plots known to be in progress. In November, one of those plots succeeded and the Ngos met their deaths in an armoured car outside Saigon.[36]

The results of the Kennedy administration's intervention in Iran were somewhat more encouraging in the short run, though ultimately disappointing. By the early sixties, American officials had become deeply concerned about Iran's future and that of her ruler. The Pahlavi monarchy continued to rest on a narrow base of support: the armed forces and bureaucracy, the landlords and some entrepreneurs. Political participation was highly restricted and corruption was rife inside the government. The economy was suffering simultaneously from inflation and recession, combined with a severe balance of payments problem and increasing inequality of incomes. The rural masses, though miserably poor, were not disaffected, but they were not yet politically mobilised. Iran's urban population, on the other hand (then 30 per cent of the country's total), was active and overwhelmingly critical of the Shah. The view in Washington, in the words of the US Ambassador in Teheran, was that 'Iran's demise was about to take place . . . that it was about to go down the drain, and we just had to take some dramatic and drastic steps.'[37]

The Eisenhower administration had considered increasing contacts with the opposition as a hedge, but the Kennedy officials decided to stick with the Shah while encouraging him to alter his policies radically in order to broaden his base of support. The administration drew up a sweeping reform programme for Iran, including economic planning, land reform, cuts in the military budget and an opening of the political system. To ensure its enactment, the Americans suggested the appointment of Ali Amini, a former Mossadegh minister who had made a good impression as Ambassador to the United States and more recently had led protests against irregularities in the 1960 elections. The Shah was not likely to show much enthusiasm for a man of Amini's background, but Washington induced him by offering $35 million in aid to tide Iran over her financial crisis, conditional on the appointment of Amini as Prime Minister.[38]

With this assistance from the United States, Amini entered the government in May 1961. Later, the Shah was able to rid himself of the independent prime minister without losing American support, but proceeded with his own reform programme, the 'White Revolution'.

Simultaneously in the Western Hemisphere, the Kennedy administration was undertaking the most ambitious effort at reformist intervention since the Second World War, the Alliance for Progress. In response to the challenge from Castro, the administration intended to shift support from the most reliable anti-Communists and use the promise of generous levels of US financial assistance to strengthen democratic leftists and foster reform to undercut the appeal of the far left. As one of the architects of the programme explained, 'We are insisting on reforms as a condition of our material support to Latin America. We would rather withhold our assistance than to [sic] participate in the maintenance of a status quo characterized by social injustice.'[39]

Overall, the Alliance's achievements were relatively modest. Reformist governments remained in power in only three Latin American countries (Chile, Columbia and Venezuela); elsewhere, the military ignored US objections and removed the civilians. Six coups occurred during the brief Kennedy Presidency, and a total of sixteen constitutional governments were overthrown in the eight years of the Alliance. In some cases, Kennedy put heavy pressure on the military to step down, but he failed in every instance except one. After Congress trimmed the administration's aid requests, the sums of money allocated were not large enough nor was the Latin Americans' degree of dependence great enough to give the President leverage sufficient to reverse the coups, particularly when they were met with public apathy, as was often the case.[40]

A complete discussion of the Alliance would be beyond the scope of this chapter. But much can be learned by comparing one of the Alliance's few successes, Venezuela, with one of its greatest disappointments, the Dominican Republic.[41]

In the latter country, as with other Latin dictatorships, the Eisenhower administration pursued a policy of 'non-intervention' until the late fifties. No steps were taken to encourage reform during most of the thirty-year dictatorship of the Trujillo family, but surplus military equipment was sold and small amounts of economic aid were provided. After Vice-President Nixon's harrowing visit to Caracas in 1958, the administration began to question its past acquiescence in dictatorial rule, and when the Castroite 14th of June Movement was organised in the Dominican Republic in 1960, the Eisenhower officials began to fear that a second Cuba might be in the making on Hispaniola. Accordingly, the United States stopped supplying arms to Rafael Trujillo in 1958 and, after the Dominican dictator was implicated in an attempt on the life of Venezuela's President in August 1960, joined with the OAS majority in applying economic sanctions to the regime. Trujillo promised to hold elections in fifteen months and made some cosmetic changes in the government that left his family's power intact.[42] One source suggests that the Eisenhower administration then went so far as to threaten a demonstration of force against Trujillo if he refused to resign, and put in motion plans for covert operations after the threat failed.[43]

Though faced with an economic crisis and eroding support among the middle and upper classes, Trujillo was still clinging to power when John Kennedy was inaugurated in 1961. American intelligence reports suggested that there was no immediate possibility of a revolt and that Trujillo would remain in power as long as the armed forces continued to support him.[44] In mid-April, the President sent veteran diplomat Robert Murphy to Santo Domingo to persuade the dictator to proceed with genuine liberalisation. The effort was unsuccessful and an extraordinary episode in the history of American diplomacy followed.[45]

A group of eight conspirators, many of them former collaborators with the regime, were interested in eliminating Trujillo but were having difficulty obtaining weapons because of the strict controls Trujillo had placed on the possession of firearms.[46] The CIA provided them with three pistols on 12 January 1961 and three carbines on 31 March. According to the report produced by the Senate Select Committee on Intelligence in 1975, the American officials knew at the time the guns were made available that they were considering an attempt on the life of Rafael Trujillo. On the night of 30 May, the plotters followed Trujillo's car along a deserted road outside the capital as he headed toward an assignation with his mistress. Around 10.30 pm, they overtook his car, opened fire and gunned down the dictator. It is not known for certain whether the weapons used were those provided by the United States. According to one account, the fatal wound was fired by a shotgun, which was not among the weapons made available earlier.[47]

It appears from the evidence at hand that President Kennedy was not fully informed about the conspiracy until May, at which time a decision was made by the National Security Council not to promote the overthrow of Trujillo until it could be ascertained what sort of government would follow him. After that decision, the conspirators' requests for machine-guns were turned down. On 29 May, the President wrote a cable to the embassy stating that the US 'cannot condone assassination as a matter of general policy' but that if the plotters went ahead anyway the US would recognise their provisional government. After the assassination, no one was reprimanded by the President.[48]

The conspirators had planned to carry out a coup after the assassination, form a provisional government and eventually hold elections which they expected to win because of the public's gratitude for their heroism. But their plans went awry when they were unable to round up the rest of the Trujillo family.[49] Trujillo's intelligence service captured and killed all but two of the gunmen and the family succeeded in reasserting its control. The Kennedy administration acquiesced at first, hoping to push President Joaquin Balaguer toward liberalisation by maintaining the economic sanctions. Balaguer and Ramfis Trujillo stated their desire to move toward democracy and took some initial steps, but the opposition grew impatient and began agitating for change in the summer. In early November, most members of the Trujillo family were persuaded to leave and crisis seemed to have passed, but on the 16th two of the late dictator's brothers returned to make one last effort to restore the family dynasty. Kennedy positioned a naval task force group three miles off the Dominican coast, plainly visible from Santo Domingo, and had jets overfly the shoreline. The brothers were then given to understand that the United States intended to do whatever was necessary to see that a provisional government was formed under Balaguer without their interference. The Trujillos were put to flight and Dominicans gathered along the coastline to shout '*Viva los Imperialistas*'.[50]

The negotiations between Balaguer and the political parties to create a provisional government broke down in November. Pressure from the American mediators saved the situation twice and eventually an interim junta dominated by the conservative National Civic Union (UCN) was formed. This 'Council of State' was immediately threatened by a coup staged on behalf of Balaguer, but the combined effects of a general strike conducted by the UCN and a threat by the US to cut off all aid reversed the coup. Once the provisional government was in place, the administration lifted the sanctions, increased US purchases of sugar and extended more aid per capita to the Dominican Republic than to any other nation in the hemisphere. When Presidential elections were held, Juan Bosch, a democratic leftist, emerged as the winner. Although the CIA had provided training to organisers in Bosch's Dominican Revolutionary Party (PRD), American officials had some reservations about Bosch.[51] Nonetheless, there was great optimism and enthusiasm. As one official declared:

The US ought to go all out to demonstrate how it can really aid in the development of democratic institutions capable of doing a good job. . . . The value of victory will be very great. It would have repercussions not only in Latin America, but in many other parts of the world as well. The US cannot afford to fail.[52]

Under the Johnson and Nixon administrations, the reformist strategy fell into disuse, and fifteen years were to pass before the next prominent effort, El Salvador. Unlike most of the other cases discussed here, the United States did not bring a reforming government to power there directly. When the planners of the October 1979 coup consulted the US embassy, they were not discouraged, but were given no assistance. The plotters took American silence as approval and they were not wrong to think so. Washington was relieved to see General Romero go and quickly promised to restore the aid that had been cut off in 1977.[53]

The colonels pledged to distribute land to the poor and put an end to military repression, and, on the strength of this programme, were able to persuade representatives from the reformist political parties (the Christian Democrats and Social Democrats) to join the cabinet. By December, however, the civilian reformers were deeply disillusioned. The right wing of the army had blocked the reforms and continued the repression and the United States seemed unwilling to put pressure on them, apparently preferring to avoid charges of interference. Late in the month, the progressive officers refused to back up the civilians in a test of wills with the conservative Defence Minister and the cabinet resigned.[54]

Three days after the dissolution of the October junta, the Christian Democrats offered to form a new government if the army would accept their programme. The military agreed, and the coalition took office on 9 January 1980. The second junta eventually succeeded where the first had failed, putting through a sweeping land reform programme and nationalisation of the banks. Two contributions of the Carter administration were vital to their success. First, the administration offered El Salvador $50 million in economic aid and $5 million in military aid, but stipulated at the outset that it would be granted only if the reform programme were enacted. Later, in February, American officials deterred a coup by warning the right-wing officers that they would face a cut-off in assistance if they toppled the junta. The decision to grant aid to the junta was controversial in view of the human rights situation in El Salvador, but seems to have given the administration the leverage it needed to make certain that the junta's commitment to reform did not slacken.[55] At least at the first stage, El Salvador, too, was a success for reformist intervention.

As we have seen, the United States has undertaken reformist intervention in at least seven domestic political crises since 1942. Of the seven, there are only two instances in which the US failed either to bring reformers to power or persuade the existing leadership to adopt significant changes. Even in Nationalist China and Diem's Vietnam some limited progress was achieved and it is conceivable that different tactics might have yielded better results. Elsewhere—in Greece, the Philippines, Iran, the Dominican Republic and El Salvador—American efforts were reasonably successful in this first phase. Again, it is important to bear in mind that these successes came in countries highly dependent on American assistance. Where the degree of dependence was more modest, as in many of the Latin American countries at the time of the Alliance for Progress, the record has been very different. But when the target country has been heavily dependent on American support, the greatest difficulty has not lain with the basic premise (the efficacy of the reforms advocated by the US) nor with the ability of the United States to bring reformers to power. The biggest obstacle to the reformist strategy, it appears, has come at the intermediate stage. Where these efforts have come to grief, and unfortunately they have done so often, it has usually been at the point of enactment and implementation. Let us look again at the historical record, first reviewing the results of American efforts and then considering the reasons why.[56]

II

In Greece, the coalition created by American intervention in 1947 was strongly influenced by the Populists, who also maintained control of the parliament, the bureaucracy, the security forces and, by one estimate, 95 per cent of the local governments. Sophoulis was later to complain that he was a 'captive Liberal' in this still conservative environment. A government of this complexion was not likely to attempt any sort of redistributive programme, and the US did not press for one, preferring a conservative economic programme that was eventually successful in curbing inflation. The coalition, then, was 'reformist' only in the most limited sense. Bringing in the Liberals broadened the government's base, making it the first of the post-war period to command widespread popular support. Even if unable to enact social or economic reforms in the short run, the cabinet was better able to rally support for the war effort and to persuade the public to accept the harsh measures necessary to check the insurgency. In the view of one historian of the period, 'the significance of this cannot be overemphasized'. Moreover, the Liberals, in combination with the US, did reduce the violations of human rights that had occurred under the Populist governments to some degree. By October, Sophoulis had released over 19,000 political prisoners and later he offered amnesty to the guerrillas.[57]

The appointment of Papagos was again 'reform' of a very limited sort. It enhanced the effectiveness of the GNA, not by turning it into a more progressive force, as in the Philippines, but by increasing its aggressiveness and improving the quality of the commanders and the morale of the troops. By November 1948, the government forces enjoyed nearly a 10:1 advantage over the guerrillas in manpower, but American officials remained apprehensive. In their minds, the army suffered from two related defects. First, many Greek politicians were able to arrange troop deployments in their own districts, which scattered the GNA across the countryside in static positions, making it impossible for the government to concentrate its forces against the insurgents. Second, many commanders seemed to be content with the arrangement and appeared hesitant to pursue the enemy. The head of the US military aid mission, General James Van Fleet, said that his advice to the Greeks upon his arrival would be simply to 'get out and fight!' Under pressure from the US mission the GNA went on the offensive in the spring of 1948 and began inflicting serious losses on the Democratic Army for the first time, but Van Fleet was still unable to eliminate incompetent or unaggressive commanders and political interference in deployments continued. As the winter of 1948–49 began, US officials were still deeply concerned about the course of the war.

The appointment of General Papagos in January 1949, with dictatorial authority over the armed forces, was a turning point. His declaration of martial law permitted the security forces to round up thousands of suspected rebel sympathisers and crushed the Communists' intelligence network. Equally importantly, he took decisive steps to improve the performance of the army, dismissing timid or ineffective commanders summarily and even going so far as to issue an order empowering officers 'to shoot on the spot anyone under his command who showed negligence or faintheartedness'. These measures, along with US aid, galvanised the dispirited government troops. Inspired at last with, to use Van Fleet's phrase, 'the will to win', they advanced on the rebels' strongholds in northern Greece in late August and dealt them the *coup de grace* on Grammos mountain.[58]

After the war, the United States wanted to see the large budget deficit reduced so that American aid could be put to more productive use. American officials proposed that this be done partly by cutting expenditures and partly by enacting a more progressive tax system. The reform programme stirred the opposition of the King and private interests, and the budget trimming measures encountered resistance from the bureaucracy and armed forces. General Plastiras agreed to the programme, but his government rested on a precarious majority in the Greek parliament and he was unable to get the assembly to act on it.[59]

Six months later, the new American Ambassador announced that he intended to be 'neutral' in Greek politics. Venizelos took this as a signal that politics as usual had returned and withdrew his party's support from Plastiras, causing the government to fall. The US then punished the new government by announcing an aid cut of $67 million, leading Venizelos to promise steps to close the deficit. The reformist effort was finally abandoned after the invasion of South Korea in June 1950. At this point the administration felt that cuts in the Greek military budget would not be prudent, and the period of reformist intervention (though not intervention in general) came to an end.[60]

In the Philippines, as in Greece, there were two general aspects to the intervention. The first, reform of the armed forces, was a stunning success. To repeat, Ramon Magsaysay was appointed Minister of Defence in September 1950 at the insistence of the United States. Magsaysay began making surprise inspections on local commanders to weed out the incompetent or corrupt. The Minister was not content to punish only small offenders and avoid provoking the powerful: eventually he dismissed the head of the armed forces and several of President Quirino's friends in the military as well. Magsaysay's vitality and courage are beyond dispute, but it seems unlikely that he could have taken steps such as these without protection from the United States. According to Magsaysay's American friend and advisor Edward Lansdale, the head of the American military mission went to President Quirino at the outset and demanded that Magsaysay be given full support. Immediately afterward, Quirino wrote a memo granting extraordinary authority to the civilian Minister of Defence: the power to promote men on the spot, to relieve others of their commands and to order courts-martial, all without consultation with the military high command. Vested with this authority, Magsaysay was able to improve the effectiveness of the government's troops in combat and, even more importantly, to curb the abuses by the security forces that had been such an important factor in the Huk's success. These changes were crucial in reversing the trend of events in the Philippines.[61]

In addition, Magsaysay, with Lansdale's advice and encouragement, devised novel and effective ways of utilising the army. It was here that the concept of 'civic action' was invented and first put into practice. The Philippine army built over 4000 schools, dug wells, gave medical assistance and even made legal services available to tenants in their disputes with landlords. One of the Minister's most innovative programmes was the Economic Development Corps (EDCOR), which was conducted by the Department of National Defence and implemented entirely by military personnel. Under this programme, approximately 1000 Huk families were settled on vacant land on Luzon and Mindinao. Though far too small in scale to ameliorate the Philippines' agrarian problem, EDCOR did prove effective in wearing down the morale of the guerrillas.[62]

Perhaps the most important of Magsaysay's unorthodox applications of the military came in the by-elections of 1951. Quirino's Liberals had won the elections two years before by blatant fraud and the Huks took full advantage of this afterwards, making 'bullets not ballots' their main propaganda slogan. Many observers had concluded that if the voting were corrupted again, the resulting demoralisation might destroy Philippine democracy. An unusual clause in the country's constitution allowed the independent Commission on Elections to solicit the aid of any group or institution in the country for the conduct of an election. After prompting from Magsaysay and Lansdale, the Commission requested the armed forces' assistance in 1951. On election day, the army helped turn out the vote and guarded the ballot boxes until the vote had been tabulated.

The United States also made a more direct contribution to the success of the electoral process. After Lansdale's urging, both the Secretary of State and the American Ambassador expressed their concern about the election, and it appears that the CIA channelled funds to two civic groups in the Philippines working to ensure a fair vote. Once he was confident that the election would go well, Lansdale forged a 'directive' from the Huk leadership calling for a boycott of the election, which was obediently implemented by many of the cadres. Over 70 per cent of the country's eligible voters then went to the polls, and the Huk's defeat was turned to discomfiture. Lansdale feels, with some justification, that the 1951 election may have been the turning-point in the defeat of the Huk insurgency.[63]

The efforts to promote social reform in the Philippines were less successful, however, again repeating the pattern in Greece. As afore-mentioned, the Quirino government passed, but did not enforce, the reform programme recommended by the Bell Mission. The best chance for effective reform came with the election of Magsaysay in 1953. Magsaysay introduced land reform bills in 1954 and 1955. The legislation ran into determined opposition from the landed interests in the Philippine House and was passed in a greatly attenuated form only after strenuous efforts by the President. Under the compromise provisions, only 1.5 per cent of the Philippine's farmland was made available, and crippling provisions made even that modest amount difficult to transfer. Magsaysay's death in a plane crash eliminated any chance of vigorous enforcement and by 1960 the percentage of tenancy had actually increased.[64]

The land reform undertaken in Vietnam during this period was equally disappointing. Disregarding American advice, Diem set the ownership ceilings quite high (at 284 acres, well above what US advisors thought necessary to achieve economies of scale), exempted non-rice properties and did not seize land held by absentee landowners. Consequently, only 10 per cent of South Vietnam's peas-antry received any land and those who did were to be given title to their property only after they had paid in full. Implementation of the reform was sluggish. The transfers did not begin until 1958, and by 1962 only one-third of the land set aside had been transferred. For most peasants, the regulations limiting rent to one quarter of the crop and guaranteeing tenure for 3–5 years meant more than the land transfer, but the effect of these was weakened by lax enforcement.[65] The slow pace of the transfers may have been partly a result of the sort of per-sonnel Diem relied upon to carry out the reform, the most egregious of whom was Minister of Agrarian Reform himself, who refused to sign leases with his own tenants as the new law required.[66] The courts set up to arbitrate tenure disputes soon came under the domination of the landlords and peasants ended up paying more than the legal limit of 25 per cent in some cases. Finally, local government officials and landlords harassed or repressed the Tenant Farmers Union and

Farmers Association organised after the reform to represent the peasants. In short, Diem's land reform programme, overly cautious at its inception and weakened further by ineffective implementation, was a totally inadequate response to the land seizures carried out by the Vietminh.[67]

Diem's removal did clear the way for a sweeping agrarian reform, though not until the early seventies. Ironically, President Thieu did not act under official pressure from the Americans—who lost interest in agrarian reform in the sixties and had actually discouraged Ky from attempting it—but on his own initiative, after seeing the gratitude of the peasants for the small amounts of land he distributed under his predecessor's reform. His 'Land to the Tiller' programme, which transferred land to over half of Vietnam's rural population, nearly eradicated the Vietcong and radically altered the nature of the war. While it was underway, recruitment by the guerrillas fell to 1000 per month from over 7000 a month in 1967 and 3500 a month even after the Tet offensive in 1968.[68] If only Diem had been persuaded to undertake a reform on this scale in the fifties, what tribulations he might have spared his country, not to say the United States! Yes, Vietnam was lost anyway, but the South was defeated not by the Vietcong, who never recovered from the thrashing they suffered during and after the Tet offensive, but by a conventional invasion by North Vietnamese regulars. Not even a programme on this scale could have protected the regime against that, any more than the US sponsored land reform would have saved South Korea from Kim Il Sung's aggression of 1950.

What might have made a difference in 1975, however, was successful reform of the armed forces, as the US had accomplished previously in Greece and the Philippines. Although the South Vietnamese army did fight well at times, there were too many signs of decay at all points for even a sympathetic observer to ignore. As early as 1965, the desertion rates for ARVN were 15 per cent per year, five to ten times as high as the enemy's. Between 1969 and 1971, ARVN combat units lost approximately one-third of their men each year through desertion, though most returned to their families and did not go over to the enemy.[69] From the beginning of the US involvement during the Kennedy administration, American advisors also complained of the lack of aggressiveness, incompetence and even treason of ARVN commanders.[70] In some areas, ARVN appeared to avoid the Vietcong deliberately or even share supplies with them. It must have seemed to US advisors at times as if the army posed a greater threat to the villagers than to the enemy. According to reports to the US command, 'many people find it difficult to consider the soldiers as their protectors', for 'the army steals, rapes, and generally treats the population in a very callous fashion'.[71]

The root of all of these problems was the quality of the officer corps. Among the top leadership, Nguyen Cao Ky was the only one who did not take advantage of his position to line his own pockets. General Dan Van Quang, the commander of the Fourth Corps, dealt in rice and opium; Generals Vinh Loc of the Second Corps and Hoang Xuan Lam of the First sold promotions and American supplies; General Nguyen Huu Co used inside information to buy up lands where US military installations were to be built; and in the spring of 1975, with the end approaching, President Thieu himself was caught trying to sneak $73 million in gold bullion out of the country.[72] Corruption spread downward from the top through the entire structure. Writing in 1967, John Paul Vann observed 'padded payrolls, the hiring out of troop labor, the theft and/or sale of material resources, the selling of jobs and promotions, the rental of military vehicles to smugglers or worse, [and] the illegal taxation of farmers and travelers'. In view of this, he found it 'surprising that the GVN [Government of Vietnam] armed forces perform as well as they do'. Generously, a number of officers also turned a blind eye to thievery by their troops. The ninth ARVN division, for example, came to be known as the 'chicken division': a comment not on their fighting spirit, but on their habit of pilfering fowl.[73]

In addition to the venality, however, the unwillingness of most of their superiors to expose themselves to risk could not have inspired the average infantryman to much sacrifice. To cite just one statistic, between 1954 and 1966 only one ARVN officer lost his life in battle. For both these reasons, it is not surprising that investigations of the deserters from combat units found that complaints about the leadership, along with homesickness and feelings of family responsibility, were the most important factors in their decision to return home. Moreover, Vietnamese studies showed a clear (negative) relationship for combat units between the level of desertion and the quality of the commander.[74]

These problems first developed in the fifties. In order to protect himself from coups, Diem began promoting in the armed forces on the basis of personal loyalty rather than professional merit and then compounded the difficulties this created by stressing the avoidance of casualties almost to the exclusion of anything else. The mediocrities advanced by Diem were so eager to please that they routinely designed battle plans permitting the enemy a route of escape. Even when the battles were going well, the political officers were reluctant to close on the Vietcong and were unable to inflict decisive defeats. The most infamous of these incidents was at Ap Bac in 1963, where ARVN surrounded a much smaller Vietcong force but allowed them to slip away, losing five helicopters in the process.[75]

Most of these characteristics were still visible after Diem's overthrow in 1963. By the seventies, US reports found virtually no connection between success on the battlefield and promotion, and no discernible policy on the part of the government to locate or develop capable leadership. Quite to the contrary, there was an actual shortage of officers between the ranks of captain and colonel by 1968 (because promotions were not being made, essentially for political reasons), and posts were continuing to go to corrupt or incompetent candidates.[76]

There were periodic attempts on the part of the South Vietnamese government to address some aspects of this problem, but none of them brought any fundamental improvement. General Ky anounced an anti-corruption drive in 1965–66, but the effort resulted in only one arrest, a businessman whom the Chinese community reportedly offered up as a scapegoat. Ky's 'Anti-Fraud and Corruption League' was later disbanded by Thieu on (amply justified) charges of fraud and corruption. The campaign was received with some amusement by the cynics in Saigon, but there is reason to think that Ky sincerely wanted to end the abuses. The difficulty was that his power ultimately rested on corruption and he could not eliminate it without endangering his own rule. Ky could not easily dismiss inept or venal local officials because they had usually purchased their positions or owed them to local commanders he could not afford to ignore. His own right-hand man, Colonel Nguyen Ngoc Loan, ran the extortion racket in Saigon.[77]

The US advisory command was well aware of these deficiencies and attempts were made to persuade the Vietnamese to correct them. The results, however, were consistently disappointing. During the Diem period, US exhortations to the timid political officers were nearly always ignored. The three men respected most by the US military mission were all placed in inferior posts and the field commander esteemed most highly by the Americans, Colonel Pham Van Dong, was convinced that the US recommendation had actually hurt his chances for promotion to general.[78] US efforts later, under Thieu, never produced anything more than limited improvement. Some of the worst offenders were removed, but they frequently cropped up again in other positions, and Thieu continued to appoint and promote largely on the basis of political reliability. US officials, concludes General Westmoreland's former Vice Chief-of-Staff, 'influenced Thieu very little in the selection of top military leaders'.[79]

Why was the United States unsuccessful in encouraging military reform in Vietnam? Accounts differ on this point. According to Douglas Blaufarb, the United States made 'extraordinary' efforts to convince the South Vietnamese government, especially under Thieu, to reform ARVN. The problem was that the Vietnamese dictator's resistance could not be overcome:

> Thieu could not change the system without putting his own position in serious jeopardy. His first political constituency was the military: if he attempted to strip it of power and privilege and access to wealth, he risked the development of a serious opposition to his leadership within the ranks of the armed forces which could eventually bring him down. He seems to have considered more than once replacing his military base with a more open and broadly supported structure, but in the end he shrank from the risk.[80]

Other observers contend, however, that US advisors were hesitant to draw up critical reports on their Vietnamese counterparts for fear that it might reflect badly on their own work or run counter to the official optimism about the progress of the war.[81] CORDS, the US agency in charge of pacification, overcame this tendency through a highly effective set of procedures for US advisors in dealing with local officials. Among other things, CORDS called for a yearly report on each Vietnamese official and encouraged US advisors to call for the replacement of those they could prove to be incompetent. CORDS successfully used the information collected to press the Thieu government into removing nearly all of the worst province and district heads in 1969–70.[82]

Despite the programme's success, the US advisory command failed to apply it elsewhere, for reasons the public record does not reveal.[83] Perhaps if they had, ARVN could have been transformed into a force capable of defending the South after the departure of the Americans. But one must take into account the political circumstances that made CORDS's achievements possible. In May 1968, Tran Van Huong launched an anti-corruption campaign that eliminated half of the province chiefs in Vietnam, many of them, no doubt, those identified by CORDS. Though Huong's motives were also honourable, most of the officials he dismissed were followers of former President Ky, which suggests that Thieu manipulated the campaign to strengthen himself at the expense of his most serious rival. Huong spoke often of the need to attack corruption at the higher levels, but never attempted to go after high-level officials or officers.[84]

If the CORDS approach, or some other method, had forced Thieu to depoliticise appointments in the armed forces, it might have made all the difference. Studies undertaken by the Defense Department in 1969 and 1970 concluded that leadership was the key factor in the success or failure of ARVN units—statistically, changes there brought four times as much improvement in performance as changes in the quality of the troops; and the few changes in command achieved later in the war produced dramatic results.[85] Whatever the reasons, the consequences of the US failure to bring about reform in ARVN were eventually fatal. In the last round of fighting in Vietnam, the South Vietnamese army put three times as many men in the field as the enemy, was equipped with twice the artillery and armour, and (despite the failure of Congress to send emergency aid) fired twelve times as much ammunition by rifle and machine-gun and nine times as much by artillery. Yet even these advantages were not enough to save a country defended by an army whose morale had been drained by the spectacle of conspicuous corruption, from the top on down.[86]

Despite the Kennedy officials' high hopes, the reformist strategy was eventually thwarted in the Dominican Republic as well. Juan Bosch inherited a difficult situation there after his election in December 1962. The country suffered from high rates of unemployment and a skewed distribution of land, but was also deeply in debt. To the puzzlement of the US embassy, the supposedly leftist Bosch gave first priority to the country's fiscal problems and did manage to balance the budget by June. In the meantime, though, the unemployed, who had expected a swift improvement in their lot, were rapidly losing faith. Moreover, land reform was moving at a snail's pace. By July, only 40 families had been settled on the land seized from the Trujillo family. The pace picked up some in August, but Bosch still transferred 25 per cent less land than the conservative transition regime that preceded him. The slow pace of reform resulted mostly from administrative incompetence, though resistance from the oligarchy also contributed.[87]

All in all, this was not exactly Roosevelt's hundred days, as the liberal American Ambassador, John Martin, remarked. At the same time, however, Bosch continued the radical rhetoric that had already alarmed the upper classes. After the promulgation of a new constitution granting the government sweeping powers to expropriate property, the Dominican oligarchs began an active campaign to persuade the military to remove Bosch. The basis of the campaign was the charge that Bosch was dangerously soft on Communism. Ambassador Martin advised the Dominican President to protect himself from the oligarchy's demagoguery by cracking down on the Communists but Bosch's democratic scruples were too strong and he did nothing to shield himself from the charges.[88] Alternatively, Bosch might have tried to purge his opponents in the armed forces, but he was afraid of triggering a coup and reluctant to act in the absence of strong US support. Thus, Bosch failed either to appease or weaken his enemies.

Ambassador Martin worked strenuously to head off a coup, even offering to accompany Bosch to confront its leaders.[89] Nevertheless, the Dominican military sent Bosch into exile on 25 September 1963, setting the stage for the tragic events that were to follow two years later.

Could Bosch have been saved? One possibility would have been to carry out a thorough purge of the armed forces, either under the Council of State or during Bosch's Presidency. According to Ambassador Martin's account, he (Martin) advised the Dominicans against attempts at purging the army on two occasions. The US tried instead to change the military's attitude by training and civic action programmes. Although both Bosch and the Council dismissed a few soldiers, neither was willing to attempt a large-scale purge without American backing.

US officials hesitated in part because of the practical difficulties. Nearly everyone in the Dominican armed forces had collaborated with Trujillo to some extent, so it would have been difficult to separate Trujillistas from non-Trujillistas. But more importantly, the North Americans had concluded that the short-term risks of a purge were greater than the longer-term risks of doing nothing. When members of the Council of State came to him with plans for a purge in 1962, Martin spoke for his colleagues in saying that while they were sympathetic, they did not want to see the Council 'huff and puff and blow itself over'. Later, in February 1963, Martin told Bosch that the armed forces seemed quiescent and willing to follow the United States' lead, at least for the present, and ought not to be provoked. US officials mistakenly believed that the Dominican military was becoming accustomed to a democratic, apolitical existence and that it would be best if Bosch did nothing to impede this transition.[90] The view on both occasions seemed to be that there were other matters of greater moment and that the government ought not to endanger itself over a secondary issue. This caution may have been understandable but in the view of some observers the unwillingness to run risks before the fall of 1963 ultimately finished Bosch.[91]

The second question that can be raised is whether the United States did all that was possible to reverse the coup. The administration strongly condemned the military's seizure of power and suspended diplomatic relations within hours. All aid programmes were cancelled and the Ambassador and the heads of the aid missions were recalled.[92] In the negotiations that followed, the US officials did not try to persuade the Dominican military to accept the return of Bosch but did ask them in October to withdraw in favour of another PRD figure. The leaders of the junta were so upset at this suggestion that they lodged a grievance with the Organization of American States (OAS) about American intervention and demanded that the official who had made the suggestion depart. Later, US officials sensed that their influence was limited and scaled down their demands to elections by December 1964 and representation for the PRD in the government. Eventually, the US had to settle for a promise that elections would be held before 1966 and recognised the regime as it was on 14 December 1963. Economic and military aid were restored in January and February.[93]

It has been suggested that the Dominican armed forces were gambling that the United States would have to back down eventually for the same reasons for which they had yielded previously after coups in Argentina and Peru.[94] In both cases, the Kennedy officials would have preferred to see democratic governments in power, but once the military intervened, they became concerned that prolonged sanctions might create an economic crisis or that cuts in military aid would reduce the effectiveness of the armed forces. Either step ran the risk of opening the way for the Communists. Fearing that, the administration had given in on both occasions and recognised the military goverments. As Kennedy himself had said after the death of Trujillo:

> There are three possibilities, in descending order of preference: a decent democratic regime, a continuation of the Trujillo regime or a Castro regime. We ought to aim at the first, but we really can't renounce the second until we are sure that we can avoid the third.[95]

Thus, the recent past suggested to the Dominican military that their country's potential vulnerability to Communist subversion could be turned to their advantage in dealing with the United States. They concluded that the US would not be willing to run the risks of a protracted confrontation and decided to wait Washington out. In this respect, the junta enjoyed especially good fortune when the Castroite 14th of June Movement launched an insurrection in late November. The army was able to suppress the rebels easily, but the abortive uprising strengthened their hand against the administration by creating pressure in Congress for recognition.[96]

This was not the only factor in the US capitulation, however. Martin himself was highly sceptical of the reports coming to him about the strength of the guerrillas but foresaw other difficulties. Apart from the 14th of June Movement, the coup had met with apathy in the Dominican Republic, so US officials had few allies inside the country to assist them. The Ambassador feared that the military triumvirate formed after the coup might be replaced by a harsher military dictatorship and was also concerned that a tough US stand might encourage the Dominican young to rise up and fight in a futile cause. Finally, most European governments had already recognised the regime; the longer the US waited the greater would be the loss of face when it finally had to give in.[97]

For these reasons, then, the Kennedy administration's 'Caribbean showcase for democracy' lay in ruins nine months after its inception. But 500 miles to the south, on the other shore of that sea, events were to follow a different course.

Romulo Betancourt won the first elections after the fall of the dictator Marcos Perez Jimenez and announced his intention to enact land reform shortly after taking office in February 1959. The Venezuelan President faced a situation similar to the one Bosch had to cope with in the Dominican Republic, but handled it more skilfully. The radical left was eager to foil his attempts at reform, fearing that he would eliminate any hope they had of mobilising support for a revolutionary takeover. At the same time, the willingness of the armed forces and the right to permit him to continue in office could not be taken for granted.

Betancourt dealt with this dilemma by doing all he could to avoid alarming the conservative forces. He invited the Christian Democrats, who had better ties to business, into a coalition and adopted policies that did not threaten the private sector. Betancourt maintained the loyalty of the armed forces by continuing large military expenditures, attending to living conditions in the services and working tirelessly to win over the officers at the personal level. On the question of land reform, Betancourt moved gradually enough not to alarm the right and paid for the land seized at current market value.[98] Unlike Bosch, the Venezuelan President managed to ward off attacks from the right long enough to enact reform measures that would eventually defeat the left. Although the programme was not vast in scale (it affected just 5 per cent of the nation's land and benefited about 20 per cent of the agricultural workers directly), it served its political purpose very well. When the Communists tried to spur the peasantry to revolt in 1962, peasants joined with the military to defeat them in two provinces and turned over the guerrillas' leader to the government. As a result, the uprising was quashed with relative ease.[99]

The United States did not bring Romulo Betancourt to power in Venezuela and did not have to convince him to introduce reform once in office, but the Kennedy administration did play a small, though perhaps significant, role in making it possible for him to carry out his programme. Previously, the United States had not assigned Venezuelan loan requests high priority because of the country's oil wealth. The administration, in keeping with the rationale of the Alliance for Progress, gave Betancourt generous financial support ($60 million in the first year of the Alliance), but their intangible contributions may have been more important. Kennedy gave a visible demonstration of his commitment to Betancourt in his visit to Caracas in December 1961 and American officials also worked behind the scenes to persuade the Venezuelan military not to stand in the way of his reform programme. On one occasion the American Ambassador learned that the Defence Minister, General Antonio Briceno Linares, was an admirer of Adlai Stevenson. The administration then arranged for Stevenson to meet Briceno and convey the message that he '[stood] as sentinel at the gate of Venezuelan democracy'. The general is said to have carried a letter Stevenson later wrote on his own person, 'close to his heart', for years afterward.[100]

Although it is not clear from the public record how much credit one ought to assign the United States, Venezuela is one of the few unambiguous successes for American policy mentioned in this study. The outcome in Iran, on the other hand, is more difficult to assess. The Kennedy officials had an ambitious agenda for that country. They intended to encourage reform while simultaneously persuading the Shah to trim the military budget and move towards a more democratic political system. They had hoped to achieve this, to repeat, by securing the appointment of Ali Amini as Prime Minister and they succeeded in doing so.

Amini's efforts were at least partially successful. He initiated a land reform programme in March 1962 and also began a campaign against corruption. During his visit to Washington in April, the Shah was persuaded to trim the armed forces from 200,000 to 150,000. The Plan Organisation favoured by the administration did not receive the support they had hoped for, but Amini did carry out austerity measures, including curbs on luxury imports, to redress the balance of payments problem.[101] With regard to social and economic policy, then, American officials had some reason to be pleased by 1962. Iranian politics, however, was another matter.

Shortly after taking office, Amini admonished the Shah that Iran's legislature, the *Majlis*, was dominated by the landlords and would block any significant efforts at agrarian reform. Land reform measures had in fact been introduced twice before by his predecessors and gutted by the legislature on both occasions. The Shah accepted Amini's advice, closed the *Majlis* and put through the land reform by royal decree.[102]

The Prime Minister had served under Mossadegh and still had contacts with the National Front (the leading middle-class opposition group), so there was hope in some quarters that he would be able to reconcile the Shah and the opposition. In 1961, he lifted the restraints on freedom of expression and assembly, but the National Front responded by putting 70,000 demonstrators in the streets in May to call for new elections and Amini quickly ran out of patience with them. Two months later he forbade the Front from holding additional public meetings, arrested most of its leadership and cracked down on two Teheran papers.[103]

Amini had argued from the outset that the best way for the Shah to preserve the monarchy was for him to remove himself from day-to-day politics and let more responsibility rest with the Prime Minister, and Washington concurred. But the Shah was not content to reign without ruling. Though constrained to grant authority to a forceful and independent Prime Minister in May 1961, he retained control over the armed forces and resisted Amini's efforts to cut their budget. In July 1962, Amini resigned over that issue, complaining as well about the lack of US budgetary support, and was replaced by the Shah's friend and associate Assadollah Alam. Alam also explored the possibility of an accommodation with the opposition but the National Front continued to insist that the Shah reduce his role to that of constitutional monarch, a proposition the Shah was not prepared to entertain.[104]

From the experience of 1961–62, Iran's monarch drew two conclusions. The first was that the National Front was implacable and that further efforts at conciliation would be fruitless; thereafter he relied on repression. The second was that no one must be permitted to upstage him politically. Thus, Hassan Arsanjani, who had won considerable popularity as the chief administrator of the land reform, was dismissed, and after his departure the Shah saw to it that he alone was seen as the motivating force behind the reform programme.[105] In January 1963, the Shah resumed his previous position of open leadership, promulgating a six-point reform programme entitled the 'White Revolution'. It included, among other things, an extension of the land reform begun by Amini (though in a more moderate form) and promises of profit-sharing for Iran's industrial workers. The programme received an overwhelming endorsement two weeks later in a referendum in which Iranian women voted for the first time.

The White Revolution did not win universal acceptance, however. In particular, it included a number of steps objectionable to Iran's Shi'ite clergy: expropriation of the *awqaf* (estates under the control of the clergy, which were to be used for charitable purposes), the secularisation of education and women's rights. Ayatollah Behbehani warned the Shah not to touch the clergy's lands in January 1963 and rioters attempted to intimidate women voters at the polls during the referendum. Undaunted, the Shah appeared in person in Qom on 24 January 1963 to distribute the region's *awqaf* estates. In the late spring, the followers of a previously obscure cleric named Ruhollah Khomeini denounced the White Revolution from their pulpits, inspiring large numbers of people to take to the streets of Teheran and other cities on 4–6 June in protest. On the second day the National Front joined in and the Shah was facing the most serious threat to his authority since 1953.[106] Unlike 1953 and 1979, he responded decisively and unleashed the armed forces, who fired on the rioters, killing approximately 1000 of them. Khomeini was jailed and the next elections produced a docile *Majilis*.[107]

Thus, the Shah emerged from the crisis of the early sixties more firmly entrenched than ever. The land reform was beginning to win some peasant support for the regime, but more importantly the outcome of the June uprising had proved to anyone who had doubted it that the army was prepared to kill to keep the Shah on his throne. The urban middle-class and clerical opposition had not been reconciled to the regime, but they had been thoroughly cowed. The 'new political synthesis' sought by the United States had not come about and Iran remained as authoritarian as before.[108]

From the perspective of the eighties, it is only natural to wonder whether greater American pressure could have produced a lasting accommodation between the Shah and the National Front that would have precluded a takeover by Khomeini's forces later. We will never know for certain, of course, but such an arrangement would have been difficult to achieve for a number of reasons. First, the Shah was upset about what he viewed as a lack of support from the United States and disappointed with the amount of aid he was receiving. It seemed unlikely to US officials that he could be convinced to cut the military budget, a step American officials thought essential, unless he remained confident in American support. Too many suggestions or too much arm-twisting might have led the Shah to dig in his heals on the budget question.[109] Second, the Shah told the Soviets in September 1962 that he would not permit foreign missile bases in his country. This was not a serious setback for the US, since the development of the Polaris submarine had reduced the utility of such bases, but Washington surmised the Shah was making the point that he had alternatives if he were pressed too hard.[110] Third, the closure of the *Majlis* by the Shah and Amini was politically defensible. The legislature had already sidetracked two reform initiatives and was still dominated by the landlords. Finally, the National Front did not respond to the overtures of Amini and Alam and thus must share the blame with the Shah for the eventual outcome. Even if the conditions they set for participation in the government are not to be questioned as unrealistic, one can still ask why it was that they decided to join Khomeini's protest against some of the very measures they had previously supported.[111]

Of course, the administration might have elected to break with the Shah altogether and work to bring the National Front to power. The objection to this was that the middle-class opposition would feel compelled to take a number of steps threatening to American interests, including withdrawing from the Central Treaty Organisation (CENTO) and squeezing the oil companies. It was also feared that a National Front government, as under Mossadegh, would open up opportunities for the Tudeh (Communist) party. The National Front, according to an intelligence report written in 1961, would offer 'the long run advantages of a more popularly based regime, but the cost does not appear to be worth the advantages'.[112]

Over a period of years, though, one would have expected the Shah's land reform to win him the support of the peasantry, which might have been enough to offset the continued opposition he faced in the cities.[113] The reform was rapid—16 per cent of Iran's villages were transferred by September 1963; and it was effective—in the areas affected by the reform observers found that the peasants enjoyed 'greatly' improved incomes, diets and standards of living very soon after the transfers had taken place. The benefits were also widespread. By the programme's end in 1971, approximately 92 per cent of Iran's 2.1 million tenant farmers had received land.[114] Yet in 1978, the villagers did not, as one might have expected, rally to the support of the Shah. What accounts for this?

Despite the reform, many of the rural poor remained destitute. None of the 1 million agricultural labourers benefited, and three-quarters of the tenants who did received plots smaller than 7 hectares, the size thought to be necessary to maintain a family of 5 at subsistence level.[115] This did not result from excessive caution on the government's part.[116] Prior to the reform, 5 per cent of the population of Iran owned 95 per cent of the land; after it, only half of arable land was held by absentee landowners. The problem was that rural Iran was so overpopulated that it would have been impossible to satisfy everyone regardless of how the land was distributed. If, for example, Iran's arable land had been distributed equally to all the landless (including the remaining tenants and agricultural workers), each family would have ended up with just 4.7 hectares.[117]

This was an underlying problem for which the Shah cannot be blamed and about which he could have done little. But serious questions can be raised about his agricultural policies during the implementation of the reform and after. Rather than leaving the peasants to organise production themselves, the Shah required them to join co-operatives established by the state and dominated by state officials. Thus, the beneficiaries of the reform found that they had been freed from the grip of the landlords only to be subjected to the caprices of government bureaucrats. Among other things, the government also failed to provide adequate credit to the peasants and allowed agricultural prices to lag far behind the rapidly increasing costs of production in the early seventies.[118] Probably the most damaging policy of all, though, was the Shah's promotion of large-scale farming in the last decade of his rule.

In the late sixties, the Shah became convinced that economies of scale were needed to boost production in agriculture. To achieve this, he coerced about 300,000 peasants to trade in their lands to state-owned farm corporations in return for shares and employment in the firms and compelled another 75,000 to sell their land to private agribusinesses. For the most part, the peasants resented being deprived of their lands in this way and did not consider the slips of paper issued to them adequate compensation for what they perceived to be a return to the status of farm labourer. Ironically, the large farms actually turned out to be less productive than small peasant plots even though they were favoured in the allocation of credit and were usually operating on better land. By these means, as Powelson and Stock put it, 'the Shah emasculated his own reform'.[119]

Finally, let us turn back to El Salvador, the most recent, and in some ways the most difficult to interpret of these cases. To repeat, the January junta announced a three-stage land reform programme under pressure from and with the support of the United States on 6 March 1980. Implementation of phase I of the reform began immediately and was nearly complete by the end of the summer. The army occupied *haciendas* larger than 500 hectares (1235 acres), compensated the owners with long-term bonds and established 517 co-operative farms. This phase transferred 15 per cent of El Salvador's total agricultural land (including 60 per cent of the best land) and eventually benefited 31,000 landless peasants. Phase II was to transfer farms between 100 and 500 hectares (247–1235 acres) on the same basis as phase I. The plans were announced along with the first phase in March but implementation was postponed. Phase III was to transfer all rented land not subject to phases I and II directly to sharecroppers (up to a maximum of 7 hectares), who were to pay for the land over a period of 30 years. It is said that the Salvadoran government adopted phase III only under heavy pressure and after promises of assistance from the US. Nevertheless, on 28 April 1980, tenant farmers were told that the land they were farming was theirs and that they could dispose of the crops as they wished. If all of these provisions had been carried out, approximately 60 per cent of El Salvador's landless peasants would have received land.[120]

As a price for the acquiescence of the right in this sweeping redistribution, the progressive officers permitted the repression that had been exercised under General Romero to continue and even intensify. By the end of the year, 10,000 had died in El Salvador, most of them victims of rightist members of the armed forces or the death squads. The Christian Democratic members of the government were powerless to restrain the killers and the progressives gradually lost influence within the junta, the turning-point coming when their leader, Colonel Majano, was forced to resign in December.[121]

The killings subsided over the next two years but the land reform programme ran into serious trouble. The death squads killed approximately 5000 peasants in 1980, largely with the intention of blocking reform by means of intimidation. Regrettably, the intimidation appears to have been effective. A survey by the Agency for International Development (AID) in 1984 found that one-third of those who had filed under phase III of the reform were not working their land because they had been 'threatened, evicted, or had disappeared' and over half those who were eligible had not applied. The reform programme received an additional and quite unexpected blow in 1982 when the reactionary parties won control of El Salvador's legislature. Although the Reagan administration was able to prevent Roberto d'Aubuisson, the rightist leader, from becoming President, his party still had enough strength in the assembly to do the programme serious damage. The conservatives abrogated phase II, drove many of the co-operatives into debt by denying them credit and technical assistance and prevented at least 58,000 of those eligible under phase III from claiming their land by refusing to extend the deadline for application for titles.[122]

Despite their sharply differing ideological perspectives, in the end the responses of the Carter and Reagan administrations to this frustrating and at times horrifying situation were not that dissimilar. Carter granted the January junta $5.7 million in aid early in 1980 without receiving assurances about human rights, contrary to the advice of El Salvador's Archbishop Romero. During 1980, political murder took place at a rate greater than even the infamous *Matanza* of the thirties. Despite pressure from Ambassador White, the junta apparently did little or nothing to halt the slaughter. The administration, however, stopped short of breaking off aid until December, when four American nuns were murdered by a Salvadoran death squad. The next day, the administration suspended all economic and military assistance to the country and demanded that steps be taken to curb the violence and bring the killers of the nuns to justice. What followed was a complex restructuring of the Salvadoran government which has been variously described as a victory for the moderates and a move to the right. Carter then restored economic aid on 17 December. Some critics felt that the administration should not have been satisfied with such meagre progress and ought to have held out for more, but by then Jimmy Carter was a lame duck and the Salvadoran right expected the winner of the 1980 election to view their case with greater sympathy. If the administration had pressed them harder, the rightists probably would have just waited Carter out.[123]

If the extreme right had expected a free ride with the Reagan administration, however, they must have been disappointed. In March of 1981, the President stated his support for the land reform and expressed his opposition to a coup. Ambassador Dean Hinton also moved on several occasions to block attempts to expel the Christian Democrats from the government. But Reagan did seek a military victory and assumed that one could be had fairly soon if the requisite equipment were made available to the Salvadoran army. In March, the administration provided $25 million in military assistance and 56 military advisors. By the end of the fiscal year in September, El Salvador was the third largest recipient of US assistance. The human rights abuses continued over the next two years, though at a reduced level, but the administration 'certified' to Congress every six months that progress was being made, in keeping with the procedure set up by the legislative branch.[124]

In July 1983 the certification law expired and President Reagan unwisely threatened to veto any new legislation conditioning aid on the observance of human rights. Coincidentally or not, death squad activity began increasing again, though not at the rate of 1980. *Tutela Legal*, a Catholic agency, estimated that 5339 civilians lost their lives in political killings in 1983. Prior to this time, the Reagan administration's position was that the war ought to be won first, then progress could be made on human rights; by late 1983, Reagan officials had come round to the view that the war could not be won unless the human rights situation were improved. Thus, in the last two months of the year, the administration warned the Salvadorans through several channels that aid might be cut off if the killings were not curtailed and some of the worst perpetrators (who were identified on a list the administration passed on to the Salvadoran armed forces personally via Vice President Bush) were not expelled from the military. None of the men named was brought to justice, but death squad murders did decline substantially in the following months. According to *Tutela Legal*, the deaths in the first 6 months of 1984 numbered 185, as opposed to 810 for January through June 1983, while disappearances fell from 326 to 139. The administration expressed its approval by asking Congress to increase economic and military aid in February.[125]

Both administrations faced a dilemma in El Salvador. They wanted a democratic government to hold on to power and enact reforms to satisfy the people's demands and pre-empt the left, while respecting human rights. At the same time, they sought to strengthen the Salvadoran armed forces in order to prevent a leftist victory and eventually to drive the Farabundo Martí National Liberation Front (FMLN) from the field. The only way to prevent the worst (a guerrilla victory) from happening was to give the army the tools to do the job, which meant a continuation of military aid and avoidance of measures that might reduce their effectiveness as a fighting force. But if the army were left alone, it might continue to abuse human rights and block reform; in effect, it could prevent the reformist strategy from working. Yet the only way to address this problem would be by threatening to cut off military aid or attempt a radical restructuring of the military, either of which could incapacitate the army and open the way for the guerrillas. The offenders, of course, were well aware of this, which lead them to discount American threats to withdraw support. In this way, the attempts by both administrations to prevent the worst from happening in El Salvador also made it more difficult for them to achieve their preferred solution. The good, one might say, became the enemy of the best.

Some observers concluded in the early eighties that this dilemma was insoluble and that the United States was headed either for defeat in El Salvador or, as the fashionable phrase went, 'another Vietnam'.[126] The picture at present is mixed, but the worst predictions have not come to pass and there is now some cause for hope. First, though abuses of political prisoners continue and there have been charges of air attacks against civilians by government aircraft, the number of political killings has fallen from around 800 per month in 1980 to fewer than 30 per month, many of which are committed by the rebels.[127] Thus far, the land reform programme has transferred 22 per cent of El Salvador's agricultural land to some 83,000 families, less than the 220,000 originally planned, but still 25 per cent of the rural landless population. Serious problems remain: the number of landless remains alarmingly high (approximately half the rural population); some of the plots distributed under phase III are too small to sustain a family or permit crop rotation; and the production of export crops has diminished, as a consequence of the debt burden left by compensation, sabotage by the guerrillas, the prolonged uncertainty over phase II and a lack of technical assistance.[128]

Still, to put this in perspective one must imagine what El Salvador's future might have been had the junta, the Christian Democrats and the United States not achieved at least as much as they did. In January 1980, leftist groups were able to persuade over 100,000 peasants to travel to the capital for mass demonstrations. As former Ambassador Robert White later observed, 'everyone to whom I spoke in the Washington intelligence community, in the Pentagon, and in the State Department said "you will be back within a month . . . El Salvador is lost"'. But in May of the same year, a few weeks after the promulgation of the programme, only 2000 demonstrators rallied for the left in San Salvador and the FMLN's call for peasant support in the 'final offensive' in early 1981 went largely unanswered.[129] By 1986, the guerrillas' control over territory had shrunk from one-third to somewhere between one-eighth and one-tenth of the country and they were beginning to find it difficult to recruit. At the time of writing, there is no prospect of an early end to the civil war, but even the guerrillas acknowledge that they have no chance of taking power in the near future.[130]

III

Two assertions began this chapter and both have now been fully vindicated. First, the United States has undertaken intervention on behalf of reform on at least eight occasions since 1944. In many instances, it is true, the attempt at reform was combined with efforts to achieve a military victory over leftist insurgents. But one ought not to forget that in Greece, the Philippines and El Salvador the military solution was sought, as a result of pressure from the US, by means less abusive than the regimes would have used if left to themselves.

Second, reform has proven to be politically effective and in some circumstances it may have been indispensible. To summarise briefly, where US pressure or support made possible major changes at a propitious moment (Greece, the Philippines, Iran, Venezuela and El Salvador), the governments survived the immediate crisis; where reforms did not take place or came too late (China, Vietnam and the Dominican Republic), they eventually collapsed. A strong case can also be made that in Greece, the Philippines and El Salvador the introduction of the US-sponsored reforms marked the turning-point in the struggle and was the decisive factor in the ultimate outcome.

In no case but Venezuela, however, where the US role was minimal, has the entire agenda of the United States been enacted. In Greece and the Philippines the armed forces were transformed into effective fighting forces but most of the social reforms advocated by the United States were not put into effect and played little or no role in the defeat of the Communists. In Vietnam and Iran, conversely, the leaders carried out land reform but refused to act on the other issues (the army in Vietnam; liberalisation of the political system in Iran). More recently, abuses by the Salvadoran armed forces have been reduced but not eliminated and phase II of the original programme has not been carried out. In addition, the stability gained by partial reform was not lasting in Iran and the Philippines and neither the land reform nor the reduction in death squad activity has yet brought an end to the Salvadoran civil war. Finally, little reform of either sort was achieved in China and the Dominican Republic.

Thus, despite the demonstrable effectiveness of reform, US efforts to foster it have seldom achieved more than partial success, though in a number of situations partial success was enough. Let us conclude, then, by considering what obstacles have stood in the way.

In general, the greatest difficulties have not occurred at the first stage, where the US must prevail upon the government to adopt a reform programme. The United States was able to put reformers in positions of authority in Greece, the Philippines, Iran and the Dominican Republic and keep them there in the face of opposition in Venezuela and El Salvador. Even in the difficult cases of Nationalist China and Vietnam it can be argued that better results might have been attained if different tactics had been used to influence the government. The second stage, that of enactment and implementation, is the one that has proved to be the most difficult. It was there that conservative forces stymied reforms in Greece, the Philippines, Vietnam, the Dominican Republic and more recently in El Salvador. Four factors seem to be involved in determining whether the reformers are able to overcome opposition at either stage.

To begin with, the United States has not always stayed with
the reformist policy. This has occurred for many different reasons.
Roosevelt backed away from confrontation with Chiang Kai-shek on
the misguided counsel of Hurley. In the Dominican Republic, the
Kennedy administration actually delivered only one-sixth as much
economic aid to Juan Bosch as it had to the more conservative
transition government, but this was partly the fault of Bosch, who
stalled the United States for a time to demonstrate his independence.
By the time Bosch had become interested in American assistance,
Washington had grown impatient with his hypersensitive nationalism,
his unwillingness to support US initiatives in the hemisphere and
the administrative incompetence of his government.[131] The Truman
administration broke off the effort to trim the military budget in
Greece with the outbreak of the Korean war, concluding that
the increased international danger had made it impossible to cut
defence spending.[132] Finally, Magsaysay won the Presidency at the
beginning of the Eisenhower administration. The new administration
was apparently less interested in promoting land reform than its predecessor, for the Eisenhower officials made no visible effort to effect
the passage of Magsaysay's programme in the Philippine legislature.

But even if Washington were to persevere, serious difficulties
would remain. First, it is obvious, yet important, to note that the
chances of success for reformist intervention are strongly affected
by the quality of the leadership that the United States has to work
with in a given country. Men like Magsaysay and the Shah had the
courage and foresight to run short-term risks to build a better future,
while Chiang and Diem were unwilling to disrupt the networks of
corruption and favouritism that kept them in power, even though
that course was to prove lethal in the long run. After Diem's
removal, effective leadership never emerged in Vietnam; Thieu, the
most prominent of the successors, went forward with the Land to the
Tiller programme without US support but was no more willing to
risk reform of the army than his predecessors. Washington found an
able general, Papagos, to rally the Greek National Army, but could
not locate civilian leadership of the same calibre and after the failure
of Plastiras probably concluded that all Greek politicians were more
or less alike and that it made no sense to try to promote one over
another. The two Caribbean leaders, Betancourt and Bosch, faced
similar situations in the early sixties. Both were trying to implement
reform programmes while facing serious threats from the right. But
while Betancourt managed to reassure his potential opposition on

the right without yielding completely on matters of substance, Bosch frightened the rich of his country with his rhetoric without actually doing anything to improve the lot of the Dominican poor. The point, simply put, is that unless the United States is prepared to run these countries as virtual colonies, it is heavily dependent on the local leadership. Where effective local leadership is missing, reformist intervention may well falter.

The difficulties for a strategy of reformist intervention seem to multiply when one considers the compatibility of reform with other goals sought by the United States. Earlier studies of reform in the third world have arrived at the discouraging conclusion that it is difficult to put through far-reaching reform in a less developed country as long as the regime remains democratic.[133] That view, unfortunately, is corroborated by the cases reviewed here. In Greece, states William McNeill:

> The left-center politicians grouped around General Plastiras had no idea of governmental modernization *à l'Americain*. Rather, their assumption was the same as that of politicians of the right; that Greek society and economy should operate autonomously as usual; that is, manage public services in such a way as to reward friends and punish enemies, and thus create a network of clients who could vote them back into office when elections became necessary. . . . Radical restructuring of the Greek economy could not be carried through as long as the government administrative machine remained democratic, that is, responsive to special pressures and traditional values.[134]

In the Philippines, the landlord class was much better organised than the peasantry, leaving the President little chance to enact his programme in the absence of strong support from the Eisenhower administration; in the end, Magsaysay's programme died in the legislature. The Shah of Iran, on the other hand, closed down the *Majlis* on Amini's advice and put through his reform without opposition from the landlords. In El Salvador, the reforms were announced and partially enacted by a military dominated junta. When elections were held in 1982, at the insistence of the United States, they produced a legislature with a conservative majority that repealed part of the programme and interfered with the implementation of the rest.

Of the eight cases under study, only Venezuela was clearly successful in combining democracy and reform. Betancourt paid relatively generous compensation to the landlords while making the land available to the peasants for free. This cost $100 million, but Betancourt was able to accomplish it without a large increase in taxation because of the country's substantial oil wealth, a windfall seldom available in these situations.[135] The timing of Venezuela's land reform was also different from that in some of the other cases. Several years earlier, the right and many in the military would have lumped Betancourt together with the Communists. But after the beginning of the Communist insurgency in 1962, Betancourt could plausibly present himself as the only alternative to a Venezuelan Castro. The military and much of the right seemed to have accepted this argument, and that, combined with Betancourt's astute cultivation of the armed forces and the restraining hand of the United States, made it possible for Betancourt to put through the modest land reform that was more effective in defeating the Communists than even the best conceived counter-insurgency campaign.[136]

By contrast, the United States promoted reform in the Philippines and Greece after the left had been defeated and in the Dominican Republic before the left had become dangerous. The efforts failed in all three cases. What this suggests is that the privileged groups will be more willing to acquiesce in reforms that affect them adversely when the danger from the far left is great enough to make moderate changes acceptable as a lesser evil. This pressure from the left is greatest, of course, at a time when the far left stands some chance of taking power by violent means.

This logic suggests that the best time to undertake reformist intervention is when the regime is facing armed resistance from the left. But it may not be totally persuasive, for there is another consideration. The basic aim of American policy in all these cases has been to prevent the Communists from taking power. In the long run, reform is the best means of doing so, but in the meantime the US must rely on the armed forces to forestall a guerrilla victory. (Or, as Dean Rusk once put it, 'Vitamins will improve a man's health over a period of months, but they will not save his life if he is set upon by thugs in a dark alley.') When the United States is allied with a 'political' army or one that collaborates with the privileged classes to maintain the status quo, it may face the sort of dilemma already described above: if the US attempts to reform the army or compel them to acquiesce in social reforms they oppose they may resist, assuming that in the end the Americans will have no choice but to back down since the army's contribution is essential if the leftist rebels are to be defeated; if the US carries out the threat, the army may be decisively weakened; if not, they will continue along the well-worn path to defeat; and even if they agree to the reform, there is the risk that the attempt to restructure the army during wartime may reduce its effectiveness. It was this dilemma that lay behind the failure to induce Diem to reform in Vietnam and the hesitation of the Kennedy administration to purge the Dominican armed forces; and it is this same difficulty that has complicated the more recent efforts to restrain the Salvadoran army.

We are left, then, with two difficult questions. Is it possible to achieve democracy, military victory and reform in unstable countries all at the same time? If not, which ought to be sacrificed?

Notes

1. Certainly not all advice, however. For example, the early training of the South Vietnamese army, which stressed conventional tactics rather than counter-insurgency.
2. Roy Prosterman, 'IRI: A Simplified Predictive Index of Rural Instability', *Comparative Politics*, 8 (April 1976), pp. 339–53.
3. Samuel Huntington, *Political Order in Changing Societies* (New Haven: Yale University Press, 1968), p. 375; see also Hung-Chiao Tai, *Land Reform and Politics* (Berkeley: University of California Press, 1974), pp. 440–6.
4. Douglas Blaufarb, *The Counterinsurgency Era* (New York: Free Press, 1977), pp. 303–4.
5. This situation differs to some extent from the others discussed here in that foreign invasion, not domestic revolt, was the greatest danger to the government at the time, at least in the eyes of the Americans. I include it here because the problem the United States faced in China is analagous to the others, especially Vietnam, because of the great historical importance of the events and because of the significance of the outcome in this period for the civil war to come.
6. Theodore White and Analee Jacoby, *Thunder Out of China* (New York: William Sloane, 1961), pp. 139–40; Hsi-Sheng Ch'i, *Nationalist China at War* (Ann Arbor: University of Michigan Press, 1982), p. 97; Herbert Feis, *The China Tangle* (Princeton: Princeton University Press, 1953), pp. 37, 45–6, 60.
7. Paul Varg, *The Closing of the Door* (East Lansing: Michigan State University Press, 1973), pp. 66, 77; White and Jacoby, *Thunder Out of China*, pp. 129–30, 139–40; Ch'i, *Nationalist China at War*, pp. 87, 92–3, 98; Michael Schaller, *The United States Crusade in China* (New York: Columbia University Press, 1979), pp. 104–5.
8. Tang Tsou, *America's Failure in China* (Chicago: University of Chicago Press, 1963), pp. 75–7, 111–12, 376–7; Schaller, *US Crusade*, pp. 101, 104–6; Ch'i, *Nationalist China at War*, pp. 86, 99; Feis, *China Tangle*, pp. 46, 53–4.

9. Feis, *China Tangle*, pp. 60–5, 69, 168–9; Schaller, *US Crusade*, pp. 106–14, 121–5, 132–8; Varg, *Closing of Door*, pp. 54–5, 90–1; Tsou, *America's Failure*, pp. 78–85, 99–100, 107–8.
10. Ch'i, *Nationalist China at War*, p. 108; Schaller, *US Crusade*, pp. 147, 155–8, 163–6; Feis, *China Tangle*, pp. 133, 166.
11. Ch'i, *Nationalist China at War*, p. 109; Feis, *China Tangle*, pp. 171–3, 185, 190; Tsou, *America's Failure*, pp. 113–16; Schaller, *US Crusade*, pp. 164–5.
12. Tsou, *America's Failure*, pp. 116–17; Feis, *China Tangle*, pp. 189–92.
13. Tsou, *America's Failure*, p. 122.
14. Ch'i, *Nationalist China at War*, pp. 111–13; Feis, *China Tangle*, pp. 202–4; Tsou, *America's Failure*, pp. 86–7. Wedemeyer's hand was also strengthened by the increased flow of US aid to China in 1945.
15. Ch'i, *Nationalist China at War*, pp. 107–8; Schaller, *US Crusade*, pp. 105, 126; Feis, *China Tangle*, p. 171; Tsou, *America's Failure*, pp. 103–5.
16. Tsou, *America's Failure*, pp. 117–22. According to Tang Tsou, Chiang himself had said in 1937 that any Chinese government making peace with Japan on terms other than a return to the status quo *ante bellum* would have been 'swept out by the tide of public opinion'. If Chiang had chosen to break with the US, there were other military leaders—and not just the Communists—with whom Washington could have dealt (pp. 121–2).
17. Quoted in Joseph Jones, *The Fifteen Weeks* (New York: Viking, 1955), p. 271.
18. Richard Barnet, *Intervention and Revolution* (New York: New American Library, 1972), p. 132; John Iatrides, 'Civil War 1945–9: National and International Aspects', in John Iatrides (ed.), *Greece in the 1940s* (Hanover, New Hampshire: University Press of New England, 1981), p. 197.
19. Iatrides, 'Civil War', pp. 197–9; Edgar O'Ballance, *The Greek Civil War* (London: Faber, 1966), p. 218.
20. Lawrence Wittner, *American Intervention in Greece 1943–49* (New York: Columbia University Press, 1982), p. 115.
21. Wittner, *American Intervention in Greece*, p. 249.
22. Wittner, *American Intervention in Greece*, pp. 123–7; Iatrides, 'Civil War', pp. 213–14.
23. Stephan Rousseas, *The Death of a Democracy* (New York: Grove Press, 1967), pp. 93–4; Constantine Tsoucalas, *The Greek Tragedy* (Baltimore: Penguin, 1969), p. 121.
24. Robert Aura Smith, *Philippine Freedom* (New York: Columbia University Press, 1958), pp. 130–1, 137–8, 144–5; Beth Day, *The Philippines* (New York: B. M. Evans, distributed by Lippincott, 1974), pp. 129–33; Eduardo Lachira, *Huk: Philippine Agrarian Society in Revolt* (New York: Praeger, 1971), pp. 41–3; Robert Asprey, *War in the Shadows* (Garden City, New Jersey: Doubleday, 1975), pp. 144–5; Benedict Kervliet, *The Huk Rebellion: A Study of Peasant Revolt in the Philippines* (Berkeley: University of California Press, 1977), pp. 194–8, 204, 210, 218–19, 265.

25. R. A. Smith, *Philippine Freedom*, pp. 156–7; Frances Starner, *Magsaysay and the Philippine Peasantry* (Berkeley: University of California Press, 1961), p. 26.

26. R.A. Smith, *Philippine Freedom*, pp. 131–2; Stephen Shalom, *The United States and the Philippines* (Philadelphia: Institute for the Study of Human Issues, 1981), pp. 82–3.

27. Starner, *Magsaysay*, p. 138; Shalom, *US and the Philippines*, pp. 83–5; contradicted by Hernando Abaya, *The Untold Philippines Story* (Quezon City: Malaya Books, 1967), p. 63.

28. Shalom, *US and the Philippines*, pp. 89–92; Starner, *Magsaysay*, pp. 32–4; Abaya, *Untold Story*, p. 157.

29. Robert Shaplen, *The Lost Revolution* (New York: Harper & Row, 1965), p. 145; John Montgomery, *The Politics of Foreign Aid* (New York: Praeger, 1962), p. 124; Robert Scigliano, *South Vietnam: Nation under Stress* (Boston: Houghton Mifflin, 1964), p. 121.

30. George Kahin and John Lewis, *The United States in Vietnam* (New York: Dial Press, 1967), p. 70; Scigliano, *South Vietnam*, p. 212.

31. Frances Fitzgerald, *Fire in the Lake* (Boston: Little, Brown, 1972), pp. 87–90, 104–5; Shaplen, *Lost Revolution*, pp. 149, 157.

32. Kahin and Lewis, *US in Vietnam*, p. 131; Scigliano, *South Vietnam*, p. 185.

33. Chester Cooper, *The Lost Crusade* (Greenwich, Connecticutt: Fawcett, 1970), pp. 211–12, 225; Roger Hilsman, *To Move a Nation* (New York: Dell, 1967), p. 424; Stanley Karnow, *Vietnam: A History* (New York: Penguin, 1984), p. 251; Theodore Sorensen, *Kennedy* (New York: Harper & Row, 1965), pp. 655–7; Scigliano, *South Vietnam*, pp. 212–13; Shaplen, *Lost Revolution*, p. 154.

34. Quotation from David Halberstam, *The Making of a Quagmire* (New York: Random House, 1964), pp. 67–9; Kahin and Lewis, *US in Vietnam* pp. 139–40; Shaplen, *Lost Revolution*, pp. 154–5; Scigliano, *South Vietnam*, p. 213; Cooper, *Lost Crusade*, p. 225; Karnow, *Vietnam*, p. 213.

35. Theodore Sorensen, *Kennedy*, pp. 654–7; Karnow, *Vietnam*, pp. 263–4; Hilsman, *To Move a Nation*, 457; Halberstam, *Making of a Quagmire*, pp. 169–70, 208–9, 217–18.

36. Sorensen, *Kennedy*, pp. 657–9; Karnow, *Vietnam*, pp. 285–311.

37. Amin Saikal, *The Rise and Fall of the Shah* (Princeton: Princeton University Press, 1980), pp. 71–5.

38. Richard Cottam, *Nationalism in Iran* (Pittsburgh: Pittsburgh University Press, 1964), pp. 298–303; Saikal, *Rise and Fall of Shah*, pp. 75–6; 'Memo for Mr Komer from Kenneth Hansen', 7 May 1963 (from Declassified Documents Series, [79] 226A).

39. Tai, *Land Reform*, p. 53.

40. Edwin Lieuwen, *Generals and Presidents* (New York: Praeger, 1964), pp. 10–11, 115–17; Seyom Brown, *The Faces of Power* (New York: Columbia University Press, 1968), pp. 214–17.

41. See Juan de Onis and Jerome Levinson, *The Alliance that Lost its Way* (Chicago: Quadrangle Books, 1970). Venezuela will be discussed below, but not in this section.

42. Howard Wiarda, *Dictatorship, Development, and Disintegration: Politics and Social Change in the Dominican Republic* (Ann Arbor: Xerox University Microfilms, 1975), pp. 835–7; Larman Wilson and Pope Atkins, *The United States and the Trujillo Regime* (New Brunswick, New Jersey: Rutgers University Press, 1972), pp. 77–8, 85, 90–1, 121–3.

43. This was allegedly in May or June of 1960. Wiarda, *Dictatorship, Development, and Disintegration*, p. 837.

44. Wiarda, *Dictatorship, Development, and Disintegration*, pp. 157, 160, 163; National Security Files, Box 66 (John F. Kennedy Library, Boston Massachusetts), 'Memo from Rusk to Kennedy', 15 February 1961, p. 2; and 'Domestic Situation', 8 May 1961, pp. 4–6.

45. Atkins and Wilson, *US and Trujillo*, p. 120; Wiarda, *Dictatorship, Development, and Disintegration*, p. 837.

46. Wiarda, *Dictatorship, Development, and Disintegration*, p. 838.

47. Howard Wiarda, *Dictatorship and Development* (Gainesville, Florida: University of Florida Press, 1970), p. 170; John B. Martin, *Overtaken by Events* (New York: Doubleday, 1966), pp. 53–63; 'Texts of Alleged US Assassination Plots', *New York Times*, 21 November 1975.

48. Piero Gleijeses, *The Dominican Crisis* (Baltimore: Johns Hopkins University Press), pp. 305–7; 'Texts of Alleged US Assassination Plots', *New York Times*, 21 November 1975, p. 502–2.

49. Wiarda, *Dictatorship and Development*, p. 172; Martin, *Overtaken by Events*, pp. 53–63.

50. Jerome Slater, *Intervention and Negotiation* (New York: Harper & Row, 1970), pp. 294–7; Wiarda, *Dictatorship, Development, and Disintegration*, pp. 855–6; National Security Files, Box 66, 'Rusk Instructions to John Hill', 19 July 1961, p. 2.

51. Wiarda, *Dictatorship, Development, and Disintegration*, pp. 810–12, 857, 873; Gleijeses, *Dominican Crisis*, pp. 62–4.

52. National Security Files, Box 66, 'Memo to CIA Director', 19 March 1962, p. 10.

53. Tommie Sue Montgomery, *Revolution in El Salvador* (Boulder, Colorado: Westview Press, 1980), pp. 11–12, 19; William LeoGrande and Carla Robbins, 'Oligarchs and Officers', *Foreign Affairs*, 58 (Summer 1980), p. 1097; Tom Buckley, *Violent Neighbors* (New York: Times Books, 1984), pp. 94–5, 112–13.

54. Cynthia Arnson, *El Salvador: A Revolution Confronts the United States* (Washington: Institute for Policy Studies, 1982), pp. 43–7; Montgomery, *Revolution in El Salvador*, pp. 21–3, 163; LeoGrande and Robbins, 'Oligarchs and Officers', p. 1094.

55. Enrique Baloyra, *El Salvador in Transition* (Chapel Hill: University of North Carolina Press, 1982), p. 182; Jose Napoleon Duarte, with Diana Page, *Duarte: My Story* (New York: Putnam and Sons, 1986), pp. 107–13; Alan Riding, 'The US Role in El Salvador', *New York Times*, 13 March 1980; Alan Riding, 'Salvador Military Said to Block Effort by Junta to Impose Changes', *New York Times*, 22 February 1980.

56. Vietnam would probably have to be classified as a failure even though some reforms were enacted because the reforms under Diem were so

modest in relation to the problems the regime faced. Venezuela was also a success, but the US did not bring the reformer (Romulo Betancourt) to power, though, as will be explained below, did play a small role in keeping him there.

57. George Kousoulas, *Revolution and Defeat: The Story of the Greek Communist Party* (London: Oxford University Press, 1965), pp. 254–5; Wittner, *American Intervention in Greece*, pp. 113–14, 139–40, 169–80; Iatrides, 'Civil War 1945–9', p. 148. The quotation was from Kousoulas. Wittner, a left–wing critic of US foreign policy, argues that the United States acquiesced in many of the harsh measures undertaken by the Greek government. His book is informative despite his point of view, but on the human rights question it is important to remember three things Wittner either does not make clear or plays down: (1) the detentions carried out by the government in 1947, which resulted in the internment of over 36,000 by the end of July (Wittner, pp. 138–9), may have been ineffective as well as abusive, but those in 1949 destroyed the intelligence network of the Democratic Army and made a significant contribution to the government's victory (Edward Wainhouse, 'Guerrilla War in Greece', in Franklin Osanka [ed.], *Modern Guerrilla Warfare* [Glencoe, New York: Free Press, 1962], pp. 225–6); (2) the United States did bring pressure to bear on the government in the fall of 1948, earlier than Wittner notes, when the Truman administration threatened to cut off aid over the issue of the detentions (C. M. Woodhouse, *The Struggle for Greece* [London: Hart, Davis and MacGibbon, 1976], p. 245); and (3) the government's measures, though harsh, were not on the same scale as those of the Democratic Army. O'Ballance notes (*Greek Civil War*, p. 153) that the Greek government reported that the Democratic Army (DA) had killed about 45,000 civilians between October 1944 and September 1947, as opposed to 4000 members of the security forces, and he believes that the figures are 'broadly correct'. Wittner estimates (pp. 144–8) that the government executed 3136 persons, some of whom were conscientious objectors. He also says (pp. 140–2) that 20,000 of those detained were acquitted by the courts. Here, as is generally the rule, Dr Kirkpatrick's distinction between authoritarian and totalitarian movements holds up.

58. Wittner, *American Intervention in Greece*, pp. 242–3, 250. Iatrides, 'Civil War 1945–9', pp. 213–14; O'Ballance, *Greek Civil War*, p. 213; Wainhouse, 'Guerrilla War in Greece', pp. 221–2; Woodhouse, *Struggle for Greece*, pp. 236–8; Kousoulas, *Revolution and Defeat*, p. 265; and not least of all, Alexander Papagos, 'Guerrilla Warfare', in Franklin Osanka (ed.), *Modern Guerrilla Warfare* (Glencoe, New York: Free Press, 1962), p. 239. This account has stressed the importance of the Papagos appointment. There were other factors in the government's victory, and some accounts would place greater emphasis on them. First, the United States made available $353·6 million in military aid to Greece by the end of 1949, including hundreds of planes and thousands of artillery pieces. US aid also allowed the government to double the size of its forces, but by 1948 the problem was no longer

expanding the GNA but increasing its effectiveness. The armaments themselves probably came too late to be decisive (Woodhouse, p. 237; Wittner, p. 253; Kousoulas, p. 258; Iatrides, p. 216). Second, Tito closed the border between Yugoslavia and Greece in July, depriving the rebels of a staging ground outside the reach of the government. They were still free to use Albanian and Bulgarian soil, however, so this in itself could not have been the difference (Wittner, pp. 252; Woodhouse, pp. 276–7; O'Ballance, pp. 210, 218–19). Third, the Democratic Army unwisely changed to conventional tactics in 1949, thus exposing themselves to the superior firepower and manpower of the government. This was quite significant, but bear in mind that if the GNA had remained as ineffective as before (indeed, this is what Zakhariadis, their commander, expected), the gamble might have paid off (O'Ballance, pp. 212–13, 219–20; Woodhouse, pp. 276–7).

59. L. S. Stavrianos, *Greece: American Dilemma and Opportunity* (Chicago: Henry Regnery, 1952), pp. 217–19.

60. William McNeill, *Greece: American Aid in Action* (New York: Twentieth Century Fund, 1957), p. 63; Stavrianos, *Greece*, pp. 218–19.

61. Edward Lansdale, *In the Midst of Wars* (New York: Harper & Row, 1972), pp. 43–4; Blaufarb, *Counterinsurgency Era*, p. 29; Kerkvliet, *Huk Rebellion*, pp. 207–8, 238–41, 265–6.

62. Lansdale, *In the Midst of Wars*, pp. 47–57, 70ff; Blaufarb, *Counterinsurgency Era*, pp. 30–3; Kerkvliet, *Huk Rebellion*, p. 239.

63. Lansdale, *In the Midst of Wars*, pp. 28, 89–93; Blaufarb, *Counterinsurgency Era*, pp. 39–40; Kerkvliet, *Huk Rebellion*, p. 239.

64. Russell King, *Land Reform: A World Survey* (Boulder, Colorado: Westview Press, 1977), pp. 320–1; Tai, *Land Reform*, pp. 167–71.

65. Kahin and Lewis, *US in Vietnam*, p. 105; Scigliano, *South Vietnam*, pp. 122–3; Shaplen, *Lost Revolution*, p. 145.

66. Montgomery, *Politics of Foreign Aid*, p. 126.

67. Shaplen, *Lost Revolution*, pp. 146–7; Kahin and Lewis, *US in Vietnam*, p. 103.

68. Roy Prosterman, 'Land to the Tiller', *Asian Survey*, 10 (August 1970), pp. 756–8; Roy Prosterman, 'Land Reform and the El Salvador Crisis', *International Security*, vol. 6, no. 1 (Summer 1981), p. 58; Elizabeth Pond, 'Viet Land Reform Gathers Speed', *Christian Science Monitor*, 18 June 1969, p. 5.

69. Thomas Thayer, *War without Fronts: The American Experience in Vietnam* (Boulder, Colorado: Westview Press, 1985), pp. 74–5; Guenter Lewy, *America in Vietnam* (New York: Oxford University Press, 1978), p. 172; Sorensen, *Kennedy*, p. 653; Kahin and Lewis, US in Vietnam, pp. 331–2. 14 percent returned to military control after desertion.

70. Bruce Palmer, *The 25-Year War: America's Role in Vietnam* (New York: Simon & Schuster, 1984), pp. 56–7; Allen Goodman, 'Dynamics of the US—South Vietnamese Alliance: What Went Wrong', in Peter Braestrup (ed.), *Vietnam in History* (Washington, D.C.: University Press of America, 1984), p. 92; David Halberstam, *Making of a Quagmire*, pp. 140–1, 175.

71. Guenter Lewy, *America in Vietnam*, p. 178.

72. Fitzgerald, *Fire in the Lake*, pp. 311–12; Joseph Treaster, 'Paper Army', *Harpers*, 251 (July 1975), p. 63.
73. Quoted in Lewy, *America in Vietnam*, pp. 171, 178.
74. Thayer, *War without Fronts*, p. 75; Lewy, *America in Vietnam*, pp. 172–3.
75. Halberstam, *Making of a Quagmire*, pp. 59, 82, 146, 179, 182, 301–2.
76. Thayer, *War without Fronts*, pp. 67–9; Lewy, *America in Vietnam*, p. 217.
77. Fitzgerald, *Fire in the Lake*, p. 312.
78. Halberstam, *Making of a Quagmire*, pp. 139–40, 145–6.
79. Quotation from Palmer, *25-Year War*, p. 56; see also Thayer, *War without Fronts*, p. 62; Goodman, 'Dynamics of the US—South Vietnamese Alliance', p. 96; Lewy, *America in Vietnam*, pp. 170, 217.
80. Blaufarb, *Counterinsurgency Era*, p. 304.
81. Lewy, *America in Vietnam*, pp. 168–9; Thayer, *War without Fronts*, pp. 62–5 provides examples. General Palmer seems to agree but does not provide details: '[The United States] lacked adequate intelligence concerning South Vietnamese leaders and their activities' (*25-Year War*, p. 56).
82. Lewy, *America in Vietnam*, pp. 124, 170; Thayer, *War without Fronts*, pp. 69–70.
83. Thayer, *War without Fronts*, pp. 69–70.
84. Allen Goodman, *Politics in War* (Cambridge, Massachusetts: Harvard University Press, 1973), pp. 100–1.
85. Thayer, *War without Fronts*, pp. 61–3; Halberstam, *Making of a Quagmire*, p. 100.
86. Treaster, 'Paper Army', p. 64; Joseph Buttinger, *Vietnam: The Unforgettable Tragedy* (New York: Horizon Press, 1979), p. 148.
87. Arthur Schlesinger, *A Thousand Days* (Boston: Houghton Mifflin, 1965), p. 773; Wiarda, *Dictatorship, Development, and Disintegration*, p. 1460; Martin, *Overtaken by Events*, pp. 91–2; Dan Kurzman, *Santo Domingo: The Revolt of the Damned* (New York: Putnam, 1965), pp. 82–3.
88. Kurzman, *Santo Domingo*, pp. 88–9, 92–100; Martin, *Overtaken by Events*, pp. 456–8, 555–63; Wiarda, *Dictatorship, Development, and Disintegration*, pp. 1619, 1624. This is the most charitable interpretation. Some American officials thought Bosch had made a deal with the Communists permitting them to operate as long as there was no violence (National Security Files, Box 66, 'Memo for Bundy, from William Brubeck', 4 June 1963, p. 1).
89. Abraham Lowenthal, *The Dominican Intervention* (Cambridge, Massachusetts: Harvard University Press, 1972), p. 15; Martin, *Overtaken by Events*, pp. 568–72.
90. Martin, *Overtaken by Events*, pp. 114–19, 323; Atkins and Wilson, *US and Trujillo*, pp. 139–40; Gleijeses, *Dominican Crisis*, pp. 75–6, 104; National Security Files, Box 66, 'Briefing Paper for President Bosch's visit to the US', 2 January 1963, p. 8, and 'President Bosch and Internal Security in the Dominican Republic', 7 June 1963, points 11–13.
91. See especially Gleijeses, *Dominican Crisis*, p. 285.

92. The US did not send in the fleet, as had been done in earlier crises, but Bosch had stated his opposition to that step. Wiarda, *Dictatorship, Development, and Disintegration*, p. 886. Ambassador Martin was told that this would not be possible, though, for the reason that the show of force would be ineffective that late (Martin, *Overtaken by Events*, p. 570).

93. Lowenthal, *Dominican Intervention*, p. 16; Martin, *Overtaken by Events*, pp. 608, 615–16, 631; Wiarda, *Dictatorship, Development, and Disintegration*, pp. 888–9; Lieuwen, *Generals and Presidents*, p. 62; Edwin Lieuwen, *US Policy in Latin America* (New York: Praeger, 1965), p. 105.

94. By Gleijeses, *Dominican Crisis*, pp. 108–14, 285–6.

95. Quoted in Arthur Schlesinger, *Thousand Days*, p. 769.

96. Slater is especially critical of US policy, *Intervention and Revolution*, pp. 15–17; Lieuwen, *US Policy*, p. 105; Wiarda, *Dictatorship, Development, and Disintegration*, pp. 888–9.

97. Martin, *Overtaken by Events*, pp. 611–13, 629–31 and also Martin's cable in the National Security Files, Box 66, 11 June 1963, pp. 3, 7, 12. Also, earlier CIA reports were not alarmist about the strength of the Communists. National Security Files, Box 66, 'President Bosch and Internal Security in the Dominican Republic', points 3 and 17.

98. Robert Bond, 'Venezuela's Role in International Affairs', pp. 232–4; and Daniel Levine, 'Venezuelan Politics: Past and Future', both in Robert Bond (ed.), *Contemporary Venezuela* (New York: New York University Press, 1977); also Robert Alexander, The *Venezuelan Democratic Revolution* (New Brunswick, New Jersey: Rutgers University Press, 1964), pp. 5–6, 106–11, 115.

99. John Martz, *Accion Democratica: Evolution of a Modern Political Party in Venezuela* (Princeton: Princeton University Press, 1966), p. 113, 311–12; Levinson and de Onis, *Alliance that Lost its Way*, pp. 231–2; Alexander, *Venezuelan Democratic Revolution*, p. 183.

100. Charles Ameringer, 'The Foreign Policy of Venezuelan Democracy', in John Martz and David Myers (eds), Venezuela: *The Democratic Experience* (New York: Praeger, 1977), p. 342; John B. Martin, *US Policy in the Caribbean* (Boulder, Colorado: Westview Press, 1978), pp. 70–1; Alexander, *Venezuelan Democratic Revolution*, pp. 77–9.

101. Saikal, *Rise and Fall of Shah*, pp. 76–7; Richard Preece, 'US Policy toward Iran 1942–79' (Unpublished Manuscript), p. 67; 'Premier of Iran Warns Wealthy to Change Ways', *New York Times*, 9 November 1961; 'Reforms in Iran Stir Resistance', *New York Times*, 3 August 1961; 'Reformer Quits as Iran's Premier', *New York Times*, 19 July 1962; National Security Files, Box 340, 'The Iranian Situation', 10 April 1963, p. 17.

102. Marvin Zonis, *The Political Elite of Iran* (Princeton: Princeton University Press, 1971), p. 57; E. A. Bayne, *Persian Kingship in Transition* (New York: American Universities Field Staff, 1968), p. 192; Helmut Richards, 'America's Shah, Shahanshah's Iran', *MERIP Reports*, 40, p. 17; Saikal, *Rise and Fall of Shah*, pp. 76–7; Eric Hooglund, *Land and Revolution in Iran 1960–1980* (Austin: University of Texas Press, 1982), p. 46.

103. Cuyler Young, 'Iran in Continuing Crisis', *Foreign Affairs*, 40 (January 1962), pp. 287–8; Richards, 'America's Shah', p. 16.
104. Young, 'Iran in Continuing Crisis', pp. 287–9; Zonis, *Political Elite*, p. 59; Preece, 'US Policy toward Iran', pp. 68–9; Barry Rubin, *Paved with Good Intentions* (New York: Oxford University Press, 1980), p. 108; Cottam, *Nationalism in Iran*, p. 305.
105. Saikal, *Rise and Fall of Shah*, pp. 77–9; Zonis, *Political Elite*, pp. 73–4; Young, 'Iran in Continuing Crisis', pp. 285–6; Richards, 'America's Shah', p. 17.
106. Cottam, *Nationalism in Iran*, p. 308; Preece, 'US Policy toward Iran', p. 70; Hafez Farmayan, 'Politics during the Sixties' in Ehsan Yar-Shatar (ed.), *Iran Faces the Seventies* (New York: Praeger,1971), pp. 104–7.
107. Figure from Robert Graham, *The Illusion of Power* (New York: St Martin's, 1980), p. 69; Zonis puts the toll at 5–10,000, *Political Elite*, p. 63.
108. Hooglund, *Land and Revolution*, pp. 47, 98; Cottam, *Nationalism in Iran*, pp. 306–7; Richards, 'America's Shah', p. 16; the term 'political synthesis' is taken from 'Memo for Mr Komer' in National Security Files, Box 340, p. 1.
109. 'Proposed Approach to the Shah', National Security Files, Box 340, p. 2.
110. 'The Internal Political Situation in Iran', 11 February 1961, p. 6 (Declassified Documents series, [78] 80D); Preece, 'US Policy toward Iran', p. 69.
111. Zonis, *Political Elite*, pp. 73–5; Young, 'Iran in Continuing Crisis', pp. 285–6; Richards, 'America's Shah', p. 17.
112. 'The Internal Political Situation in Iran', p. 9.
113. Along the lines suggested by Huntington, *Political Order in Changing Societies*, chapter 6.
114. Hooglund, *Land and Revolution*, pp. 72–3, 141, 146–9; 'The Iranian Situation: A Special Intelligence Estimate', submitted by the Central Intelligence Agency, 10 April 1963, National Security Files, Box 340, pp. 2–3; Ann Lambton, 'Land Reform and the Rural Conservative System', in Ehsar Yar-Shatar (ed.), *Iran Faces the Seventies*, pp. 23–4; Russel King, *Land Reform: A World Survey*, pp. 408–10.
115. Hoogland, *Land and Revolution*, pp. 77–8, 99.
116. One qualification is necessary here. The land reform proceeded at a rapid pace for the first year. In January 1963, the Shah became more receptive to the pleas from the landlords, perhaps under Alam's influence. The next phase of the reform was less radical: it regulated the terms of tenancy rather than redistributing land. The transfers had raised expectations, however, and in the late sixties rural unrest led the Shah to pass a law requiring the sale of land to all tenants holding long-term leases. Implementation of the 1969 statute was less aggressive than that of the 1962 law, but still led to the large-scale transfers noted in the text (Hooglund, *Land and Revolution*, pp. 53–72).
117. John Powelson and Richard Stock, *The Peasant Betrayed: Agriculture and Land Reform in the Third World* (Boston: Oelgeschlager, Gunn,

and Hain, 1987), p. 68; Hooglund, *Land and Revolution*, pp. 79–81, 99.

118. Powelson and Stock, *Peasant Betrayed*, pp. 71–4, 76–7; Hooglund, *Land and Revolution*, pp. 46, 59–60, 106–11, 138.

119. Powelson and Stock, *Peasant Betrayed*, p. 75–6, quotation from p. 67. Also Hooglund, *Land and Revolution*, pp. 85–7.

120. Roy Prosterman and Jeffrey Riedinger, *Land Reform and Democratic Development* (Baltimore: Johns Hopkins University Press, 1987), pp. 151–7, 170; Powelson and Stock, *Peasant Betrayed*, pp. 230–3; Liisa North, *Bitter Grounds: Roots of Revolt in El Salvador* (Westport, Connecticutt: Lawrence Hill and Co., 1985), p. 85; Buckley, *Violent Neighbors*, pp. 116–19. Duarte explains his reservations about phase II in Duarte, pp. 164–6.

121. Montgomery, *Revolution in El Salvador*, p. 177; Lydia Chavez, 'El Salvador', *New York Times Magazine*, 11 December 1983, p. 77; 'El Salvador Factions Scramble for Reagan Attention', *Christian Science Monitor*, 29 December 1983.

122. Enrique Baloyra, *El Salvador in Transition*, pp. 139, 142; Enrique Baloyra, 'Political Change in El Salvador', *Current History*, 83 (February 1984), p. 55; Prosterman and Riedinger, *Land Reform and Democratic Development*, p. 163; North, *Bitter Grounds*, p. 106; Stock and Powelson, *Peasant Betrayed*, pp. 231–3; 'Salvador Land Reform Plowed under by Rightists', *Christian Science Monitor*, 18 October 1983; 'Critics Cast New Doubt on Reform in El Salvador', *Christian Science Monitor*, 6 February 1984; 'Salvador Land Reform in Trouble', *Christian Science Monitor*, 4 October 1983.

123. Raymond Bonner, *Weakness and Deceit* (New York: Times Books, 1984), pp. 221–2; Baloyra, *El Salvador in Transition*, pp. 114–16; Arnson, *El Salvador*, pp. 65–6; Robert Pastor, 'Winning Through Negotiations', *New Republic*, 26 (December 1982), pp. 14–16; Christopher Dickey, 'Behind the Death Squads', *New Republic*, 26 (December 1986) pp. 19–20.

124. Arnson, *El Salvador*, p. 77; Baloyra, *El Salvador in Transition*, pp. 123–4; Montgomery, *Revolution in El Salvador*, pp. 180, 184; Richard Meisler, 'El Salvador: The State of Seige Continues', *New York Times Magazine*, 20 February 1983, p. 38; Prosterman and Riedinger, *Land Reform and Democratic Development*, p. 159; Buckley, *Violent Neighbors*, p. 133.

125. Meisler, 'The State of Seige Continues', p. 39; Dickey, 'Behind the Death Squads', pp. 20–1; Chavez, 'El Salvador', p. 54; Baloyra, 'Political Change in El Salvador', pp. 55–7; 'Attacking the Death Squads', *Newsweek*, 16 January 1984, p. 27; 'Easing up on El Salvador', *Newsweek*, 13 February 1984, pp. 32–3; Bonner, *Weakness and Deceit*, p. 365; North, *Bitter Grounds*, pp. 108–11.

126. Bonner, *Weakness and Deceit*, p. 367 is particularly pessimistic. See also Christopher Dickey, quoted in North, *Bitter Grounds*, pp. 107–8, and Steffan Schmidt, *El Salvador: America's Next Vietnam?* (Salisbury, North Carolina: Documentary Publications, 1983), pp. 129–31.

127. 'Abuses by Both Sides Continuing in El Salvador', *New York Times*, 26 August 1986.
128. 'Land for Salvador's Poor to Many, Bitter Victory', *New York Times*, 28 September 1987, p. 1; Prosterman and Riedinger, *Land Reform and Democratic Development*, pp. 157, 170.
129. Prosterman and Riedinger, *Land Reform and Democratic Development*, pp. 147–8, 157; Duarte, *Duarte*, pp. 162–3.
130. 'After Parades and Promises, Duarte Flounders', *New York Times*, 16 February 1987; 'Salvador Rebels Learn to Dodge Bullets', *New York Times*, 5 January 1986. An alternative explanation for the limited success would be that large amounts of US aid in a small country have made a military solution possible. By early 1987 the US had given a total of $2.5 billion in assistance to El Salvador. In military aid alone (see'Parades and Promises' above), the US provided $35.5 million in 1981, $81 million in 1982 and again in 1983, and $196 million in 1984. The Salvadoran army quadrupled in size, but apparently had not become more professional as of 1984. Morale and discipline remained unimpressive: the army contined to rely on large-scale manoeuvers, eschewed night fighting and took the weekends off (Buckley, *Violent Neighbors*, p. 299; North, *Bitter Grounds*, p. 116).
131. Kurzman, *Santo Domingo*, pp. 80, 84–5.
132. Stavrianos, *Greece*, pp. 218–19.
133. See Tai, *Land Reform*, pp. 472ff, 496; Huntington, *Political Order in Changing Societies*, pp. 388ff.
134. William McNeill, *The Metamorphosis of Modern Greece* (Chicago: University of Chicago Press, 1978), pp. 94–6.
135. Levinson and de Onis, *Alliance that Lost its Way*, pp. 231–3.
136. Levine, 'Venezuelan Politics', pp. 13, 19–20; Alexander, *Venezuelan Democratic Revolution*, pp. 116–17, 122–3.

2 The Perils of Liberalisation

'The most perilous time for a bad government is when it seeks to mend its ways.'

—Alexis de Tocqueville[1]

The Carter administration's human rights policy had a number of successes to its credit, of which the administration and the American public can be justly proud. But there was another side to the policy, which no evaluation can neglect. On two occasions, the liberalisation programmes pressed on friendly authoritarian governments by the United States ran out of control, leading to their overthrow and replacement by regimes hostile to the US and even less solicitous about the human rights of their peoples.

The experience of the Carter years raises a crucial question for the proponents of a human rights policy: can a dictatorial regime loosen its grip over the population without losing control? I intend to explore that question here by examining four attempts by autocratic governments to liberalise, two of which succeeded and two of which did not. 'Success', in this context, can mean different things to different people. The leaders of these four regimes may have differed in their ultimate aims and their determination to stay in power, but none of them had any intention of stepping down in the near future. In each case, liberalisation was undertaken to stabilise authoritarian rule by making it less burdensome for the public and was not originally intended to evolve into full democratisation.[2] If democracy is the end result of the changes initiated by authoritarian leaders, as it was in one of the cases to be examined here, liberalisation cannot exactly be called a 'success' from the regime's perspective, though such an outcome would be even better than a limited liberalisation from the American viewpoint. But what both the US and the regime's rulers want to avoid above all else is a deterioration of the liberalisation process into bloody revolution, leading to a victory of the most extreme elements of the opposition. Hence, I will define as a success any serious liberalisation that does lead to violent upheaval of this sort, whether it leads all the way to democracy or not.[3]

The first case to consider is Franco's Spain. At the height of the repression after the civil war, some 270,000 opponents of the Nationalists were held in prison camps. The Civil Guard placed machine-guns at important crossroads and pairs of armed Guardsmen patrolled the highways, while the army remained garrisoned outside major cities. Spain, in the words of one historian, 'resembled a conquered land'.[4] Beginning in 1945, Franco permitted a gradual amelioration of conditions over the next fifteen years. The Civil Guard's visibility throughout the countryside was reduced and amnesties were announced on nine occasions. A large number of exiles returned home, and by the sixties the number of political prisoners had fallen to between 500 and 1500.[5] In its formative period in the late thirties, the regime had banned all political parties except the official *Falange Espanol Tradicionalista y de las JONS* as well as independent trade unions. (The workers, in theory, received representation in the corporatist syndicates set up for each industry.) In the fifties and sixties, Franco relaxed the strict controls over labour and allowed moderate opposition groups to carry on a few activities without hindrance, though strict limits on the freedom of public assembly remained in force.[6] Finally, the Minister of Information eliminated prior censorship of printed materials in 1966. The Spanish media reacted cautiously at first, but by the seventies opposition views were widely reported and even Marxist literature was freely available in bookstores.[7] In short, Franco succeeded in gradually easing his controls on Spanish life over a span of nearly thirty years without endangering his regime. In this sense the policy was successful, though it apparently did not win the loyalty of the public, for Franco's regime died with him.

Liberalisation was also attempted in Communist Hungary in the fifties. Here the Stalinist period was perhaps the grimmest in all of Eastern Europe. It came to an abrupt end in 1953 when the death of Stalin brought a collective leadership to power in Moscow that sought to relieve some of the miseries the dictator had caused in their own country, and then imposed the changes on their satellites as well. In Hungary, the Soviet leaders forced Matyas Rakosi to step aside and let Imre Nagy modify the Stalinist system Rakosi had erected. Nagy released the Communist political prisoners, permitted peasants to withdraw from collective farms and attempted to upgrade living standards. Then, early in 1955, the balance of political forces shifted in the Kremlin and Rakosi was put back in control, but prevented by his sponsors from utilising the harsh methods to which he was accustomed. Neither Rakosi nor his successor, Erno Gero, was able to break the revolutionary momentum that built up in Hungary in 1956 and the Russians were forced to intervene in the summer of that year to save the situation. Hungary, of course, we would have to categorise as a complete failure.[8]

The third case is the Shah of Iran's ill-fated liberalisation of the late seventies. The Shah proceeded on two tracks. The first was an expansion of political participation through the creation of a new political party, the *Rastakhiz* ('Resurgence' party), in 1975. Previously, effective participation had been limited to a small circle of 3–400. Though the Resurgence party made no effort to attract opposition elements, it did manage to recruit some 5–6 million members in 2 years. The second track was a relaxation of controls over freedoms of press, assembly and expression in 1977, which had the immediate effect of stimulating the opposition to action. For reasons we shall discuss below, the Shah was unable to control or co-opt this opposition, which expanded and radicalised, developing into a full-fledged revolutionary movement by 1978.[9]

Finally, there is Brazil, which can now be classified as a success. Brazil's liberalisation was begun by General Ernesto Geisel in 1974 under the label *distensao*, or 'decompression'. Geisel's first step was to permit an opposition party, the Brazilian Democratic Movement, to compete in congressional elections in that year, and the MDB did surprisingly well. In 1975, Geisel dismissed a general for abuses that had taken place under his command, and made considerable progress in curbing violations of human rights. After a temporary reversal in 1977, Geisel began to dismantle the legislative underpinnings of the military dictatorship, the Institutional Acts, in 1978. General Joao Baptista Figueiredo succeeded Geisel in January of the next year and continued the policy of gradual liberalisation. By 1980, the last of the political prisoners had been freed; direct municipal, congressional and gubernatorial elections were held in 1982; and finally, in 1985, Brazil's Electoral College ended the period of military rule when it chose a member of the opposition party as President.[10]

Thus, among these four cases we see two relatively successful liberalisations, Brazil and Spain, and two that ended in disaster, Hungary and Iran. What explains the difference? At least five factors come to mind: the nature of the opposition; the regime's past, that is, the evils it has committed; the state of the economy as liberalisation takes place; the role played by outside powers in the process; and finally, the tactics used by the regime. I propose to take these up in turn.

The first factor to take into account is the sort of opposition the regime faces. From the government's standpoint, liberalisation would probably be easiest if the opposition were weak and moderate, and most difficult if it were strong and radical. ('Moderate' here would imply that the opposition would be willing to settle for modest improvements, more willing to wait for the government to proceed to see what will develop and less likely to resort to violence.) Any number of things could affect the disposition of the regime's opponents, but two would seem to be especially important. One would be the personal qualities of the opposition's leadership. Some men would be inclined, for personal reasons, to seek confrontation with the government, others to seek accommodation. One obvious case in point would be the Ayatollah Khomeini, who lost a son in what he assumed was an assassination sponsored by the National Security and Information Organisation (SAVAK), and later stubbornly opposed any suggestion of compromise with the Shah during the revolution. In addition, the leaders of some oppositions are able to overcome the differences between themselves, or at least paper them over for the time being, while others cannot stop quarrelling and thereby reduce their effectiveness. The Spanish exiles, for example, were not able to overcome the divisions between Communists and non-Communists in the early years and failed to form a government in exile, which would have improved their chances of attracting foreign assistance considerably, and the clash between the Communists and non-Communists (as well as other divisions) continued to bedevil the Spanish opposition's efforts later.[11]

The country's political culture probably also influences the mood of the opposition in an important way. Various observers have speculated that Iranians may still be influenced to an important extent by their Zoroastrian beginnings. It is possible that the Manichean belief in extremes of good and evil has made it difficult for Persians to conceive of their opponents in less than satanic terms, and thus made compromise difficult. The political culture of Brazil appears to be quite different, both among political elites and the masses. Brazilian elites have long prided themselves on their pragmatism and adaptability, so much so that the word 'Machiavellian' is not necessarily pejorative in Brazil, and Brazilians of the lower class emerged from one recent study as remarkably patient and longsuffering. The urban slum dwellers interviewed by Janice Perlman in the early seventies credited the government with the intention of 'doing its best to understand and help people like themselves' and seemed to possess 'the aspirations of a bourgeoisie, the perseverance of pioneers, and the values of patriots'. If this is so, one would expect liberalisation to go more smoothly in Brazil than Iran, other things being equal.[12]

To some extent, then, the prospects for political decompression are affected by accidents of personality and political culture that are beyond the control of the liberalising leaders. But the opposition to autocratic governments does not evolve in a vacuum. The next question we must ask, then, is to what extent the actions of the regime, both in the past and as liberalisation is underway, shape the sort of opposition that it has to deal with.[13]

Let us consider first the question of how bad the dictatorship was at its height and what effect this may have later. In both Spain and Hungary, repression took place on a massive scale. As I mentioned above, the victors in the Spanish civil war placed about 270,000 Republicans in prison camps by 1940. Many of the prisoners died of disease or malnutrition, and of those released, some 140,000 were assigned the status of 'conditional liberty', a kind of political parole that strictly circumscribed opposition activity.[14] But the victors in the civil war were not content merely to jail the defeated. Exactly how many victims the repression eventually claimed is still a matter of dispute. The most conservative estimate is that of Ramon Salas Larrazabal, who states that 16,763 were shot in 1939 and 1940. Others have maintained that as many as 200,000 may have died as a result of the Nationalist repression after the civil war, in addition to the 200,000 executed during the conflict.[15]

In Rakosi's Hungary, the situation was equally grim. The regime's determination to expand industry at all costs led to a fall of living standards of 15–20 per cent, as well as chronic shortages in urban areas. Nearly one-third of the farms were collectivised by 1953, precipitating a decline in food production which, along with the forced requisitions, created conditions of near starvation in the countryside. Rakosi's rule was buttressed, as elsewhere, by secret police terror. His State Security Authority (AVH) not only employed 100,000 policemen directly, but also created a vast network of informers and spies. (According to captured documents, the AVH's files contained information on at least one million Hungarians, one-tenth of the country's population.) Between 150 and 200,000 people were held in forced labour camps at the nadir of the repression in the early fifties. It is thought that about 2000 victims were shot immediately; many more must have died under torture or in the camps, but the exact number is not known. As in the USSR, purges were employed against the Communist party itself. Rakosi purged 200,000 members of the Hungarian party, the most famous of whom was the former Interior Minister, Laszlo Rajk. Rajk was arrested in 1949 and put through a show trial reminiscent of Stalin's productions of the 1930s in which fabricated evidence was introduced linking the victim to a plot with 'foreign imperialists' to restore capitalism in Hungary. Rajk and some others were hanged on 15 October 1949 and a reign of terror against much of the Hungarian party followed.[16]

The Shah of Iran's regime was somewhat less brutal than these, but still relied heavily on the mailed fist. Amnesty International reported in the mid-seventies that the Shah held between 25,000 and 100,000 political prisoners. Torture was practised 'routinely' during interrogation and political enemies were also executed frequently. (Amnesty knew of 15 in the first two months of 1976.) Further, the repression was directed even at non-violent opposition.[17] In particular, the regime had turned its attention toward the clergy in the early seventies. In the years that followed, the secret police infiltrated mosque meetings, the clergy's lands were expropriated, and mullahs were arrested, imprisoned and even executed 'regularly', according to Iran specialist James Bill. This intensification of repression, Bill has concluded, gave Iran's Shi'ite clergy little choice but to fight back to ensure their survival.[18]

Brazil is clearly the mildest dictatorship of the four. The 'Institutional Acts' declared by the military in the early years of their rule allowed the government to suspend the political rights of men they considered dangerous and dismiss elected officials without replacing them. In all 1577 Brazilians were punished in this way, including 6 Senators and 110 Deputies, which reduced the Congress to a rubber stamp by 1970. Like many of her neighbours, Brazil faced a growing threat from urban terrorists at this time, and the military dealt with it successfully by making a pre-emptive sweep in November 1970 in which 5000 to 10,000 suspects were arrested. The number of 'disappeared', however, was much less than elsewhere—35 in 1971, 9 in 1975 and none afterward. Also, it should be noted that the foundations of the 'economic miracle' of the later sixties were laid by an austerity policy that reduced the minimum wage by 20 per cent in real terms in the mid-sixties and sharply increased the inequality of income.[19]

What, then, is the relationship between a regime's past and its prospects for liberalisation? It would certainly be plausible to assume that the worse the degree of repression, the more difficulty a government would have in letting up. But this seems not to be the case. Liberalisation failed in an extremely harsh dictatorship, Hungary, but succeeded to some extent in Spain, which was scarcely any better. Liberalisation worked best in the mildest dictatorship, Brazil, but broke down in Iran where the abuses were not as great as in Hungary or Spain. The relationship is evidently more complicated than one would imagine.

A partial answer is provided by Machiavelli:

> one ought to be both feared and loved, but as it is difficult for the two to go together, it is much safer to be feared than loved, if one of the two has to be wanting.[20]

Brutality practised on the scale of a Rakosi or a Franco obviously creates hatred for the perpetrators, but it also creates fear. From the perspective of the tyrant, things may go reasonably well as long as the fear is greater than the hatred, and we can be quite certain that the peoples of Spain and Hungary were in no hurry to repeat the experiences of the civil war and Stalinism. Writers on Spain have stressed that the most important explanation of the stability of the fifties under Franco was the desire of most of the Spanish to avoid another civil war. Franco did not enjoy enthusiastic support at this time by any means, but the public mood was more one of apathy than seething discontent.[21] In Hungary, most scholars, though sympathetic to the 1956 revolution, admit that there was little evidence of popular discontent until quite soon before the revolution's outbreak.[22]

In other words, large-scale terror may create political stability by cowing the public for some time to come. It may also stabilise the situation by eliminating the potential leadership of the opposition. Franco's terror of the forties drove many of the surviving opposition leaders into exile, where they never managed to overcome their divisions. The repression that continued at home was extremely effective—in 1953 the entire leadership of the Socialist underground was arrested—and the opposition never regained a firm toehold within Spain.[23] The Shah, on the other hand, harassed the Shi'ite clergy throughout the seventies, but never eliminated the mosque network. The mosques remained, as one opposition leader recalled, 'sanctuaries where we met, talked, prepared, organised, and grew'.[24]

Whatever the Shah's intentions, Iran never became a totalitarian society. This brings to mind another admonition from Machiavelli:

> [enemies] . . . must either be destroyed, or conciliated by benefits. Any other course will be useless; and above all, half measures should be avoided, these being most dangerous, as proved by the Samnites, who, when they hemmed the Romans in between the Caudine forks, disregarded the advice of an old man, who counselled them either to let the Romans depart honorably, or to kill them all. And by taking the middle course of disarming them and obliging them to pass under a yoke, they let them depart with shame and rage in their hearts.[25]

The regime's past is important in one other respect. The ruler or rulers may inherit what we might call 'skeletons in the closet', that is, acts of which the public is unaware, which could be extremely damaging if they were to become known. This is a situation where de Tocqueville's dictum applies with particular urgency—in a creditable effort to make amends and serve justice, a government might unintentionally deal itself a mortal blow. In Hungary, Imre Nagy got Moscow's permission to release the remaining Communist political prisoners (though thousands of non-Communists still languished in jail). This was perhaps the most important single precipitant of the revolution. The tales told by those released evoked a strong sense of shame among the many Hungarian intellectuals who had previously lent their services to the government in writing apologies for Rakosi's brutality. The intellectuals became the strongest defenders of Nagy's 'New Course' and the focus of the opposition once Rakosi returned to power. In addition, Moscow inadvertently created even greater problems for Rakosi later in forcing him to admit publicly that Rajk had been framed.[26]

One solution to this problem, other than continuing to keep the skeleton in the closet, is to satisfy the public's demand for justice by conspicuously punishing someone who can be held accountable for the past abuses. Machiavelli gives a cynical account of this strategy in chapter 7 of *The Prince*, where he describes how Remirro de Orco was made to serve as a fall guy for Cesare Borgia. On this point, though, Machiavelli is less convincing. The Shah hoped to appease the public in 1978 by sacrificing General Nassiri, the head of SAVAK, but the tactic backfired, demoralising the Shah's supporters more than it satisfied the public. The reasons are not far to seek—Iranians held the Shah, not Nassiri, responsible for what had happened. If a man is to play the role of fall guy, the deception must be more convincing.[27] On the other hand, situations where a change of personnel takes place within a regime are at least potentially manageable. If the Russians, for example, had demanded that Nagy give Rakosi a punishment of appropriate severity, they might have been forestalled by the Hungarian revolution.[28]

The third general factor which might explain the success or failure of liberalisation is the state of the economy. Again, there is an obvious and plausible hypothesis: liberalisation is more likely to go smoothly during a time of prosperity. The experience of Spain lends some support to this notion. The Spanish economy did not recover from the ravages of the civil war in the forties, and much of the population continued to live at a subsistence level. Production remained only 70 per cent of what it had been in the republic. The vivid memories of the civil war and fear of Franco's security forces kept the lid on for many years, but opposition finally broke out in 1951 when a general strike in Barcelona triggered a wave of protest elsewhere. Luckily for the regime, the economy began improving the next year and Spain enjoyed prosperity for the rest of the decade. Most scholars think that the favourable economic climate had much to do with the apathetic mood of Spain in the fifties, and may have given the regime the confidence to undertake the liberalisation measures mentioned above in the mid-sixties.[29]

Prosperity has two possible disadvantages, however. The first is that it brings tight labour markets that may tempt labour to take advantage of its increased leverage to wring more from management by the use of strikes. Franco did face some trouble temporarily in the mid-fifties when workers in a number of cities braved the regime's prohibition on strikes. That crisis was defused by the granting of enormous wage increases that lead to serious inflation by the late fifties. The government arrested the inflation by imposing a stiff austerity programme in 1959, laying the foundation for a sustained boom that lasted till the early seventies. In the next decade, industrial production tripled and GDP per capita rose from $300 to $2446 (1957–1974). Once again, prosperity increased the militance of the Spanish working class. Strikes for economic motives were eventually legalised, and in the seventies Spain became one of the five most strike-prone nations in Europe (measured in days lost), ranking along with Britain and Italy.[30]

It could be argued, however, that the increase in striking posed no threat to the regime and in fact may have helped stabilise it. Most of the strikes concerned economic or labour questions such as wages, working conditions, benefits or the election of union officials. Few of them were directed toward broader political issues and the workers remained largely apathetic about politics. (A poll conducted in 1973 found that only 12 per cent of them could be classified as 'very interested' in politics.) The apathetic mood of the Spanish workers was a severe handicap to opposition organisers.[31]

The second danger of prosperity is one identified first by de Tocqueville and restated more recently by James Davies.[32] The risk is that good times will generate rising expectations, creating great danger for the regime should the economy fail temporarily. According to this 'J-curve' theory, those countries suffering an economic decline after a prolonged period of prosperity will be the most vulnerable to revolution.

Iran would seem to fit the theory. The Shah's liberalisation came at a time when Iran's oil boom was ending and his efforts to stem inflation were creating unemployment among the urban masses and resentment among the bazaar, or traditional merchant class. But Generals Geisel and Figueiredo carried out their decompression after the Brazilian economic miracle had failed and the economy was running into its now infamous debt problems, though Geisel may have eased his difficulties to some extent by coupling liberalisation with efforts to improve the lot of Brazil's poor. In Spain, as we noted, the general prosperity the country enjoyed was interrupted on two occasions, when the regime imposed an austerity programme in 1959 and during the recession of 1967. Both these downturns were preceded by some steps at liberalisation, yet in neither case did the liberalisation run into serious difficulties. In Hungary, Nagy raised standards of living some 15 per cent by slowing the pace of industrialisation and allowing peasants to leave the collectives. When Rakosi returned, he was not permitted by his Soviet sponsors to shift course completely, and things remained better than they had been during Rakosi's first tenure in office.[33]

The J-curve theory may be the best general explanation of the relationship between the state of the economy and political stability, but it seems to be a relatively poor predictor of the fate of liberalisation. Overall, the effects of the economic situation on liberalisation have been uneven and less important than one might have guessed. Uninterrupted prosperity is probably preferable to anything else, but improved economic conditions did not save the situation in

Hungary and the worsening conditions did not prevent the Brazilian decompression from succeeding.

A fourth possible explanation, and, as it turns out, an important one, is the role played by outside powers in the liberalisation. The two most successful cases, Brazil and Spain, are instances where liberalisation proceeded with relatively little outside interference; in Hungary and Iran, outside powers played a significant role in the events, to their regret later.[34]

Outside powers may affect the course of liberalisation in two ways. They may alter the expectations of the public about what the government will tolerate, or they may constrain the government, either actively or unintentionally, and thus weaken its ability to deal with growing opposition. The Soviets in Hungary and the Americans in Iran produced both effects.

One of the turning-points in Hungary was Khrushchev's 'secret speech' in which he condemned Stalin's purges on the grounds that they had weakened the Soviet Communist Party. Prior to the speech, Hungarian intellectuals had hesitated to attack Rakosi for fear of being branded 'anti-party'. The speech was interpreted in Hungary as a green light to speak freely about the abuses that had taken place under Hungary's version of Stalinism, and criticism intensified in 1956 to the point where one writer was likening Rakosi to Judas and the noted Marxist philosopher Lukács was speaking of the 'bankruptcy' of Hungarian Marxism.[35]

By this time, the intellectuals were beginning to attract a popular following and Rakosi was becoming concerned. The one virtue of liberalisation from the tyrant's perspective, as Mao showed in the 'Hundred Flowers campaign', is that it encourages one's enemies to make themselves visible. In late June, Rakosi drew up an enemies list of 400 names and proposed that they be arrested as soon as possible. But on 17 July, Anastas Mikoyan arrived in Budapest and bid Rakosi step down. Rakosi's successor, Gero, made a few concessions and did not deliver the crushing blow Rakosi had planned, presumably because of the Russian's objections. In the view of Paul Kecskemeti, Rakosi probably could have broken the revolutionary momentum if he had been allowed to work his will. In staying his hand the Russians created a crisis which only the Red Army could resolve to their satisfaction.[36]

Shaul Bakhash has reminded us that, notwithstanding the polemics of certain critics of the Carter administration, the Shah, not Jimmy Carter, lost Iran.[37] Bakhash is right, for reasons I will discuss later, but the American role was still significant, if less important than the Soviet role in Hungary. First, the Carter human rights policies did encourage the Shah's opposition. For evidence on this point we need only consult the opposition members themselves. As Mehdi Bazargan, the puppet head of Khomeini's first government, has said, '[the revolution] was the result of 25 years of cruelty, oppression, and corruption. We did not believe the Shah when he started the liberalisation policy, but when Carter's human rights drive lifted the hope of the people, all the built up pressure exploded.' Karim Sanjabi, a veteran National Front leader, told a journalist that 'President Carter's words on human rights were what originally raised the people's hopes and gave them courage to defy the dictatorship.' Richard Falk, a vocal critic of American foreign policy, reports that he was told on a visit to Iran that the religious opposition was also emboldened by the human rights policy.[38]

The effects of President Carter's policy on the Shah are somewhat more difficult to gauge. According to one account, the Shah is said to have complained during the crisis in 1978 that 'the Americans will not give me a free hand to settle this crisis in my own way', and in his memoirs suggests that the United States 'wanted me out' after a point.[39] On the basis of such statements, some critics of the Carter administration have contended that the United States demoralised the Shah and prevented him from taking firm action to contain his opposition. On the other hand, former government officials have pointed out that President Carter praised the Shah effusively during his January 1978 visit to Iran and made declarations of support so frequently during the revolution that the Shah actually requested Washington to ease up at one juncture.[40] I will not attempt to resolve this dispute here. My own view is that Ambassador William Sullivan's inability to confirm the statements of support from Washington (because he had no clear instructions to do so) probably did shake the Shah's confidence, but it is also true that the Shah undertook liberalisation largely on his own initiative, without a clear roadmap and without the willingness he had shown in 1963 to shed blood to save his throne. As Sullivan has explained, the Shah's illness not only reduced his effectiveness as an executive, but also increased his inhibitions about the use of force. Facing death, the Shah did not want to be remembered as a sanguinary tyrant and did not use force as freely as he had in 1963, when an estimated 1000 supporters of Khomeini died in an unsuccessful revolt.[41]

One effect of the human rights policy is indisputable, however. The Human Rights Bureau in the State Department embargoed riot control equipment to Iran for several months in 1978, and the equipment was missed. The Japanese Ambassador remarked during the crisis that 'the Tokyo riot squad could handle any disturbance in this country with their duty squad'. Lacking such equipment and training, the Shah's forces had a choice between firing on the demonstrators or firing over their heads.[42]

Particularly in the case of Hungary, the influence of foreign powers is related to the last, and most important, factor—the tactics adopted by the rulers. Liberalisation creates at least three dangers for the government: (1) the slackening of controls may allow the opposition to operate more effectively; (2) the people may begin to anticipate further change at a faster rate than the regime can deliver it or set higher standards for the government; and (3) the public and the opposition may lose their fear of the regime and risk acts of defiance that would have been considered too dangerous before. The fundamental dilemma faced by liberalising autocrats is how to hold these dangers in check without damaging the credibility of liberalisation. If the regime is too cautious, the people may become cynical about the prospects for improvement; if the regime loosens the reins too quickly, the process may run out of control. The ability of the government to cope with this dilemma is the key to the success or failure of liberalisation.

These dangers are all too apparent in the cases discussed here. In Hungary, as we have seen, de-Stalinisation led to the alienation of most of the intellectuals, who became the cutting edge of the revolution. In the view of one American official in Teheran, the changes introduced by the Shah 'led to the rebirth of the revolutionary movement'. Far from appeasing the opposition, 'increased political leeway encouraged [them] to press for even more'.[43] In Brazil, General Geisel was rewarded for his willingness to permit an opposition to run in the 1974 Congressional elections with a defeat for the governing party.[44] Liberalisation, then, often leads to a strengthening of the opposition, at least in the short run. If liberalisation is to continue, the government will have to develop some strategy for dealing with this.

Franco's solution was to permit significant liberalisation in some aspects of Spanish life but not in others and, in general, to err on the side of caution. Specifically, controls were lifted on the press and unions, but the opposition was not permitted to operate freely until the seventies. Originally, the Falangists had hoped to overcome class struggle by creating syndicates where representatives of labour and management would meet to achieve both justice and productivity. Labour gave up the right to strike or organise independent unions under the plan, but was to be compensated by restrictions on management's rights of dismissal. The Labour Ministry saw that the workers' interests were not ignored totally, but in practice the denial of the right to strike and the system of indirect elections meant that the system functioned more as a means of control than of representation for the workers and did not win their confidence.[45] In the late fifties, two changes were made. Larger numbers of *enlaces*, the representatives directly elected by the workers, were created and a form of collective bargaining was introduced at the local level. In the mid-sixties, the *enlaces* were instrumental in forming the independent Workers' Commissions that provided the leadership for the resumption of strike activity. The government declared the Commissions illegal and arrested the leaders, but was unwilling or unable to suppress them, and ended up with a great increase in the number of strikes. As I argued above, however, this may not have been an entirely bad thing from the regime's perspective, since the Commissions' efforts went mostly into economic, not political protests.[46]

Franco tried harder and was more successful in preventing the growth of overtly political opposition. *FET y de las JONS* continued to be the country's only legal political organisation, and the ban on competing parties was enforced. However, the regime permitted opposition moderates to conduct political discussions in their homes, travel inside and outside the country, and publish abroad and eventually at home as well. Thus, the moderates came to enjoy a sort of twilight existence Juan Linz has characterised as 'alegal'. Far from endangering the regime, the limited toleration afforded the alegal opposition, in Linz's view, actually helped undercut their support. As he put it in 1973:

> Their freedom permits their activity to be visible to the government but not necessarily to any large constituency, and this allows the government to co-opt and corrupt them, to know their weaknesses and failings. On the other hand, this freedom creates a subtle gratitude and dependence on those in power that limits their contestation activities. This in turn transforms them, in the view of many opponents of the system, into a sham opposition, [which] weakens their legitimacy as an alternative.[47]

For the opposition the government considered more dangerous, there was still repression. In the regime's later stage the methods were not extremely harsh, especially by the standards set earlier. By the sixties, 'only the most active and directly subversive political opponents were arrested, almost none were shot', as one observer explained. The mature dictatorship had a variety of other means at its disposal to keep opponents in line—revoking drivers' licences, interfering with careers, etc—so Franco could afford to forego some of the old brutality. In its immediate purpose the repression was effective. The Socialist party, which was to play a leading role later, had virtually no organisation inside of Spain at the time of the dictator's death. But Franco's reliance on apathy and demobilisation as a means of achieving stability also meant that the regime did not put down deeper roots.[48]

In the late sixties, two years after the most dramatic moves toward liberalisation the regime was to make, Spain began experiencing the same unrest as much of the rest of Western Europe. Basque terrorists began a campaign of sabotage, armed robbery and assassination in 1968, and Franco responded by declaring a 'state of exception' (exempting the authorities from the guarantees against arbitrary arrest promulgated in 1945) in the province of Guipuzcoa. At the same time, a number of opposition groups lodged protests over the remaining parts of Franco's repressive apparatus. A petition was signed by 1300 intellectuals decrying the use of torture by the police, women relatives of the jailed leaders of the Workers' Commissions held sit-ins in churches in the large cities, and lawyers' associations in Madrid and Barcelona called for the abolition of the special courts used for political cases. Finally, in January 1969, a severe wave of student protest broke out at the University of Madrid. On the 24th, Franco extended the state of exception to the entire country. The harsh measures contained the protest, but in one observer's words, 'the state of exception was a catastrophic blow to the [regime's] long efforts to achieve legitimacy. . . . Franco's government had proved far more dramatically than the opposition that the country was still a police dictatorship.'[49]

If Franco's liberalisation failed to win over the public and build enough support to allow the regime to survive the death of its founder, at least it prevented the worst from happening (from the regime's standpoint). In Hungary, Soviet policy was so poorly conceived that it transformed what may well have been a manageable situation into a revolution.[50] The first mistake was in replacing Nagy at a time when his 'New Course' seemed to be winning some support for the regime.[51] Next, having brought back to power a man many Hungarians perceived (quite correctly) as a murderer, the Russians failed to exploit the one asset Rakosi possessed—his ability to strike fear into the hearts of potential opponents. According to Paul Kecskemeti:

> [The revolution] was a delayed reaction to all the negative experiences of the past, a reaction released when elements of weakness appeared in the image of the regime.[52]

That the people of Hungary bore the Communist regime immense hatred is amply evident from the spontaneous attacks on all symbols of Communist authority that broke out in Budapest in the summer of 1956.[53] But the Hungarians dared to express this only after the Russians tied Rakosi's hands.

The Soviet's constraining of Rakosi was important in a more specific sense. One thing a liberalising government must guard against is the spread of disaffection from limited 'elite' groups to a broader audience. The effects of the easing of censorship in Spain, for example, were offset by the regime's continued control over television, which reached a much wider audience than the print media. When controls were lifted on censorship of the press in Brazil in 1978, articles began appearing on torture and other abuses of power that had taken place earlier. But as in Spain, television and radio remained under close government supervision, so the damage was contained.[54] In Hungary, as I have said, the ferment began with the intellectuals at a time when the public was sullen but quiescent. The two major forums for the intellectuals became the Petofi Circle, a debating club that Rakosi permitted within the Federation of Working Youth, and *Irodalmi Ujsag*, the official literary journal. By the summer of 1956, the previously innocuous publication was selling out on the newstands and the Petofi Circle was drawing crowds in their thousands to its meetings. Either Rakosi was slow to grasp the importance of these developments or the Russians again held him back. In any case, these two maverick Communist institutions played a key role in the transmission of ideas from the intellectuals to the people as a whole. By June, a 'revolutionary spirit' was taking hold of the entire country. As Khrushchev remarked later, 'if ten or so Hungarian writers had been shot at the right moment, the revolution would never have occurred'.[55]

Finally, Khrushchev's success in defusing an equally threatening situation in Poland suggests that the Soviets missed one last chance to stave off the tragedy of 1956 when they brought in Gero, a man closely associated with Rakosi, rather than returning Nagy to power.[56]

Perhaps more than any other case, the Shah's failure in Iran illustrates the difficulties a ruler faces in mixing concession and repression, for where some leaders might have alienated the opposition in trying to control their protests and others might have lost control in attempting to win them over, the Shah managed to do both simultaneously.

As of August 1977, Iran's future was still open.[57] At this time, only the far left and a few extremists in the clergy ruled out compromise with the government. The moderate opposition was still suspicious, but had convinced the radicals to abstain from violence while they explored the possibilities for peaceful change. Unfortunately, the government took a number of steps in late 1977 that undercut the moderates. The first was the arrest of a Teheran Ayatollah, Mahmoud Taleqani, in August. Taleqani was tried secretly, contradicting the earlier pledges that trials would now be held in public. Throughout the early fall, the dissidents succeeded in attracting growing numbers of people to their meetings. The regime's response was uneven. SAVAK monitored all the meetings, but sometimes broke them up, and sometimes did not. After some of the gatherings were vandalised, the police were told to 'control' the meetings but not 'disrupt' them. Finally, in late November, 200 government thugs arrived at a large gathering at the home of a moderate leader and roughed up the guests. According to John Stempel, 'the attack helped to destroy the hope of moderate dissidents that there could be evolution to an acceptable political society'. The last straw for many moderates was the massacre at Jaleh Square on 8 September 1978, when government forces fired on a large crowd that refused to disperse, killing approximately 300–400. After the massacre, several of the moderates began to say that the Shah would have to go. Over the next two months, the monarch offered the moderate opposition the opportunity to form a cabinet as long as it was done under his aegis. He found no takers.[58]

While a number of the Shah's acts offended the moderates, the Shah managed at the same time to strengthen his most implacable enemies. One example of this was his release of political prisoners at the height of the crisis. Not only did the release, as in Hungary, lead to increased public awareness of past abuses, it also provided the extremists with new leadership. Included in the 1500 that were set free were Tudeh union officials who played a key role in organising the crippling strikes that were so important to the revolutionary cause, and guerrilla leaders who mobilised their forces for the decisive street fighting.[59]

But the Shah's cause was lost, more than for any other reason, because the monarch was unable to use force effectively to curb the extreme opposition. During the summer of 1978, the regime practised exactly the sort of 'half measures' Machiavelli cautions all rulers to avoid. SAVAK and other security forces would crack down on rioters one day and free them the next, reinforcing their hatred of the regime without precluding them from venting it. At two decisive points later—the declaration of martial law in September and the formation of a military government in November—the opposition drew back to avoid a confrontation with the armed forces. Despite Khomeini's braggadocio, the revolutionaries seemed in no hurry to lay down their lives. But on both occasions, the Shah failed to respond firmly. After the disaster at Jaleh Square, the Shah told his soldiers not to fire on demonstrators. In November, the army was instructed to fire into the air and kill the opposition only in self-defence. The streets were quiet for a time in both cases, but once the army's orders became clear, the opposition lost its fear and began to resume its activities. By December, the Shah had lost what support he had in public opinion and the morale of the armed forces was cracking.[60]

In Brazil, the government's strategy was much more successful. Throughout 1975–7, Geisel continued to use the Institutional Acts to deprive opposition figures of their political rights. The progress of decompression in Brazil was so uneven that critics said the country moved two steps back for every one forward. But Geisel himself had warned that it would be so. The pace, he explained, would be 'slow, gradual, and sane' in order to avoid 'inconvenient, premature, or imprudent' changes. The use of repression would remain 'widespread and flexible'.[61] According to David Fleischer and Robert Wesson, Figueiredo adopted a similar approach:

> The process was consequently gradual and limited, subject to a delicate balance between pressures for fuller democracy and fears of a loss of control. Stronger demands, as the parties pushed for ever new concessions, and radical speeches, as deputies tested the limits of official toleration, made the government hesitate or grip the reins more tightly. . . . President Figueiredo and his ministers continued their commitment to democratisation as a necessity for the country; however, Figueiredo wanted to move at his own initiative, not that of Congress, and concessions were to be made on the government's terms.[62]

The Brazilian strategy seemed to be designed to prevent expectations from rising too rapidly and to maintain the people's awe of the government. If the concessions were granted under pressure, the government would seem to be acting from weakness and that could encourage further demands. If the government were seen as acting on its own timetable and not being stampeded, the likelihood was less that the concessions would be destabilising.[63]

The one danger of this strategy was that the Brazilian public would lose patience with the slow pace of change or lose confidence in the intentions of the leadership. There was, however, one convincing reason for giving the government a chance: the most likely alternative seemed worse. As one opposition member told an American journalist in 1975, 'maybe it's better to go along with Geisel's slow decompression than to provoke a new clampdown by the hardliners', and that seemed to be the predominant mood in Brazil at that time.[64] In the sixties, the military's hardliners had reacted to what they took to be an increase in the threat from the opposition by demanding, and getting, a severe tightening of the dictatorship by the more moderate President Castello Branco. The hardliners were still a force to be reckoned with in Brazil in the seventies, and the opposition was well aware of this. This division in the armed forces, then, may have been a boon to decompression in that it allowed Geisel and Figueiredo to proceed slowly enough to maintain control without generating complete scepticism about their ultimate intentions.

Obviously, the existence of a strong threat from the far right is not an unmixed blessing. The Papadopoulos regime in Greece experienced virtually no public dissent from its beginning in 1967 till 1973. In August of that year, Papadopoulos cancelled martial law in Athens, freed several political prisoners and promised some further steps toward democracy in the future. Three months later, the first outbreak of violent protest since 1967 occurred when students and workers seized control of the Polytechnic University in Athens. Hardline elements under the leadership of Dimitrios Ioannides decided that liberalisation had gone far enough, and removed Papadopoulos.[65]

That this did not happen in Brazil was due in large part to the skill of the liberalising Generals. At times, Geisel moved aggressively to eliminate possible opponents of his policies, taking commands away from those who opposed his policies or even putting them under protective arrest. A particularly important instance occurred in October 1977 when the Minister of the Army, a potential hardline rival to Figueiredo, was dismissed in an atmosphere of high tension, though without incident.[66] On the other hand, Geisel, as I have already stressed, was firm enough with the opposition to avoid charges of weakness. In 1977, he adopted the 'April Package', which altered the electoral competition to the benefit of the pro-government National Renovating Alliance (ARENA) party. The promulgation of the April Package touched off an upsurge in political protest in Brazil and was condemned by representatives from many leading groups in Brazil.[67]

Even so, the success of the Brazilian liberalisers may ultimately have rested on chance. On 30 April 1981, an explosion took place outside a large convention centre in Rio de Janeiro on the day a popular music concert was scheduled, killing an army intelligence officer and severely wounding another. It was rumoured in Brazil that the hardliners in the military had intended to stage an apparent terrorist attack during the concert and then use it as a pretext to seize power from Figueiredo. The President preferred not to provoke the hardliners, and no serious investigation of the incident was undertaken. (The surviving participant, for example, was never interviewed.) The moderate opposition rallied to Figueiredo, and decompression continued on course.[68]

To sum up, liberalisation seems most likely to be successful when it is not undertaken as a result of outside pressure, when the economic climate is favourable, when it aims at a transformation of the autocracy and not just its amelioration, and when the regime has avoided the half-measures that Machiavelli warned of. A regime is probably best off when it has as little to apologise about as possible, but rulers who are sufficiently ruthless may enhance the prospects for liberalisation in the future by liquidating the opposition thoroughly and instilling terror in their publics. (I hope that it goes without saying that in noting this I am not condoning it.) Regimes in which a perpetrator can be identified and punished may have an easier time satisfying their people's desire for justice than ones in which the ruler himself can not evade responsibility.

All of the factors above, however, are less important than the tactics the government uses in dealing with the question of how to deter and contain protest without destroying the credibility of liberalisation. In both Spain and Brazil, the regime moved slowly and gradually, careful to preserve the image that it was dealing from a position of strength. As I indicated, the liberalisers in the Brazilian military may well have been aided by the visible division in their ranks, with the existence of the hardliners allowing Geisel to escape the blame for the slow pace of decompression.

De Tocqueville was surely right to stress the dangers a repressive government faces when it begins to treat its people better. But there is also wisdom in John Locke's observation that

> Revolutions happen not upon every little mismanagement in public affairs. Great mistakes in the ruling part, many wrong and inconvenient laws, and all the slips of human frailty will be born by the People, without mutiny or murmur.[69]

It is still surprising how strong a case one can make that things could have been different in the two cases that I have classified as failures, Iran and Hungary. In both of these, it was only after the government's actions had caused the people to lose both their fear and their hope that the people took up arms against their rulers.

The implications of this for the United States and its foreign policy are not obvious. It would be difficult, of course, to interpret the record above as justification for an aggressive human rights policy of the kind advocated by some in the Carter administration. On the other hand, if, as I have suggested, the Hungarian and Iranian revolutions were brought about to an important extent (though certainly not entirely) by tactical mistakes, our conclusions need not be completely pessimistic about the possibilities of improving conditions in other countries without damaging American interests.

The United States, in my view, need not abandon all efforts to persuade friendly governments to liberalise, but must pursue this aim with a greater understanding of the dangers a bad government faces as it tries to change its ways. In particular, it ought to be borne in mind that concessions that appear to be made from weakness are more likely to be destabilising, and that successful liberalisation may require some tactical retreats, as it did in Brazil.

It may be said in objection that bad governments deserve to 'fail' and that justice is best served when they do. This is undoubtedly true in some cases. Some of the rulers discussed here probably did deserve to end their days on this earth swinging from a lamp post. But our major moral concern should not be seeing that the leaders get what is coming to them, but rather doing what we can to minimise the suffering of those living under oppressive rule. Here, I only want to remind the reader that revolution is, and ought to be, a desperate remedy, a means of the last resort. The toll taken in most revolutions in recent history is ample evidence of that. More importantly, history has often mocked those who have given their lives to the cause of freedom by replacing one tyrannical government with another that is no better, and frequently worse. How often has that happened in this century? Russia, China, Cuba, Vietnam, Iran and now perhaps one or more countries in Central America—the record is not encouraging.

In many instances, then, gradual liberalisation may be the best hope, as well as the option most consistent with American interests. In such cases, improvements may be best achieved by the use of Machiavellian tactics in support of Lockean ends.

Notes

1. Alexis de Tocqueville, *The Old Regime and the French Revolution* (New York: Doubleday, 1955), pp. 176–7.
2. There would seem to be no question about the ultimate aims of Franco and the Hungarian communists. The Shah's conception is not entirely clear, though I believe he would have been reluctant to reduce the Iranian monarchy to a merely ceremonial role. Two readers of this book have argued that the Brazilian generals differed from the others in their willingness to contemplate leaving office very early on. According to several of the contributors to the best account of the Brazilian liberalisation I have seen, however, Generals Geisel and Figueiredo did not initially intend to restore democracy. See Wayne Selcher, 'Introduction', p. 4; Enrique Baloyra, 'From Moment to Moment: The Political Transition in Brazil, 1977–1981', pp. 17, 33, 36, 48, 50; Donald Share and Scott Mainwaring, 'Transitions through Transaction: Democratisation in Brazil and Spain', p. 201; all in Wayne Selcher (ed.), *Political Liberalisation in Brazil: Dynamics, Dilemmas, and Future Prospects* (Boulder, Colorado: Westview, 1986).
3. This definition is thus neutral on the regime's definition of success and the United States' view. The definition I will use here differs from that of Robert Dahl, who concentrates on the first possibility—regime maintenance, not regime transformation—in the introduction he wrote to *Regimes and Oppositions* (New Haven, Connecticutt.: Yale University Press, 1973) pp. 16–17, which he also edited.
4. John Coverdale, *The Political Transformation of Spain after Franco* (New York: Praeger, 1979), p. 13; Richard Herr, *Spain* (Englewood Cliffs, New Jersey: Prentice-Hall, 1971), pp. 212–13.
5. Juan Linz, 'Opposition to and under an Authoritarian Regime', in Robert Dahl (ed), *Regimes and Oppositions* (New Haven: Yale University Press, 1973), p. 174.
6. Jose Amodia, *Franco's Political Legacy* (London: Penguin, 1977), p. 182; Coverdale, *The Political Transformation of Spain*, p. 18.
7. Amodia, *Franco's Political Legacy*, p. 186; Linz, 'Opposition to and under an Authoritarian Regime', pp. 175, 211; Coverdale, *The Political Transformation of Spain*, p. 9. Stanley Payne, *Franco's Spain* (New

York: Thomas Crowell, 1967) pp. 109–24, 144–5; Raymond Carr and Juan Pablo Fusi Aizpura, *Spain: Dictatorship to Democracy* (London: George Allen and Unwin, 1979), pp. 138–40, 167, 193, also consulted on this paragraph.

8. By 'failure', I mean for the outside power promoting the liberalisation, in this case the USSR. These developments are widely known. My sources on Hungary are : Ferenc Vali, *Rift and Revolt in Hungary* (Cambridge, Mass.: Harvard University Press, 1961); Paul Zinner, *Revolution in Hungary* (New York: Columbia University Press,1962); and Paul Kecskemeti, *The Unexpected Revolution* (Stanford, California: Stanford University Press, 1961). The shifts in Soviet policy in Hungary are attributed to the political competition in the Kremlin in Charles Gati, 'Imre Nagy and Moscow, 1953–56', *Problems of Communism*, May–June 1986.

9. John Stempel, *Inside the Iranian Revolution* (Bloomington, Indiana: Indiana University Press, 1981).

10. David Fleischer and Robert Wesson, *Brazil in Transition* (New York: Praeger, 1983), pp. 39–40; Wayne Selcher, 'Contradictions, Dilemmas, and Actors in Brazil's *Abertura* 1979–1985' in Wayne Selcher (ed.), *Political Liberalisation in Brazil* (Boulder, Colorado.: Westview Press, 1986), p. 60.

11. Kenneth Medhurst, *Government in Spain* (New York: Pergamon, 1973), p. 35; David Gilmour, *The Transformation of Spain* (London: Quartet Books, 1985), 95, 100–1, 104; Herr, *Spain*, 231; Linz, 'Opposition to and under an Authoritarian Regime', pp. 222–3.

12. Peter McDonough, *Power and Ideology in Brazil* (Princeton: Princeton University Press, 1981), p. 14; Janice Perlman quoted in Riordan Roett, *Brazil: Politics in a Patrimonial Society* (New York: Praeger, 1978), p. 51; Marvin Zonis, *The Political Elite of Iran* (Princeton: Princeton University Press, 1971), pp. 73–5; Cuyler Young, 'Iran in Continuing Crisis', *Foreign Affairs*, 40 (January, 1962), pp. 285–6.

13. The contributors to the *Regimes and Oppositions* volume also raise this issue, though they provide somewhat different answers than I. See Linz, 'Opposition to and under an Authoritarian Regime', pp. 221, 237, 257; and Dahl, 'Introduction', pp. 4, 13.

14. Linz, 'Opposition to and under an Authoritarian Regime', pp. 230–1; Herr, *Spain*, p. 212; Payne, *Franco's Spain*, pp. 109–112; Gabriel Jackson, *The Spanish Republic and the Civil War 1931–39* (Princeton: Princeton, University Press, 1965), p. 537.

15. Ramon Salas Larrazabal, *Perdidas de la Guerra Civil* (Barcelona: Editorial Planeta, 1977), pp. 387–88, 428–9.
    Salas Larrazabal also says that half a million people fled Spain early in 1939, and that 190,000 remained abroad indefinitely (pp. 83–4). He estimates that 23,000 people were executed from 1939–61. As indicated above, most of the executions were in the first two years (pp. 428–29). Gabriel Jackson is the source of the 200,000 and 200,000 estimate, pp. 536–9. He notes that a significant percentage

of the deaths after the war came when the prison camps filled up so quickly that the Nationalists were unable to provide food for their captives.

In *An Explanation of Spain* (New York: Random House, 1964), pp. 250–2, Elena de La Souchere observes that the regime's own records list 107,000 violent deaths in 1939–41, as opposed to only 22,500 in 1932–35. She takes this as 'an implicit recognition of 84,000 capital executions'. But she thinks that the actual total is probably much higher, since the overall number of deaths between 1939 and 1941 was 220,000 greater than during the three years immediately before the civil war. Salas Larrazabal agrees that the figure is broadly correct, but argues that the number of violent deaths recorded increased rapidly after the civil war because the government was catching up on the registration of deaths that had occurred earlier, and that the total number of deaths increased between 1939 and 1940 because of famine and wounds suffered during the war (pp. 384, 395). Miss de La Souchere, on the other hand, suggests that a large number of political executions may have been disguised in the official records as 'deaths from illness'. She says that survivors from the prisons in Madrid remember 500 or 600 executions per day throughout 1939–40, which would produce a total of about 60,000 in the capital alone. Salas Larrazabal's reasoning is plausible and his research appears to be thorough, but his background suggests that some scepticism about his conclusions may be in order. Salas Larrazabal is a colonel in the Spanish armed forces. He fought with Franco in the civil war and later fought with Hitler on the eastern front. His conclusion, however, does not sound like a whitewash: 'the truth, the awful truth, is that the number of political executions that occurred between the dates of January 1, 1939 and December 31, 1959 . . . was exactly 22,716, a chilling figure that does not need to be exaggerated in order to indicate the extent and importance of the repression.'

16. Vali, *Rift and Revolt*, pp. 58–64, 82–4, 87; Kecskemeti, *The Unexpected Revolution*, pp. 41, 18. The production of food grains in 1950–54 was actually somewhat less than 1911–15, although the population was then 25 per cent greater (Vali, p. 87). Hungarian economist Ivan Berend has estimated that the real wages of Hungarian workers fell 20 per cent during the first plan in Hungary (cited in Chris Harmon, *Bureaucracy and Revolution in Eastern Europe* [London: Pluto Press, 1974]).

The figures on the AVH and the numbers killed and imprisoned are taken from David Pryce-Jones, *The Hungarian Revolution* (London: Ernest Benn Ltd, 1969), pp. 41, 43.

17. Amnesty International, *International Report*, 1975–6, pp. 182–8.

18. James Bill, 'Power and Religion in Revolutionary Iran', *Middle East Journal*, 36 (Winter 1982), pp. 24–8.

19. Peter Flynn, *Brazil: A Political Analysis* (Boulder: Westview, 1978), pp. 385–87; Howard Handelman and Thomas Sanders (eds.), *Military Government and the Movement toward Democracy in Latin America* (Bloomington: Indiana University Press, 1981), pp. 192, 196; David Vital,

'If Brazil Has Hope, It All Rests with Strongmen', *New York Times*, 26 March 1978.

Brazil's population in 1966 was 83 million; Iran's in 1980, 38 million; Hungary's in 1950, 9 million; and Spain's in 1939, 25.5 million. Hence, Rakosi jailed between 1 and 1.5 per cent of his country's population, while Franco jailed 1 per cent and did away with perhaps 0.5 per cent (assuming Elena de La Souchere's figures are roughly accurate and that many of the deaths above the 84,000 figure were caused by disease). The Shah, in contrast, held no more than 0.3 per cent of the population in prison, and in Brazil the figures were miniscule in comparison to the other cases, especially the first two. Population figures taken from *Cross-Polity Time-Series Data*.

20. *The Prince*, chapter 17, Luigi Ricci (trans.) (New York: Modern Library, 1940).

21. See Herbert Matthews, *The Yoke and the Arrows* (New York: G. Braziller, 1961), pp. 120–1; Carr and Fusi, *Spain: Dictatorship to Democracy*, pp. 35–6, 47; Payne, *Franco's Spain*, pp. 117, 119; Gilmour, *The Transformation of Spain*, pp. 17, 24.

This mood continued for a very long time. As late as the mid–sixties, a clear majority of those polled, including 59 per cent of the working class, chose 'peace' as the most important goal for Spain. In total 67 per cent of the Spanish women cited 'peace' and 48 per cent of the Spanish men did also; for the men, 'justice' was a distant second at 20 per cent, and 'freedom' was the choice of only 4 per cent. (Linz, 'Opposition to and under an Authoritarian Regime', pp. 181–2.)

22. Kecskemeti, *The Unexpected Revolution*, p. 117.

23. Matthews, *The Yoke and the Arrows*, pp. 120–1; Carr and Fusi, *Spain: Dictatorship to Democracy*, pp. 135–6, 47; Payne, *Franco's Spain*, pp. 117, 119; Gilmour, *The Transformation of Spain*, pp. 83–4.

24. Sapehr Zabih, *Iran's Revolutionary Upheaval* (San Francisco: Alchemy Press, 1979), p. 20.

25. *Discourses*, Second Book, c. XXIII; also Third Book, ch. XL (Christian Detmold, trans.) (New York: Modern Library, 1940).

26. Kecskemeti, *The Unexpected Revolution*, pp. 44–5; Vali, *Rift and Revolt*, pp. 133, 143–50; Zinner, *Revolution in Hungary*, p. 170.

27. Stempel, *Inside the Iranian Revolution*, pp. 100–2, 133.

28. This is partly my own speculation, but may have been implied or stated by one of my sources on Hungary.

29. Herr, *Spain*, pp. 221, 233–5, 242, 284.

30. Herr, *Spain*, pp. 256, 259; Coverdale, *The Political Transformation of Spain*, pp. 1, 12; Linz, 'Opposition to and under an Authoritarian Regime', p. 234.

31. Coverdale, *The Political Transformation of Spain*, p. 12; Amodia, *Franco's Political Legacy*, pp. 150–3; Medhurst, *Government in Spain*, pp. 35, 38.

32. James Davies, 'Towards a Theory of Revolution,' *American Sociological Review*, XXVII (February 1962), pp. 5–19.

33. Vali, *Rift and Revolt*, pp. 164–5, 133, 174–5; Zinner, *Revolution in Hungary*, p. 177.

34. I assume that the Carter policy had little effect in Brazil because Geisel reversed course and imposed the 'April Package' just as President Carter began calling for greater respect for human rights in early 1977.

35. Zinner, *Revolution in Hungary*, p. 203; Vali, *Rift and Revolt*, pp. 224–5; Kecskemeti, *The Unexpected Revolution*, pp. 69–70.

36. Vali, *Rift and Revolt*, pp. 233–4. 244–5, 254–7; Zinner, *Revolution in Hungary*, p. 227; Kecskemeti, *The Unexpected Revolution*, p. 76; Paul Kecskemeti, 'Limits and Problems of Decompression', in *Annals of the American Academy of Political and Social Sciences*, May 1958, p. 105.

37. Shaul Bakhash, 'Who Lost Iran?', *New York Review of Books*, vol. 29, 8 (14 May 1981).

38. Quote in Nicholas Gage, 'US–Iran Links Still Strong', *New York Times*, 9 July 1978; also see Sharif Arani, 'Iran', *Dissent*, 27 (Winter 1980), p. 14; Herman Nickel, 'The US Failure in Iran', *Fortune*, 99 (12 March 1979), p. 98; Zabih, *Iran's Revolutionary Upheaval*, p. 49.

39. William Lewis and Michael Ledeen, *Debacle* (New York: Knopf, 1980), pp. 143–4, 153; William Sullivan, *Mission to Iran* (New York: Norton, 1981), pp. 156–7, 168, 191–2, 204; Mohammad Reza Pahlavi, *Answer to History* (New York: Stein & Day, 1981), pp. 161, 164–5.

40. Gary Sick, *All Fall Down: America's Tragic Encounter with Iran* (New York: Penguin, 1985) pp. 33–36.

41. See the Shah's own comments, *Answer to History*, p. 167. Also Sullivan, *Mission to Iran*, pp. 167–8, 188.

42. Stempel, *Inside the Iranian Revolution*, pp. 92, 133–4; Sullivan, *Mission to Iran*, p. 168.

43. Stempel, *Inside the Iranian Revolution*, pp. 37–8; also 56, 288.

44. Handelman and Sanders, *Military Government and the Movement toward Democracy*, pp. 151, 153.

45. Medhurst, *Government in Spain*, pp. 33–5; Amodia, *Franco's Political Legacy*, pp. 147–9; Coverdale, *The Political Transformation of Spain*, p. 17.

46. Medhurst, *Government in Spain*, p. 36, Herr, *Spain*, pp. 14–15. The regime did crack down on the Workers' Commissions after a large-scale protest in 1967, however. The Spanish Communist Party had infiltrated the bodies by that time. Gilmour, *The Transformation of Spain*, p. 93.

47. Linz, 'Opposition to and under an Authoritarian Regime', pp. 220, 216–18. Linz also suggests that the moderates were hurt by the easing of censorship. Quoting from him again, 'it might be argued that freedom of the pen, whose use requires time to explore the always uncertain limits and to fight the legal and alegal pressures that might endanger it, has wasted much of the energy of the opposition. The time that might have been invested in contacting men, building the foundations of an organization, working out tactics among many small groups, formulating specific policies for the day when power is assumed, even real conspiracy, went instead into endless arguments over whether this or that could be published without endangering the continued publication of the newspaper.' (pp. 218–19)

48. Carr and Fusi, *Spain: Dictatorship to Democracy*, pp. 165, 181; Coverdale, *The Political Transformation of Spain*, p. 18.

49. Herr, *Spain*, pp. 285–6. Medhurst gave a similar but more measured assessment in 1973: 'Events of the past decade have indicated that the more conservative elements now in power . . . will react very strongly against the manifestations of dissent which such a liberalisation program is bound to encourage.' (*Government in Spain*, p. 52)

50. The outside power here is the USSR, not the US. The reasoning about American human rights policies, then, will be based on an analogy between Khrushchev's role as liberator—an unusual role for a Soviet statesman—and the efforts of American leaders to promote liberalisation by allies of the US. The US role in Hungary was of some significance in the outbreak of the revolution, of course—tragically—but will not be discussed here.

51. Kecskemeti, 'Limits and Problems of Decompression', pp. 105; also Kecskemeti, *The Unexpected Revolution*, p. 117.

52. Kecskemeti, *The Unexpected Revolution*, p. 117.

53. Vali, *Rift and Revolt*, pp. 268–9; Kecskemeti, *The Unexpected Revolution*, p. 111.

54. Amodia, *Franco's Political Legacy*, p. 187; Robert Levine, 'Brazil's Definition of Democracy', *Current History*, 76 (February 1979), p. 83.

55. Zinner, *Revolution in Hungary*, pp. 140, 205–10; Vali, *Rift and Revolt*, pp. 220, 228–31. Khrushchev quote is the epigraph to Ned Barber, *Seven Days of Freedom* (New York: Stein & Day, 1974).

56. Kecskemeti, 'Limits and Problems', p. 105; Kecskemeti, *The Unexpected Revolution*, p. 117.

57. I am adopting the interpretation of John Stempel, *Inside the Iranian Revolution*, pp. 38–9, 265.

58. The moderates hesitated not just because of their distrust of the Shah but also because of the growing power of the Ayatollah Khomeini. By October, the moderates were intimidated by his grip on the urban masses. The growth of Khomeini's power is related to the factors discussed immediately below.

59. Zabih, *Iran's Revolutionary Upheaval*, p. 56.

60. Stempel, *Inside the Iranian Revolution*, pp. 110–11, 119–21, 134, 153; my own research confirms Stempel.

61. Quotes from Handelman and Sanders, *Military Government and the Movement toward Democracy*, pp. 155, 172–3. Information above from Riordan Roett, *Brazil: Politics in a Patrimonial Society* (New York: Praeger, 1984), p. 147–8. Riordan Roett agrees: 'The message was clear—if there was going to be liberalisation, Geisel would orchestrate it.' (p. 147). See also, Wayne Selcher, 'Introduction', pp. 1, 3; and Enrique Baloyra, 'From Moment to Moment', pp. 29–30 and Luciano Martins, 'The "Liberalisation" of Authoritarian Rule in Brazil', in Guillermo O'Donnell, Phillippe Schmitter and Laurence Whitehead (eds.), *Transitions from Authoritarian Rule: Latin America* (Baltimore: Johns Hopkins University Press, 1986), pp. 83–4.

62. Quote from Fleischer and Wesson, *Brazil in Transition*, 41. See also Martins, 'The "Liberalisation" of Authoritarian Rule in Brazil', pp. 85–7.

63. Judging by the results of these four cases, the tactics adopted by the liberalising generals in Brazil were far and away the best conceived. But before ascribing most of the credit for Brazil's success to the tactics of Geisel and Figueiredo, we need to consider an alternative explanation suggested to me by William Perry and an anonymous reader of the manuscript. As noted at the outset, the Brazilian generals did not intend, initially, to move all the way to democracy. But unlike leaders in the other three countries under study here, they apparently changed their minds once liberalisation was underway, and began relying on promises of democratisation to legitimise the continuation of their rule. It does not seem unreasonable to suggest that liberalisation undertaken to transform and not merely to mitigate the evils of the existing system has a better chance of succeeding because of its wider appeal to the opposition. There are two reasons, however, not to place the strongest emphasis on this change of goals in Brazil. First, the use of the promise of democratisation to legitimise the regime began only after Brazil's economy reached its nadir in the early eighties, and thus could not account for the generals' success up to that point. (Wayne Selcher, 'Contradictions, Dilemmas, and Actors in Brazil's *Abertura*, 1979–1985', in Wayne Selcher (ed.), *Political Liberalisation in Brazil: Dynamics, Dilemmas, and Future Prospects* [Boulder, Colorado: Westview, 1986], p. 57.) The second point will be addressed above in the next paragraph.

64. Fleischer and Wesson, *Brazil in Transition*, p. 41; *New York Times*, 25 November 1973.

65. 'The Junta Is Forced to Take Off the Velvet Gloves', *New York Times*, 25 November 1973.

66. Roett, *Brazil: Politics in a Patrimonial Society*, p. 147; Robert Levine, 'Brazil's Definition of Democracy', *Current History*, 76 (February 1979), p. 70.

67. Levine, 'Brazil's Definition', p. 63. An additional motive may have been to demonstrate to the United States that Brazil would not take direction from Washington at a time when President Carter was trying to promote human rights.

68. Robert Levine, 'Brazil's: The Dimensions of Democratisation', *Current History*, 81 (February 1982), p. 82; Roett, *Brazil: Politics in a Patrimonial Society*, p. 153.

69. *Second Treatise*, ch. xix, para. 225.

3 The Elusive Political Solution

If reformist intervention is not attempted or is not successful, the time may come when the opposition can no longer be appeased or weakened by changes in policy but can only be satisfied by a fundamental alteration of the regime itself. The past performance of the United States government in these situations has been bitterly attacked both by critics on the left and critics on the right. The experience of the recent past, however, has provided little support for either view.

According to the non-interventionist critics of US foreign policy, the usual American response to revolution has been to assist the government in suppressing the opposition either by direct or indirect means. But these writers have overlooked at least nine attempts by the United States to resolve revolutionary conflicts by means of a political solution between 1945 and 1981. More recently, a very conservative US administration has acted to remove embattled dictators in two instances and appears to be applying a similar policy elsewhere. After the experience of the Reagan years, the sixties vintage characterisation of US policy is simply no longer plausible, if indeed it ever was.

Oddly enough, the record of the Reagan Presidency also seems to belie the influential analysis of Jeane Kirkpatrick. Writing after the débâcles in Iran and Nicaragua, she warned that US efforts to assist the moderate opposition would run the risk of weakening the government and paving the way for a takeover by the radical opposition. US interests and ideals, she argued, would be best served by continued support of friendly autocrats facing rising opposition. But in the Philippines and Haiti, the Reagan administration wisely abandoned the Kirkpatrick line and helped to arrange a transition away from dictatorship. The successful outcome in both countries has lead many observers to think that Dr Kirkpatrick's pessimism about the capacity of the US to manage political change was exaggerated and that the US ought to continue to press for political solutions in the future.

Before the mood shifts too far in the optimistic direction, though, it is worth noting that the record of past US efforts is not especially

90

encouraging. The United States has attempted to end revolutions through political solutions on at least eleven occasions since the Second World War. In Cuba (1958), Lebanon (1958), Iran (1978–79), Nicaragua (1978–79), Haiti (1986) and the Philippines (1986), what I have termed the 'moderate solution' was the basis of US policy. The aim of this type of solution is to broaden or replace the existing leadership with elements of the moderate opposition, while excluding the radicals. The 'inclusive solution', on the other hand, brings in the radical opposition but attempts to limit their influence by incorporating representatives of the old regime as well as the moderates. The US helped put inclusive solutions in place in China (1944–47), Laos (1960–62), the Dominican Republic (1965–66), Vietnam (1972–75), Rhodesia-Zimbabwe (1978–80) and, depending on the definition, Yemen (1962). Excluding two situations where American troops were occupying the country (Lebanon and the Dominican Republic), there are only two or three cases—the Philippines, Zimbabwe and, if one is generous, Haiti—where a political solution consistent with US interests was achieved. If foreign policy were made on a purely actuarial basis, this record would hardly seem to justify the current optimism about the feasibility of the political solutions.

The record does not speak for itself, of course. After most of the failures, critics of US policy, many of them disappointed government officials, have argued that success could have been achieved if the United States had acted earlier or more forcefully in support of the political solution. If they are right, the prospects for the middle options during revolution may be considerably better than the record suggests. The key issues, then, would seem to be why US policy has succeeded or failed in the past and whether more skilful execution could have made a difference.

I propose to address these questions by reviewing (in section I) US policy toward the revolutions in China, Cuba, Nicaragua, Iran, the Philippines and Haiti, then considering (in section II) the reasons for the success or failure of US policy and trying to specify what sorts of circumstances are most conducive to the political solution. The narratives in the first section will show that the critics' contention about past US efforts is highly plausible; the analysis in the second will suggest that their conclusions are wrong nonetheless because they neglect the difficulties the United States is bound to encounter in persuading the right to yield. Parts I and II will be mostly, though not exclusively, concerned with the moderate solution. Part III will focus on the particular problems of the inclusive solution. The sole success in that category, Zimbabwe, will be contrasted with the failures in China, Laos and Vietnam to demonstrate when the inclusive solution can hold once it is put in place and why this is unlikely to happen frequently. Let us begin, then, with a frustrating episode now four decades distant: the United States' mediation in the Chinese civil war.

I

General Patrick Hurley, acting as Roosevelt's special emissary, arrived in China in September 1944 and soon put an end to the effort discussed in a previous chapter to compel Chiang Kai-shek to appoint General Stilwell as commander of the army. Hurley decided instead to concentrate on bringing together the Chinese Communists (CCP) and the ruling Nationalist party (KMT). On his way to China, the general had visited Moscow and come away convinced that Stalin could be persuaded to withhold support from the Communists. He reasoned that if the United States also refused to aid them, they would have no choice but to accept his preferred solution: a coalition government, but with the KMT remaining dominant. The Russians' assistance was secured at Yalta when Stalin agreed to back Chiang Kai-shek in return for restoration of the privileges the Tsars had enjoyed in Manchuria. Despite this, Hurley was unable to obtain an agreement. The CCP agreed early on to integrate their forces into a unified national army if they were allowed to participate in a coalition government, but the KMT insisted that the integration of forces be carried out before any sort of political reorganisation could occur. Rejecting the advice of the career foreign service officers in the embassy, Hurley refused to bring pressure to bear on Chiang and the deadlock continued for months.[1]

By the summer of 1945, the CCP had lost patience with the American mediator but the events set in motion by the collapse of Japanese power on the Asian mainland forced them to deal with him. In August, the Soviets pledged publicly to support the existing Nationalist government, receiving in return concessions even more generous than those at Yalta. This left Mao Tse-tung no choice but to accept an invitation he had previously declined three times to come to Chungking for another round of negotiations with Chiang and Hurley.[2] At the same time, the United States began transporting KMT troops to the north to accept the surrender of the Japanese and landed 50,000 Marines there to hold the territory until the KMT forces arrived. These steps offset the geographical advantage of the CCP, transforming the situation to the benefit of the Nationalists. Under these combined pressures, the Communists offered their first concessions in many years, dropping the demand for inclusion in a coalition and suggesting instead that a Political Consultative Commission be convoked to discuss the establishment of a multi-party system in China. The Commission convened in October but was unable to reach agreement on the more fundamental issues of the integration of the armed forces and the disposition of territory liberated from Japan. The KMT continued to insist that only the government forces be given the right to disarm the Japanese and occupy the areas cleared, while the Communists sought recognition of their control of much of north China.[3] The transport of troops was essential to enable the Nationalists to overcome the disadvantages of geography and they would have had to take a threat to suspend it very seriously, but as before, Hurley declined to press the government and the transporting continued uninterrupted through the fall. In the absence of an agreement both sides acted unilaterally to extend their control in north China and Manchuria until Hurley, exhausted by the ordeal, resigned in late November and returned to the US.[4]

President Truman contacted George Marshall on the afternoon of Hurley's resignation and asked him to continue the mediation effort. Initially, Truman administration officials were prepared to adopt the suggestions of Hurley's critics in the foreign service but in the end Marshall was instructed to threaten Chiang, though not to carry out the threats. Despite this, Marshall was still able to achieve rapid progress in the negotiations soon after his arrival on the scene in early 1946.[5]

In January and February, the two sides reached agreement on three sets of issues. A truce was declared on 10 January 1946 and put into effect three days later. Under the agreement, the Nationalists were permitted to move forces into Manchuria but all other troop movements were to cease and truce teams, including representatives of both sides and the United States, were set up to monitor the ceasefire. A sharp reduction in the level of hostilities followed. On 23 February, the two Chinese parties reached an agreement to integrate their armies within one year. The Communists accepted a ratio of 5 KMT divisions for each of theirs and also welcomed Marshall's proposal that the US retrain their officers. Finally, the Political Consultative Commission drew up a plan calling for the formation of an interim coalition government to serve until the first meeting of the National Assembly. The plan would have permitted the Communists to maintain and probably extend the control they had previously achieved over local governments. Marshall did not play a direct role in the Commission's deliberations, but did try to persuade Chiang to accept changes of the sort it was recommending and expressed his satisfaction with the Commission's work. The right wing of the KMT strongly opposed the charter while the Communists continued to insist on its implementation in the following months.[6]

On 11 March, Marshall returned to the United States to arrange a $500 million loan for China. During his absence, the Russians announced that they would complete the withdrawal of their troops from Manchuria by the end of April. This created a power vacuum in Manchuria which both sides rushed to fill. The truce teams were unable to contain the violence that ensued and the fighting spread to north China. Marshall obtained a ceasefire in June, but it lapsed on the 30th before any of the issues were settled and the fighting recommenced. The negotiations deadlocked because Chiang wanted his gains on the battlefield recognised while the Communists were willing to withdraw from areas they occupied only on the condition that the governments they had established would remain in place. In July, the Communist's representative proposed that negotiations be undertaken to form the coalition contemplated under the PCC charter. Chiang demanded in return that the Communists withdraw from the areas they controlled and hand over the government to the KMT in their home base in Kiangsu.[7]

It was apparent by this time that the Nationalists intended to use force to compel the Communists to accept their conditions and would ignore Marshall's pleas for restraint. The transport of KMT troops had been completed and Chiang no longer had as strong an incentive to placate the Americans. On 29 July, Marshall stepped up the pressure for the first time, blocking the shipment of arms and ammunition to the KMT. The embargo did not persuade Chiang to halt his offensive, at least in the short term. The Nationalists had already won much of what they had demanded earlier at the bargaining table and were still enjoying great success on the battlefield.

The mediation effort finally collapsed in October. As the KMT forces approached the Communist stronghold of Kalgan, the CCP warned Marshall that they would consider the negotiations at an end if their enemies could not be restrained. Marshall advised Chiang that he would request his own recall if Kalgan were attacked, which induced Chiang to propose a ten-day truce. The Communists answered this with the suggestion that the Nationalists abandon everything they had won since 13 January in China proper and everything since 7 June in Manchuria. The Generalissimo's forces then assailed Kalgan, taking it on the 10th. Marshall concluded thereafter that further efforts would be 'futile', and departed in early January.[8] The fate of China was now to be decided on the battlefield.

In a personal statement published shortly after his return, Marshall attributed his failure to extremists in both camps, but laid the blame particularly on 'irreconcilable groups within the Kuomintang, interested in the preservation of their feudal control of China, [who] evidently had no real intention' of implementing the agreements.[9] Critics would say, however, that if Marshall or Hurley had been willing to apply greater pressure before the summer of 1946, their resistance might have been overcome.

The problem with US policy toward the Cuban revolution, by contrast, was not the timing of US pressure, but rather the diffidence of the most influential officials about 'intervention' in Cuban domestic affairs. Fulgencio Batista had enjoyed warm relations with the United States for several years after his seizure of power in 1952. The US Ambassador in Havana, a frequent canasta partner of the dictator, was outspoken in his support of the government to the point of embarrassing his host. But Washington began rethinking the matter once armed resistance to Batista developed in 1956, both from Fidel Castro's well-publicised but not so numerous guerrillas in the Sierra Maestra and the urban-based *Directario Revolucionario* (DR). In July 1957, Earl E. T. Smith replaced the former Ambassador with instructions to 'alter the prevailing notion in Cuba that the American Ambassador [is] intervening on behalf of the government of Cuba to perpetuate the Batista dictatorship'. Smith made the change in American policy evident soon after his arrival, condemning the excessive use of force by the police against an uprising in Santiago. Later in 1957, the United States began delaying shipments of military equipment ordered by Batista and the DR concluded that American authorities 'were looking the other way as much as they possibly could' when their supporters began running guns into Cuba from the United States.[10]

The goal of US policy over the next months was to resolve Cuba's political crisis by persuading the government to hold honest elections. Batista had already scheduled an election for 1 June 1958 but insisted on maintaining a suspension of constitutional guarantees in the meantime, which made normal electoral campaigning impossible. Ambassador Smith was asked to persuade Batista to restore the guarantees and take other steps to prepare the way for elections, and also to warn the dictator that if he refused to do so he would face a cut-off in the sale of American military equipment. In late January 1958, Batista agreed to lift the suspension and end press censorship, though he did not incorporate other suggestions offered by the American Ambassador. In return, the US promised to deliver twenty armoured cars that Batista had ordered months before and enforce the neutrality laws against the guerrilla's leading arms supplier.[11]

The electoral solution still faced two serious problems, however. The first was that most of the moderate opposition remained very sceptical about any election conducted by Batista. In an attempt to remedy this, Ambassador Smith encouraged the dictator to allow observers from abroad to monitor the election and to consult with the opposition about other steps which could be taken to reassure them.[12] The other difficulty was that Castro and his followers had no interest in seeing an election take place which could render them irrelevant. Castro threatened to kill anyone who participated and the DR began a campaign of sabotage and terrorism in February in an effort to foil the electoral solution by compelling Batista to reverse his course and again suspend the guarantees.[13]

On 28 February, before Smith had received a firm commitment from Batista on the electoral procedures, the Catholic Episcopate of Cuba issued a call for a government of national unity to restore peace and order and prepare the way for elections. It was not immediately clear what the bishops had in mind. The papal nuncio told Earl Smith that they aimed at a coalition headed by Batista; the opposition at first took it to mean a provisional government without him. Batista replied emphatically that he intended to serve out his term but also appointed a new cabinet headed by Nunez Portuondo, a man highly regarded in the United States, and told Smith on 3 March 1958 that he would agree to permit outside observers during the elections. On 6 March, the Church named a four-man 'Commission of National Harmony' to mediate between the government and the opposition. Batista informed the bishops that he would participate in the proposed coalition but when the mediators contacted Castro on 10 March, the rebel leader refused to co-operate unless Batista agreed to step down. Faced with this deadlock, both the members of the Commission and Batista's new cabinet resigned. The only action taken by the United States during these discussions was to reiterate publicly the policy of non-intervention in Cuban affairs.[14]

Two days after the commission's resignation, Castro called for an all-out offensive, including a general strike, to overthrow the government. On the same day, Batista revoked the constitutional guarantees and announced plans to expand the army. In retaliation, the United States cancelled the shipment of 1950 Garand rifles on 14 March. After this point, Batista received only one additional shipment of arms from the United States; the US had, in effect, embargoed arms to Cuba.[15]

In retrospect, it is clear that this period in March 1958 was the best, and perhaps the only, opportunity that the United States and Cuban moderates would have to work out an acceptable political solution. Writing four years after, Ambassador Smith was to blame middle-level State Department officials for the failure of the Church's mediation effort. According to the former Ambassador, when the papal nuncio asked him if the United States would lend its support, he was compelled to withhold it because he had not been granted the authority. The Department would endorse the efforts only if they were successful; to do more could be seen as 'intervention'.[16] None of the State Department principals has responded publicly, but Wayne Smith, then a junior officer in Havana, has contended that the Ambassador himself must bear the greatest responsibility. He believes that the Department did not want to become associated with the bishop's plan because it did not call explicitly for Batista's resignation and they feared that the Ambassador was too sympathetic to Batista to be trusted to raise the matter with him tactfully.[17]

The documents available do not fully substantiate either account. In his cables concerning the National Harmony Commission, Ambassador Smith did not request authority to apply greater pressure to Batista. On the contrary, his communication of 4 March praised Batista's 'earnest efforts', despite the dictator's initial rejection of the proposed government of national unity.[18] After Smith received word that Batista intended to suspend the constitutional guarantees, he recommended 'continued non-intervention' and suggested only that Batista be advised to 'explore every possibility of a peaceful solution before again suspending [the] guarantees'.[19] There was no direct suggestion in either cable that Batista be pressured to broaden his government or resign. On the other hand, the State Department recommended nothing more than consultations between the government and the opposition on the elections in early March.[20]

It may be that if the United States had thrown full support behind the Church's effort some sort of political solution could have been achieved. But as Batista himself noted, the Commission made a serious tactical mistake in contacting Castro so soon, before a consensus had been built among the moderate opposition. Had they waited, or had they simply ignored the violent opposition altogether and tried to arrange an agreement between Batista and the moderates, Castro might have been left in isolation. One must bear in mind, though, that Castro would surely have done everything in his power to disrupt the elections and might well have succeeded.[21]

In any case, after the State Department received word of the suspension of the guarantees, Smith was sent a cable much more urgent in tone than anything he had received before. Secretary of State Herter and Assistant Secretary Roy R. Rubottom asked whether Batista could in fact survive and what might replace him if he did not. 'While [it is] true', they said, 'that [the] US does not desire [to] intervene [in] Cuban internal affairs, [we] believe [that the] US' special relationship to Cuba requires that we seek *by every means possible* [to] use our constructive influence with [the] Government and Opposition to help find [a] peaceful solution to [the] problem [author's italics].' But this strong statement, soon to be enforced by the arms embargo, was followed by a rather meek prescription: 'Would it be possible for Batista . . . to decide and somehow convincingly convey through [the] Church or other impartial group that elections will in fact be free and that all candidates will have [an] equal chance [to] win at [the] polls?'[22] This cable does not corroborate Wayne Smith's characterisation of the State Department as more far-sighted than the embassy. Even so, it might have provided the Ambassador with enough of an opening to pursue a political solution more aggressively if he had been so inclined.

The opportunity was not long in coming. On 14 March, Smith was told that the Joint Committee of Civic Institutions, an influential organisation of 42 religious, professional and fraternal groups, was preparing to call for Batista's resignation. Smith met with Raul de Velasco, a representative of the Joint Committee, and advised him to delay the announcement. The Ambassador wanted to make certain that they knew of Batista's promises to hold elections in the presence of impartial observers. Velasco responded that Batista had suspended the guarantees again in order to protect the head of the secret police, who had recently been indicted, and suggested that the dictator could not be trusted to conduct elections under any circumstances. 'The only solution', he told Smith, '[is] for Batista to leave.' When the civic associations made their announcement on 18 March, the US again remained uninvolved and nothing came of it.[23]

Asked to explain US policy during this period, the Director of Caribbean and Mexican affairs told the Senate Judiciary Committee three years later that 'we said we would not provide arms until they could achieve a more popular form of government, until they could show that they themselves had a formula for some for of solution . . .'. However, the United States 'would not intervene in Cuba's internal affairs . . . we could merely use good offices and try to explain our position, explaining in our own national interest that we did not want to become excessively involved in Cuban political strife. We were not thinking of dictating what would be the type of government- . . .'. These sentiments were expressed frequently by US officials in the documents available from this period.[24]

On 9 April, Castro called the general strike he had threatened earlier. The strike failed to attract much support from organised labour and collapsed without doing the regime serious harm. By the end of the month, the sugar harvest was nearly complete, arms had been purchased from the Dominican Republic and revolutionary activity outside Havana had subsided. Batista's confidence returned and the prospects for negotiations diminished to the vanishing point as Batista sought a military solution. On 24 May, Batista sent an army of at least 6–7000 into the Sierra Maestra to face Castro's guerrillas. By late June, the government forces had reduced the amount of territory in Castro's undisputed control to a mere four square miles, but they were turned back on the 29th when the rebels surrounded the 11th Battalion and inflicted a crushing defeat on Colonel Sanchez Mosquera, capturing or killing two-thirds of his men. After the rebels blunted a second offensive in late July, the army retreated from the Sierra Maestra, leaving behind hundreds of prisoners and a large quantity of weaponry. After this point it was the rebels, not the government, who were on the offensive.[25]

By late summer, it was clear to American officials that Batista was not going to have an easy time defeating the violent opposition. The question then became what attitude the United States ought to take concerning the elections, now rescheduled for November. Ambassador Smith credulously accepted Batista's pledges to hold an honest election but worried that the opposition might be too divided to defeat Batista's protégé, Andres Rivero Aguero.[26] Wieland, on the other hand, correctly foresaw that there was 'little possibility for anything resembling an acceptable election in Cuba', but was again unwilling to involve the United States more closely, despite his assessment that 'the only possibility apparent at this moment of minimizing a violent transition in Cuba is that of effecting a compromise arrangement between the Batista government and responsible leaders of an organized opposition',[27] In the end, Batista corrupted the election in what soon became known as the *cambiazo*, or 'great theft'. After some hesitation, the President-elect decided to fight it out with the guerrillas.

In late November, William Pawley, former Ambassador to Peru and Brazil and a personal friend of President Eisenhower, began lobbying for a more active American policy. Pawley's idea was to arrange a deal in which Batista would be allowed to reside in his Palm Beach mansion and his followers in Cuba would be spared from reprisals; in return, Batista would step aside in favour of a junta of pro-American moderates who would hold elections 18 months later. After this point they would be free to prosecute those guilty of fraud or abuses of power under Batista. In addition, the United States would immediately make available $10 million in arms to the new government. After meeting with Eisenhower, Pawley was referred to the State Department. They consented to send him but stipulated that he would have to go as a private citizen, and would not be permitted to speak for the President. State's reason, according to Pawley, was again the desire to avoid the appearance of intervention in Cuban politics.[28]

Pawley apparently misrepresented his status to Cuban officials in order to gain an audience with Batista, but when received on 9 December, adhered strictly to his instructions from the State Department. Batista was enraged when he found out that the proposed junta included some of his most bitter enemies and muttered to General Tabernilla afterward that he had wanted to 'kick [Pawley] out of here with my foot'.[29]

Pawley's status as private citizen put him in the same class with any number of other people advising Batista what to do. Would things have been different if he had been given official status? According to one account, Batista told Pawley one month later in exile that if he had known that the plan had Eisenhower's support, he would have gone along with it.[30]

While Pawley was in Havana, Smith and Wieland were involved in heated discussions in Washington about what to do if the mission failed. Smith felt that the choice was coming down to Batista's protégé or Castro's 26th of July Movement, which he considered Communist dominated. Wieland, for his part, was less convinced of the strength of Communists in Castro's movement but was now willing to support moderate alternatives, even if they had to employ violence to replace Rivero. At the decisive meeting in December, open rancour broke out between the two as Smith advocated sending arms to Rivero while Wieland insisted that the sooner Batista left the better.[31]

Smith lost the debate and was instructed on 23 December to advise Batista to transfer power but not to suggest any names. It was now very late in the day for the moderate forces, but two last-ditch attempts were made to assist them. First, the CIA promised support to Antonio Varona, a former prime minister, who intended to fly to Camaguey province, gain a base of support there with the backing of a disaffected army captain and then bargain with Castro for a share in power. Varona's plan went awry when he could not locate the captain and was intercepted by some of Castro's men.[32]

Support for Ramon Barquin was a more promising possibility. Barquin was a member of the *Puros* clique in the armed forces that had attempted to overthrow Batista in 1957. Although he had ties with the 26th of July Movement, he was also considered well-disposed toward the United States. The CIA provided a bribe to spring him from jail and Barquin was then able to make his way to Camp Columbia, where General Cantillo handed over command of the forces to him on 1 January 1959. Barquin's plan was to declare the army a 'revolutionary force' and order troops to hold their places against Castro, then invite President-designate Urrutia to Havana to form a government. With his 10,000 troops at Camp Columbia, Barquin could deny Castro Havana and place himself in a strong bargaining position.[33]

But as the rebel column advanced toward the capital, Barquin lost heart and handed over command of the base to the rebel commander. American officials were surprised and disappointed, but it is hard to fault him. Castro was popular in Cuba and a last-minute effort to keep him out of power would not have had wide support. The majority of Cubans seemed to be following Castro's call for a general strike. Moreover, if Barquin's bluff had been called, the odds would have been against him. As before, the rebels were outnumbered, but morale had collapsed among the government forces who had refused to engage the rebels in Santa Clara and had already surrendered several posts, contrary to Barquin's orders. At Camp Columbia, many had simply changed into civilian clothes and fled.[34]

With the departure of Batista on New Year's Eve and the failure of these last-minute gambits, the road was open for Castro, who entered Havana a week later to claim the spoils. Could this fiasco have been averted? Conservative critics of American policy believe so. If Pawley had been given a free hand or if the US had thrown support behind the efforts of the Cuban Episcopate, it might have been possible to replace Batista with a moderate successor who would have satisfied the Cubans' understandable desire for change without endangering United States' security. For now, let us withhold judgement and continue the narrative, moving next to Nicaragua.

In 1977, the Carter administration broke with the past American policy of acquiescence in the rule of the Somoza family and began an effort to prod the Nicaraguan dictator toward liberalisation. Somoza tried to appease Carter in September by lifting martial law and permitting the press to operate without censorship for the first time in three years. The administration rewarded Somoza with a military sales agreement which made it possible to release funds if his good behaviour continued. Unfortunately for Somoza, the loosening of restraints had the same effect observed so often in the previous chapter. *La Prensa*, the leading opposition newspaper, mounted a campaign against corruption; a wave of student demonstrations and labour unrest followed; and the long-dormant Sandinista National Liberation Front guerrillas re-emerged in mid-October to stage a series of attacks.[35]

Throughout 1977, the Carter officials hoped that Somoza could hold on until the election scheduled for December 1980, at which time he could be replaced by a more acceptable figure. But the situation changed fundamentally on 10 January 1978 when Pedro Joaquin Chamorro, the editor of *La Prensa*, was assassinated. Although Somoza was probably not responsible for the killing, it provided the spark that ignited the revolutionary conflagration in Nicaragua. On the day of Chamorro's funeral, 50,000 people went into the streets of Managua. Some marched peacefully in the funeral procession, others rioted and committed small acts of arson. Two days later, the Superior Council of Private Initiative (COSIP), an association of business and professional groups, called for a general strike against the regime. The lockout closed an estimated 80 per cent of the stores and factories in the larger towns temporarily, but collapsed after three weeks. One reason for the strike's failure, and the failure of the subsequent efforts in July and August, was the relative passivity of the United States.[36] The Carter administration announced in February that Nicaragua would be the only country in the world to lose its 1979 military assistance loan for human rights violations, and the State Department announced that the US favoured 'democratic government' for Nicaragua. But American officials ignored the pleas of Nicaraguan businessmen to intervene to depose Somoza and refused to involve themselves directly in negotiations at this point. Ambassador Mauricio Solaun explained later that 'our instructions were clear—follow the policy of neutrality. The embassy was to continue encouraging all parties to dialogue [sic] in search of a peaceful solution, a made-in-Nicaragua formula; we were not to serve as messengers, mediators, or guarantors of any solution.'[37]

In June, Carter sent a letter to Somoza congratulating him for inviting observers from the Inter-American Court of Human Rights to visit Nicaragua and for an amnesty he had proposed for political prisoners. The letter was intended to encourage Somoza to continue the liberalisation and was not a statement of support for the regime, as Somoza came to understand. But after the message was leaked in July, at the same time that Washington was announcing the release of $12 million in economic aid, it was taken as an indication that the United States would not break with Somoza. Critics were to charge later that Carter's letter, as in Iran, demoralised and weakened the moderates, driving them into an alliance with the left.[38]

With the failure of the moderates, the initiative shifted to the FSLN guerrillas. On 22 August, 25 Sandinistas led by Eden Pastora seized the National Palace and held its 1500 occupants hostage for 2 days before Somoza agreed to their demands and allowed them to leave. In September, the FSLN staged a full-scale military offensive. Somoza's National Guard crushed the rebels after two weeks of fighting, but resorted to brutal means in doing so. The Guard dragged boys into the streets to shoot them summarily without taking much trouble to find out whether they were rebel sympathisers or not, and heavy mortar fire destroyed large sections of several of the smaller cities, creating 30,000 refugees. Between 1500 and 3000 lives were lost in this first round of fighting.[39]

These events convinced American officials that some sort of political solution was now urgently needed. In the last two weeks of September, the Carter administration, in co-operation with the OAS, arranged to have a committee composed of representatives from Guatemala, the Dominican Republic and the United States to act as mediator. To encourage Somoza, Washington positioned a naval cruiser near the coast and cut $8 million in aid from the next year's budget.[40]

Somoza's adversary in the negotiations was the Broad Opposition Front, or FAO, an alliance of opposition political parties, labour organisations, and 'the twelve', a group of priests, intellectuals, businessmen and professionals with ties to the Sandinistas. The FAO entered the negotiations in early October intending to demand Somoza's immediate resignation and replacement by an interim junta. The only purpose of the mediation as they saw it was to provide the dictator with a way of saving face. Somoza responded that he intended to serve out his term and hold the election scheduled for 1981. In an attempt to bridge the gap, the OAS team persuaded the FAO in late October to offer a compromise: (1) Somoza would resign; but (2) representatives of the FAO and the Nationalist Liberal party (which had long been tied to the regime) would form an interim coalition government; and (3) the National Guard would be restructured, but not abolished. The representative of the twelve quit the negotiations at this point, on instructions from the Sandinistas, with the intention of fragmenting the FAO and sabotaging the negotiations. When this proposal failed to break the *impasse*, the mediators presented the FAO's original demand that Somoza leave Nicaragua. The US coupled this with pressure on the International Monetary Fund (IMF) in early November to deny Somoza $20 million in credits.[41]

In response, Somoza restated his intention to serve out his term, but raised the possibility of a plebiscite on his rule. The chief US negotiator, William Bowdler, suspected that Somoza was engaged in a negotiating ploy and advised Washington to bring all pressure to bear on him immediately to force him from office before the FAO broke apart or lost all public support. Bowdler and assistant secretary Viron Vaky thought that if the US reduced Nicaragua's beef quota in the United States and threatened to deny Somoza asylum he could be forced to capitulate. The two officials failed to convince President Carter and the negotiations continued, focusing on the details of the plebiscite. The opposition never received the assurances they sought and eventually the United States was forced to make good an earlier pledge to punish Somoza if he failed to accept the US plan.[42] On 9 February 1979, 47 American officials were recalled (more than half the official US representation in Nicaragua), and all economic and military aid to Somoza ceased, with the exception of economic aid projects benefiting the poor.[43]

Liberal critics were to say afterwards that the US did not try hard enough to remove Somoza.[44] With hindsight, one could question both the reformulation of the FAO's original proposal and the decision in November to take the plebiscite proposal seriously. But one must not overlook the pressure the US did put on Somoza, at all points. In July, in an effort to undo the unexpected effects of the Carter letter, the State Department announced that 'we are against Somoza'. Somoza states in his memoirs that he decided at this point to fight on regardless of what anyone outside Nicaragua said or did, and began his military build-up. In mid-September, William Jorden, the former Ambassador to Panama, was sent on a two-week tour to central America to set up the OAS mediation effort. Jorden told Somoza that 'the possibility of your departure from office is one of the possibilities that has to be considered. I am not saying it has to be done, I am saying it has to be considered.' In October, in his first meeting with Somoza, Bowdler simply asked the dictator 'why don't you just resign?' and the American mediator subsequently told Somoza that his instructions were to get him to leave the country.[45] In November, as aforementioned, the Carter administration blocked Nicaragua's request for a loan of $20 million from the IMF and announced publicly that the US favoured the resignation of Somoza. In late December, General Dennis McAuliffe, head of the Southern Command in Panama, accompanied Bowdler in a meeting with Somoza. McAuliffe argued that Somoza's continuation in office was abetting the Communists. 'Peace will not come', he said, 'until you have removed yourself from the presidency and the scene.' Also in late December, Bowdler presented what Somoza recalls as an 'ultimatum' that 'you, General Jose Somoza, your son, and your families must leave Nicaragua forthwith'. Finally, after hesitating for three weeks, the administration carried out its threat to break with the regime in February 1979.[46]

None of these steps convinced Somoza and the issue was now to be settled by force of arms. Once it was clear that the National Guard was in difficulty, the US proposed that an OAS peace force be introduced into Nicaragua. The proposal was rejected in the OAS and the

US then joined the majority in demanding that Somoza resign. Next, Carter officials entered into talks with various Nicaraguan factions to arrange a transition that would minimise the Sandinista's role. The details of this need not be rehearsed here; suffice it to say that this effort was no more successful than the last-minute improvisations in Cuba. On 17 July, Somoza departed, and three days later the Sandinistas had control of Managua.

Halfway around the globe, the Carter administration had been struggling to cope with an even more intractable set of circumstances. The Iranian revolution broke out in January 1978, just nine days after the departure of President Carter from Tehran. The revolutionary movement gradually gathered force over the first half of the year, went into a period of latency in the early summer, and then began building once again in August after the death of over 400 people in a fire at the Rex Theatre in Abadan. The response of the United States in the early stages was to express support for the Shah while adding that the support was predicated on a resumption of the Shah's efforts at liberalisation when circumstances permitted. The policy did not change, but was reaffirmed after the dreadful massacre at Jaleh Square on 8 September 1978.

In retrospect, it is clear that the events of early September marked a turning-point. In the following months, the Shah appointed two different governments in his efforts to stem the swelling tide of revolution. The first, headed by Jaafar Sharif-Emami, was put in place after the incident at Jaleh Square. Sharif-Emami entered into negotiations with the moderate clerical opposition in an attempt to work out a political solution that would split them off from the followers of Khomeini. The government attempted to appease the revolutionaries by adopting some elements of their programme but would not meet Ayatollah Shariatmadari's basic demand that Iran return to the 1906 constitution, which provided for a strong parliament and limited monarchy.[47] The second government, a military regime headed by General Azhari, was installed in early November after law and order broke down in the capital on the 4th and 5th. The key test for Azhari's government was whether it could contain protest in the streets during the holy month of Moharram, which began on 1 December. By the middle of the month, it was clear that the government was not going to pass that test. Azhari's curfews and bans on meetings were going unenforced and the government appeared 'powerless to preserve order'.[48] Finally, on 29 December, the Shah asked Shahpour Bakhtiar to form a new government and announced that he would take a 'rest' abroad in the near future.

The first mention of a political solution to the crisis by US officials came in late October, when Ambassador William Sullivan suggested that the Shah broaden his government by drawing some members of the moderate opposition into the cabinet. The Shah contacted two elderly members of the National Front a few days later, commenting wryly to Sullivan that one of the candidates was so deaf that he might not be able to hear the offer. The choice suggested, as a former US official put it, that the Shah was 'more interested in preserving his own absolute dominance of the political system than he was in making the opposition an offer that it could not refuse.'[49] On 2 November, Sullivan sent a cable to Washington expressing, for the first time, doubts about whether the regime would survive, and asking for guidance. After several weeks of relatively optimistic reporting from the embassy, the cable came as a shock to the White House, but it did not convince the President actively to seek an agreement with the opposition. Rather, Sullivan was instructed to tell the Shah that it was 'up to him' whether or not to pursue a political solution and that 'we are not pressing for it'. The message stated once again that 'the United States supports [the Shah] without reservation' and recognises 'the need for decisive action and leadership to restore order . . . '. Three days after the message was delivered, the Shah formed the military government under Azhari.[50]

This announcement had some calming effect and may have bought enough time for a solution. The Shah renewed his negotiations with the moderates later in November, but the talks remained deadlocked because of his refusal to surrender control of the armed forces or permit the *Majlis* to vote on their budget. Ambassador Sullivan, as before, did not involve himself closely.[51]

The possibility of putting greater pressure on the Shah to make concessions to the opposition did not receive much attention at the highest level until December. At this time, long after the most propitious moment for a political solution was past, George Ball was called in as a special consultant. Ball suggested that the Shah be advised to delegate most of his power to a 'council of notables', a coalition ranging from diehard supporters of the Shah to Khomeini's representative in Teheran, and accept the status of constitutional monarch. Ball's report to the President, presented on 15 December, was not met with immediate approval, but did prompt Carter to request the embassy to question the Shah more closely about the possibility of a political solution. Specifically, Sullivan was instructed to ask the Shah whether he would be willing to yield budgetary authority over the armed forces to the cabinet or parliament, and whether he thought that the US ought to play a larger role as intermediary with the opposition. The Ambassador was also to tell the Shah that the US had drawn up a list of names of possible candidates for a new government, and to mention them or not at his discretion. Carter's national security advisor, Zbigniew Brzezinski, feared that this would 'push the Shah into concluding that the US was pressing for a coalition government'. The Shah responded, however, that he intended to remain commander-in-chief, that budgetary authority over the army would have to be 'worked out' and that a larger role for the US in mediation would not be helpful. This answer, in addition to the combined opposition of Sullivan and Brzezinski (who seemed to agree on little else), killed the Ball plan.[52]

By the end of the month, Sullivan had concluded that the Shah was doomed, but that the minimum US goals could still be achieved if he could prevent the Iranian armed forces from being 'chewed up' by the revolution. If the military remained intact, it would not only protect the country against aggression from the USSR or Iraq but also provide some support for the moderate elements of the revolutionary movement against the religious and leftist extremists once the Shah fell. Sullivan wanted to pursue this by promoting an arrangement between the army and the religious revolutionaries. He reported that understandings had already been reached between Mehdi Bazargan, the probable head of a new government, and the armed forces, under which the latter would transfer their allegiance to Bazargan after several senior officers objectionable to the revolutionaries had left Iran. The plan collapsed on 10 January when Brzezinski, to the Ambassador's vexation, convinced Carter to cancel the meeting Sullivan had set up between an American representative and Khomeini.[53]

The President had decided instead to throw support behind Shahpour Bakhtiar, a National Front figure who replaced Azhari as prime minister in late December. The emergence of Bakhtiar may have taken US officials somewhat by surprise. After the collapse of the Ball plan, and further evidence of the Shah's hesitation, Secretary of State Vance and Brzezinski had agreed upon a compromise statement that called upon the Shah to 'choose without delay a firm military government' if an acceptable civilian government could not be put together very quickly. When Sullivan presented the message on 29 December, the Shah remarked that he 'did not have the heart' to bring down the iron fist, but reported that Shahpour Bakhtiar had agreed to make an attempt to form a government. Bakhtiar had accepted the position, though, on the condition that the Shah leave the country. The Shah, in turn, inflicted a serious political wound on the new prime minister when he refused to grant his choice to head the defence ministry, General Jam, full control of the military, leading Jam to withdraw.[54] On 3 January 1979, Carter reluctantly offered the Shah asylum in the US and committed himself tentatively to Bakhtiar. General Robert Huyser was then dispatched to Tehran with the complex and somewhat contradictory aims of rallying military support for Bakhtiar, dissuading the generals from attempting a coup in the near future, but laying the groundwork for a coup later if Bakhtiar were to falter. Huyser achieved the second objective, but neither of the others. When Khomeini returned from Paris in February to challenge the prime minister, the soldiers stayed in their barracks rather than risk their lives for the courageous but quixotic Kerensky backed by Washington. As was the case with Barquin, it is hard to fault them. Ambassador Sullivan had warned Washington in January that the armed forces would disintegrate if asked to fire on crowds to keep Bakhtiar in power, and events proved him right.[55]

In all four of the cases above, the efforts of American officials to promote a political solution to civil war collapsed and governments well disposed to the United States were overthrown by radical anti-American movements. In every instance, critics of US policy were to argue later that the disaster could have been forestalled if officials had acted differently. With the advantage of hindsight, it is not at all difficult to suggest alternative courses of action in each case which might have yielded better results. Hurley, for example, could have adopted the policy of the career foreign service officers in China and tried to coerce Chiang, perhaps even extending aid to the CCP, rather than supporting the KMT unconditionally. After August, Hurley and Marshall might have demanded specific concessions from Chiang in return for American assistance in transporting troops to north China. By the time the Truman administration was willing to use leverage against Chiang, the civil war was raging out of control.

Critics of American policy toward the Cuban revolution agree that the United States missed the best opportunities to stave off a victory by Castro in March 1958 when the United States failed to give active support either to the mediation attempted by the Catholic bishops or to the Joint Committee of Civic Institutions' call for Bastista's resignation. Castro's stature in the opposition was greatly enhanced by the defeat of the summer offensive and the odds were probably against any political solution excluding him after that point. But the best opportunity was again missed when William Pawley failed in his effort to persuade Batista to hand over power to a junta of moderates when he was not given authority to speak for the President. In both cases, the scruples of the State Department officials involved led them to think that they were right to put pressure on Batista to do something (through the arms embargo) but that they ought not to suggest what it ought to be. As a result, the United States ended up waiting until it was simply too late to stop Castro before trying to put the moderates in power.

In Iran, the US might have tried to break the deadlock in the Shah's negotiations with the moderates in the period from late October through December by making continued US support contingent on his willingness to reduce his role to that of constitutional monarch and accept a loss of control over the armed forces.[56] The transition itself did not take place until January, at which time the Ambassador was warning Washington that the Iranian armed forces could no longer be counted on to save Bakhtiar, who may have been the wrong horse anyway. Finally, Carter administration officials may have missed the best opportunity to achieve an acceptable solution in Nicaragua in failing to press Somoza to step down when COSIP held its general strike. Later, the US allowed Somoza to stall for time while he negotiated, and may have weakened the moderates by persuading them to drop their call for Somoza's immediate resignation.[57] After the failure of the moderates, the initiative shifted to the Sandinistas and the administration's last-minute efforts to strengthen moderates in the post-revolutionary junta were unavailing.

Critics of past policy, then, have contended that political solutions have failed at least in part because the United States has waited too long either to apply maximum pressure (China) or to specify what sort of solution would be acceptable (Cuba). If US officials had acted forcefully at the right moment, the critics would argue, the political solution would have had a good chance of succeeding. As we have seen, this contention is at least plausible for China, Cuba,

Nicaragua and Iran. Moreover, the Reagan administration succeeded in early 1986 in removing discredited dictators both in Haiti and the Philippines without bringing anti-American forces to power, and in so doing fostered a brief revival of enthusiasm for use of the political solution. Subsequent developments in those countries, however, as well as closer analysis of what actually happened in 1986, lead one to a more sober assessment.

For the sake of brevity, a thorough discussion of US policy toward Haiti will not be presented here. Suffice it to say that unlike some of the cases above, US officials acted expeditiously, at least up to the departure of President Duvalier. Pressure from Washington to liberalise destabilised a government that had successfully deterred public protest for years, and once the regime was tottering, US advice and influence was important in convincing the dictator to step down rather than bathe his country in blood.[58] But the Haitian solution began to disintegrate late in 1987 when the transitional government, headed by General Namphy, disbanded the independent electoral council and failed to prevent the deaths of 34 victims of a campaign of intimidation, believed by some to have been carried out by or with the complicity of some members of the army. In the end, the election scheduled for November was cancelled and the next election in January was boycotted by several of the leading candidates. The army's preferred candidate, Leslie Manigat, won the election but lasted less than six months in office. In June, Manigat and Namphy reached an *impasse* over the issue of transfers in the army. When Manigat placed Namphy under house arrest, Namphy's supporters stormed the Presidential palace and sent Manigat into exile. Namphy then named himself President.

Critics blamed the Reagan administration for not putting enough pressure on Namphy, but the administration did cut back aid to Haiti drastically after the first election fiasco in November, and this seems to have brought no discernible change in the general's attitude. After the coup in June, the US had little leverage remaining. Thus, despite the hopes raised by the swift collapse of the Duvalier regime, the developments since have provided yet another illustration of how difficult it is to make a political solution work.

The Philippines is also an ambiguous case, and not only because her future, like that of Haiti, is uncertain. In the first years of the Reagan administration, the US expressed consistent support and approval of the government of Ferdinand Marcos, assuming that the Philippine President was immovable—'the only game in town', as one anonymous official put it—and that continued use of the Subic Bay and Clark bases rested on his goodwill. The judgement itself was not unreasonable. Marcos's most formidable opponent, Benigno Aquino, acknowledged that the dictator was a 'master' of political manipulation, an opinion shared by most of his countrymen. One could question, however, the lengths to which administration spokesmen went to curry favour.[59] The US Ambassador, Michael Armacost, was so friendly with the regime that the local press nicknamed him 'Armaclose'. During a 1981 visit to the islands, Vice-President Bush told his host that 'we love your adherence to democratic principles and democratic processes. We will not leave you in isolation'. Two years later in Manila, Secretary of State George Schultz reaffirmed this support, praising Marcos's management of the government and declaring that US relations with the Philippines were 'very special'. The administration reaped the short-term gains of this approach in May 1983, successfully concluding an agreement for the continued occupation of the bases, though pledging $900 million in aid over the next five years for the privilege.[60]

As in Nicaragua, the assassination of the leading critic of the government precipitated the erosion of a position that previously had seemed almost impregnable. On 21 August 1983, immediately upon his return from years in exile, Benigno Aquino was shot dead on the tarmac of Manila airport. A month later, Marcos was facing the largest public protests he had seen since 1965, and by the fall the Philippines was entering an economic crisis that was to worsen steadily. The Reagan administration cautiously distanced itself from the Marcos regime in the weeks after the killing. In September, a State Department spokesman observed that recent events had 'beclouded' the reputation of Marcos, and in early October, Reagan cancelled a planned visit to the Far East, including the Philippines. Fearful that the cancellation might undermine the dictator, Reagan sent a letter to Marcos the following day (later released to the public) assuring him that 'I've always had confidence in your ability to handle things' and that 'relations were as warm as ever'.[61]

Over the next few months, the Philippine economy continued to deteriorate (shrinking by over 5 per cent in 1984), while the Communist insurgency led by the New People's Army (NPA) prospered at an alarming rate. By January 1985, it was estimated that the NPA controlled 20 per cent of the nation's villages. At first, these trends seemed to reinforce the President's instinctive sympathy for Marcos. During the 21 October 1984 debate with Walter Mondale, he admitted that 'there are things there in the Philippines that do not look good to us from the standpoint of democratic rights' but then asked 'what is the alternative [to the government]?' Ignoring the democratic opposition, Reagan answered his own question: 'A large Communist movement.'[62] At the same time, though, the accumulation of bad news was leading middle-level State Department officials to a reassessment, one that ended with their abandonment of the previous policy of co-operation with the regime.

The officials concluded that the death of Aquino had destroyed the political credibility of the government. Marcos was now seen as 'part of the problem' but also 'part of the solution'. The thrust of the new policy, then, was to press Marcos to introduce reforms and 'influence him to set the stage for a transition', though not to try to destabilise or overthrow him. Specifically, Marcos was to be asked to establish promotion by merit in the armed forces, to break up the economic monopolies controlled by his supporters and to permit the 'revitalisation of democratic institutions' in the Philippines. Public statements critical of the regime were made by the embassy to provide some impetus for reform and several US officials visited Manila to reinforce the message. At this point, however, the State Department was not willing to threaten Marcos explicitly with a loss of support or reduction in aid. It was hoped that the growing opposition in Congress and pressure from international banks would be enough to convince him, but there was great reluctance to make direct threats because carrying them out could weaken the government in its fight with the NPA.[63]

The difficulty with the new policy was that Marcos was not fully convinced, with some reason, that Ronald Reagan stood behind it. As a result, US officials found it 'a struggle every step of the way' to convince him to adopt the changes suggested. It was to address this problem that Senator Paul Laxalt was sent to Manila in October 1985 to deliver a handwritten note from the President expressing his concerns about the Philippines directly. The substance and results of the visit have been subject to conflicting interpretation. A senior State Department official stated later that 'Laxalt told Marcos that it was the President speaking, not just a bunch of bureaucratic mandarins. He said that reforms, particularly military reforms, were top priority. He said that Marcos had to prepare the way for others to succeed him. In sum, he convinced Marcos that he had a real problem with us.'[64] Journalist Raymond Bonner, however, alleges that whatever Laxalt was instructed to say, the practical effect of his mission was to strengthen Marcos's confidence and compound the difficulties Washington was facing in implementing the policy of reformist intervention. According to Bonner, Laxalt did not deliver a blunt message but rather assured Marcos that Ronald Reagan was still his friend, that his troubles were mostly with Congress and that these could be cleared up if he would do some of what the State Department asked and take steps to improve his image in the United States. The effect, then, was that 'Marcos was now convinced that he could bypass Bosworth, the embassy, and the State Department.'[65]

Either in Manila or later by telephone, Laxalt also took up the question of a snap Presidential election, which Marcos had considered earlier (according to some reports at the suggestion of CIA director William Casey) and dropped in August. The election, however, 'was not our priority solution', in the words of one US official.[66] As it turned out, this was virtually the only US suggestion that Marcos accepted. After 'brushing aside' nearly every other piece of American advice, Marcos came to agree with Laxalt that an early election would be 'very effective for American consumption', and announced the election over US television on 3 November.

In calling the election, Marcos was gambling that opposition divisions would make it possible for him to win re-election and get the US off his back without resorting to massive fraud, and for several weeks this appeared to be the most likely outcome. State Department officials were convinced by this time that a transition away from Marcos would eventually be necessary, but they did not expect the election to provide it. Rather, they anticipated at the outset that Marcos would win the election by such a large margin that the government's manipulations would be discounted, but that his health problems would force him into retirement in the not too distant future. In the meantime, the US would continue to criticise his failure to implement the suggested reforms as a means of distancing the US from the regime but resist efforts in Congress to reduce military assistance.[67] The administration attempted instead to use the prospect of increased levels of assistance to encourage an honest election.

These calculations were not unreasonable, but two developments in December rendered them obsolete. On 2 December, a pro-government court disregarded the findings of the independent commission and acquitted General Fabian Ver and 25 other defendants in the Aquino case.[68] Nine days later, just an hour before the deadline for registration, Cardinal Sin, supported by the United States, persuaded Salvador Laurel to run as a candidate for Vice-President on a unified opposition ticket with Corazon Aquino; their combined forces, assisted by the Catholic Church, then campaigned much more effectively than had been anticipated. Desperately, Marcos resorted to force and fraud on 7 February despite the presence of foreign observers, damaging his legitimacy and credibility fatally in so doing.[69]

Four days after the election, the administration's most serious mistake during the crisis was committed by the President himself. In response to a question posed at a news conference, Reagan volunteered that 'it could have been that [violence and fraud] was occurring on both sides'. Again, there is some difference of opinion about what policy or disposition underlay the President's curious statement. Bonner argues that the White House had decided at this point to stick with Marcos despite the outcome of the election, and that the President may actually have believed what he said, having been misled by his wife who had close ties with Imelda Marcos.[70] The other possibility is that the administration was attempting to maintain neutrality between the two sides in order to work out a compromise. According to this interpretation, it was for this purpose that veteran mediator Philip Habib was sent to the Philippines the next day. The compromise the administration had in mind would have involved Marcos's continuation in office 'for a while', perhaps in a coalition with the opposition.[71] Bonner believes that Habib was sent in part because the conservative White House staff, particularly Donald Regan, had come to feel that the embassy was too strongly opposed to Marcos to be trusted. Secretary Schultz and other senior State Department officials acquiesced in the mission on the assumption that Habib could be counted upon to convince the President to disregard the advice of Regan and break with the regime. On this view, Habib's mission was not to persuade Aquino to reach a deal with Marcos but only to assess the situation. Both sides in the debate in Washington assumed that Habib would strengthen their case upon his return.[72]

The Philippine opposition seems to have concluded that Habib's instructions were to convince them to reach some sort of accommodation with Marcos, and Mrs Aquino wanted no part of this. She declared on 10 February that she intended 'to take power', and reiterated this forcefully in her meeting with Habib six days later. On the 16th, she announced a campaign of civil disobedience to drive Marcos from the Malacanang Palace.[73]

If matters had remained as they were, a difficult deadlock might have ensued. Mrs Aquino was adamant, Marcos was not likely to depart of his own accord and the administration seemed unwilling to put pressure on him.[74] We can only speculate about what would have emerged from this situation, but the dangers are quite apparent. Fortunately, the stalemate was broken on the evening of 22 February when Juan Ponce Enrile and Fidel Ramos mutinied against Marcos and were joined by about 200 other soldiers at Camp Aguinaldo in Quezon City. The revolt attracted both military and civilian support over the next three days, compelling Marcos to depart on the 25th. Clearly, most of the credit for this nearly bloodless revolution must go to Enrile and Marcos, as well as Corazon Aquino, Cardinal Sin and the many other civilians and soldiers who risked their lives for Philippine democracy. What was the role of the United States in these events?

A representative of Enrile contacted the US embassy on the afternoon of 22 February and asked the US to take steps to protect Enrile, who felt that he was in immediate danger. According to the account of a Canadian journalist, Bryan Johnson, the embassy refused to do so at this early stage, apparently because they were unwilling to antagonise Marcos when the outcome was still in doubt. Johnson reports that this fence-sitting engendered considerable bitterness on the part of the rebels later.[75] The administration did not delay long in coming to their support, however. On Sunday morning (the 23rd), Ambassador Stephen Bosworth read to Marcos the first official pronouncement issued by the White House after the coup: 'these statements strongly reinforce our concerns that the recent elections were marred by fraud, perpetrated overwhelmingly by the ruling party. . . . Many authoritative voices in the Philippines have been raised in support of non-violence. We support these voices and expect them to be respected.' At the Bosworth's suggestion, the White House also began urging Marcos privately to observe restraint. These statements were issued before the Loyalist forces advanced toward Camp Crame and were repulsed by the throng of civilians. The US warnings did not prevent Marcos and Ver from attacking, but did contribute to their fatal hesitation before launching the attack, which will be discussed in greater detail below. Later in the day, Marcos cancelled a strafing run by helicopter gunships from the 15th Strike Wing out of concern for the US reaction. As of the next morning, the Loyalist side held the advantage in firepower and Marcos was still in a very strong position. At this point a personal note was delivered to Marcos from Reagan threatening the cessation of military assistance from the US if heavy weapons were used against the rebels. The weapons were not fired, though the US warning itself was not the reason.[76]

On Sunday afternoon (Washington time), President Reagan, apparently still undecided about whether Marcos ought to go or to stay, met with his closest advisors. The White House chief-of-staff, Donald Regan, argued once again that Aquino was not a reliable alternative, but the President was finally convinced by Habib that 'the Marcos era has ended'. Marcos was then advised through private channels that the US believed he ought to step down to spare his country the danger of civil war.[77]

By the evening of the 24th, it was clear that Marcos was beaten, but there was still some danger that he would lash out with his remaining forces or stubbornly prolong the crisis. The White House called for Marcos's resignation publicly and repeated an earlier offer of asylum to the dictator and his family, but warned that the offer might be withdrawn if force were used.[78] Finally, in the early morning hours of the 25th in Manila, Marcos called Laxalt on the phone and asked if Reagan truly wanted him to leave. Laxalt drove to the White House and consulted with the President, then called Marcos back three hours later and advised him to 'cut and cut cleanly. The time has come.' After a long silence, Marcos replied that he was 'very, very disappointed', and hung up the phone.[79] That evening, the Marcos family loaded suitcases stuffed with jewellery, furs and currency into US helicopters and fled from Malacanang Palace. The Marcos era in the Philippines had come to an abrupt and inglorious end.

It is not my purpose here to deny the Reagan officials all credit for the successful transition to democracy in the Philippines. But were their actions that much more skilful or more timely than their predecessors? In the last phases of the crisis, US officials did play a constructive role in restraining Marcos and expediting his departure, but at many points beforehand they were not any quicker to react than their predecessors. The administration was hesitant to break with Marcos after the assassination, so much so that the President felt it necessary to write a letter of reassurance to Marcos after the Aquino murder. The administration's staunch support of Marcos earlier made it more difficult to convince him to enact the reforms they suggested in 1985. At that point they were not willing to take steps to remove Marcos or even to threaten him explicitly with a loss of US assistance. The February election proved to be the key to the transition and surely would never have taken place without American pressure; but the State Department did not place an especially high priority on it before the Laxalt visit and at least initially did not expect it to provide a solution to the crisis. After the large-scale fraud and violence were apparent to everyone, the administration did not try to force Marcos's resignation at once, but appeared to be aiming at a compromise wholly unacceptable to the opposition. The potentially dangerous stalemate that seemed to be developing was broken by the rebellion of Enrile and Ramos, which the administration did support, but only after hesitating briefly. President Reagan himself did not decide to press for Marcos's departure until the afternoon of 23 February. What if the opposition had remained divided and Marcos had won the election? What if Enrile and Ramos had not mutinied against Marcos? Is it not possible that critics would now be saying many of the same things about the US response in the Philippines that they had said earlier about policy in China, Cuba, Iran and Nicaragua?

II

In all four of the failures discussed above, as well as in the Philippines, critics of United States policy have argued that US policy-makers waited too long to promote a political solution actively (as in Cuba), or to apply the maximum extent of their leverage (as in China). What accounts for this hesitation? On some occasions, the full extent of the problem has not become clear to senior officials until too late. In the late summer and fall of 1978, the Carter administration was involved in the Camp David negotiations, the normalisation of relations with China and the final details of the SALT II treaty with the USSR. Ambassador Sullivan did not send the sort of cable that would redirect top level attention away from such pressing matters until 2 November, at which time it was already very late to attempt a political solution. Afterwards, President Carter complained, in words that leaked to the public, of the inadequate intelligence he was provided with. President Reagan, on the other hand, received early warning from the embassy and other US sources (nearly two years in the case of the Philippines and several months in Haiti) that Marcos and Duvalier were in deep trouble. It goes without saying that timely warning is of great importance in handling these situations. The question of how to improve intelligence collection and assessment, however, is best left for another time.

There are two additional reasons for these delays, and, unlike the intelligence failures, efforts to eliminate them would most likely be controversial. Conservative officials usually have little confidence in the success of US mediation and believe that the dictator may be all that stands between them and a victory of the anti-Western forces. If so, US efforts to effect a political solution may fail to bring the moderates to power but still weaken the government enough to remove the last firm barrier to the extreme opposition. This concern leads conservatives to oppose the political solution and delay its implementation until it is too late for it to succeed, thus making their fear that the best will be the enemy of the good self-fulfilling. The clearest example of this would be Zbigniew Brzezinski's staunch, and not entirely unreasonable, opposition to the proposals of Sullivan and Ball in the Iran crisis. Earl Smith may also have played this role later in 1958, though his memoir denies it. This may also explain the (fortunately less significant) reluctance of Reagan administration officials to go all out against Marcos until after the military revolt.

Liberal officials, on the other hand, are often reluctant to involve the US so closely in the domestic affairs of other countries. President Carter himself is probably the best example of this. In late March 1978, President Perez of Venezuela admonished Carter that developments in Nicaragua bore an ominous resemblance to those in Cuba two decades before. Carter agreed, but replied that he would 'have a difficult time proposing direct action by the US to bring about Somoza's downfall'. As we have seen, US passivity was particularly damaging in this instance, because it came at a time when the Nicaraguan moderates still held the initiative. In November, William Bowdler warned the President that if Somoza were not soon persuaded to turn the government over to the FAO, the Sandinistas would end up in power in Managua. Carter again objected that the United States would be telling another country what kind of government it ought to have or that he would be telling another sitting President that he had to leave. The next month, after George Ball had presented his suggestions on Iran, the President commented once again that he was not prepared to 'tell another head of state what to do', and refused to press the Shah to do as Ball suggested. This sort of reluctance also appears to have been an important influence on US policy toward the Cuban revolution.[80]

Suppose that American officials overcame their hesitations of this sort and acted promptly in support of the political solution. Would success come more frequently than it has in the past? Perhaps so, but much would still depend on underlying conditions shaped by the dynamics of the revolutionary process and largely beyond the control of the United States.

Revolutions can be thought of as an intersection of two trends. The first is the tendency for the strength of the extremists to grow in the opposition as time passes. This is likely to occur because of public outrage at the steps the leader feels he must take to hold on to power, because the dictator deliberately tries to weaken the centre in order to maintain the support of the United States and moderate opinion at home, because the violent opposition proves more effective in redressing the grievances of the people, or simply because the radicals are the ones who have the guns in what is becoming a violent environment. Second, there is a decline over time in the strength, discipline and morale of the armed forces and police. The longer they are exposed to revolutionary crowds and the more they are asked to risk their lives or commit morally questionable acts to defend the regime, the greater their hesitation is likely to be. In the end, if the revolution is successful, they will break altogether. A political solution of either sort requires a favourable conjunction of these two trends. The earlier the radicalisation of the opposition begins, or the later the security forces weaken, the more difficult it will be for the United States to achieve a successful outcome.

Let us consider first the balance of strength between opposition moderates and radicals as a factor in the success or failure of political solutions. In two of the cases where American mediation failed, Iran and China, the moderates were so weak even at the outset that there was never much hope for political solution of any sort. In Iran the Shah offered to draw the moderate opposition into the government in October, at a time when it was far from certain that he would not survive. He found no takers anywhere. One member of the moderate opposition explained why: 'none of us dares disagree with [Khomeini] in public [now] . . . it would be political suicide'. Karim Sanjabi, one of the leading figures in the National Front, threw in his lot with Khomeini in late October, observing that he could not command a majority in a free election and that the Ayatollah was now master of Iran's urban masses. Indeed, as early as May, American journalists estimated that the clergy had become dominant in the opposition movement, although the Ayatollah Shariatmadari, a relative moderate, was as popular as Khomeini for many months.[81]

In China, there was a small third force between the KMT and CCP, the Democratic League, an amalgam of members of several minor parties formed in 1939. The League's programme was to end the period of KMT 'tutelage', negotiate an agreement between the KMT and CCP to merge their armies and form a coalition, and then establish democratic institutions and freedoms in China. Most of the League's members were Westernised intellectuals, especially academics, though there were also a few bureaucrats, professionals and businessmen among them. Marshall was impressed with many of the liberal leaders—he referred to them as 'a splendid group of men' in his parting speech—but none of the centre parties had a large popular following and, unlike the KMT and CCP, none possessed an army. The centre was also divided. Some of the parties in the alliance were so closely associated with the larger parties that they could not be considered truly independent. In late 1946 the alliance finally split apart altogether when the China Youth League and most of the Social Democratic Party decided to join the National Assembly while the other parties honoured the Communists' boycott. Marshall attempted, without success, to persuade moderate Chinese to organise a unified liberal party to offset the extremists in the larger parties, but the moderates remained weak and divided. When he left China in January 1947, Marshall remarked that 'the salvation of the situation . . . would be the assumption of leadership by the liberals in the Government and in the minority parties', but recognised that 'as yet [they] lack the political power to exercise a controlling influence'.[82]

Under the circumstances obtaining in Iran and China, what I have termed the 'moderate solution' would have been difficult or impossible. It was still conceivable that a political solution of another sort could have been substituted, but the odds of it succeeding would have been very small for reasons that will become clearer below. The situation in Haiti, on the other hand, was deceptive: that is, apparently favourable for a political solution in the short run, but with longer-term and largely unrecognised problems looming ahead. Years of repression there had laid waste to the entire political spectrum, so there was little organisation of any kind other than the government, the Church and the armed forces. One positive result was that the far left was very weak (it was estimated that the Communist party had only about 300 members in early 1986); hence, the Reagan administration could press Duvalier to ease up and eventually to leave without having to worry about bringing anti-American radicals to power in the near future, a luxury Carter officials did not have in 1978–9. The problem was that there was no clear moderate alternative to the regime. As a result, even a leading opposition figure had to concede in December 1985 that intervention by the armed forces 'was not the best solution, but the only solution'.[83] In early 1986, this did not seem a fatal handicap; by the time of this writing, however, General Namphy has obviously become reluctant to permit the emergence of an independent civilian government and the prospects for democracy in Haiti appear increasingly dim.

The pattern in Nicaragua and Cuba was very different from any of the cases above in that there was substantial moderate opinion and organisation at the outset. Thus, the eventual outcome in these two countries belies the sensible but incomplete observation that the political solution is possible when a strong third force is present. In Nicaragua, there was a solid, well-organised centre, led by COSIP, but it began losing ground to the left very early in the crisis. One journalist found that in May 1978, only a short while after the failure of the first strike, the Sandinistas were already the country's strongest political force. In late August, Somoza began what appeared to be a concerted attack on the moderate opposition by revoking the charter of the largest business associations and arranging for the Central Bank to call in loans to businesses involved in the strikes. Fifty moderate leaders, including Adolfo Calero of the Conservative Party, were rounded up in that week, and another 550–750 moderates were subsequently jailed. Rather than intimidating the opposition, the death and devastation of the next month only served to accelerate the radicalisation of the public, especially the young, and expand the FSLN's base of recruitment. 'Everybody had a relative or friend killed in the struggle', a leading Sandinista later observed. 'There was a great thirst for revenge.' Thus, by January 1979, when the FAO called for a demonstration on the anniversary of Chamorro's murder, 90 per cent of the participants were affiliated with the United People's Movement (MPU), a group having links with the FSLN. 'The problem with the groups that remain in the FAO', a Nicaraguan politician told journalist Bernard Diederich in early 1979, 'is that they represent nobody.'[84]

The situation was probably less unfavourable in Cuba, but still difficult. By the time of the Pawley mission in November it may have been too late to achieve a moderate solution. Castro's influence had been greatly enhanced by the guerrillas' successful stand against the vastly larger forces of the Cuban army. When the opposition gathered in Caracas in late July to sign a pact of unity, it was he they named 'commander-in-chief'. But if the transition had occurred before the failure of the summer offensive, a moderate or coalition government would have had considerable popular support. At this time, as Wayne Smith puts it, 'the Cuban people wanted Batista out; they did not necessarily want Castro in'.[85] If credible elections had been held on schedule in the spring of 1958, the Cubans might have been able to rid themselves of the Batista dictatorship without saddling themselves with a worse one. There were two obstacles, however. First, many of the Cuban young had lost confidence in the older generation of Cuban politicians the elections would have brought back to power. No less than half a million of the young eligible to vote in 1958 failed to register. Second, Castro and the Revolutionary Directorate were determined to thwart the electoral solution. When the US convinced Batista to lift martial law in order to create a proper climate for elections, they began a campaign of terror that made it impossible to hold the election, not just in Batista's eyes, but also in the judgement of William Wieland of the State Department, Carlos Marquez Sterling (one of Batista's two opponents in the election) and several civic groups in Cuba.[86] Whatever the views of most Cubans, one segment of the public seemed indifferent to the elections and an armed minority intended to prevent them.

One might think that the Philippines, a country with a democratic tradition, an influential Catholic Church and close ties to the United States, was especially fertile ground for a moderate political solution. But the danger of a radicalisation of the opposition was present even there. Journalist Lewis Simons reports that in 1984 the moderate, middle-class 'yellows' who had taken to the streets in protest were already involved in a 'growing contest for control of the crowds' with the Communist 'reds'. The moderates still had the upper hand at that time, but they 'quickly realised that they faced the very real danger of being taken over by the far left'. In October 1985, a moderate Philippine economist claimed that, as in Nicaragua, '[there was] a significant increase in sympathy [for the Communists] among the business community and professionals'. 'There is no doubt that the businessmen are allowing themselves to be deceived,' he added, 'but this shows how desperate they are.'[87]

The Philippines escaped the fate of Cuba and Nicaragua, at least for the time being, because of a series of events that were by no means inevitable or even likely. To imagine how different the results might have been we have only to ask a few counterfactual questions. First, what if Aquino and Laurel had not allied and Marcos had won the election handily, as most observers expected? US officials thought that Marcos would soon have to resign anyway because of his health problems and that a transition could be worked out at that point. But there was still the danger that he or others would attempt to perpetuate the regime under Imelda, General Ver or through some other means. If so, how much faith would the Filipinos have retained in democracy and how much would the NPA have benefited?

Second, what if Enrile and Ramos had not risked their lives in resisting Marcos? The administration, at least up to the point of their defection, did not seem to be willing to take steps to force Marcos out and Mrs Aquino made it clear that she would not acquiesce in his corruption of the election. A prolonged test of wills in the streets would have followed. Would this have remained peaceful? That was the intent of Cardinal Sin and Mrs Aquino, but there were armed anti-Marcos groups in the streets as well, and the discipline and restraint of the armed forces may or may not have held up in a long series of confrontations. Further, would a campaign of civil disobedience have succeeded against a determined dictator who maintained the allegiance of most of the armed forces? If not, Aquino would have been compelled to choose between allying with the NPA or risking losing her supporters to them.

To review, then, the moderates were weak at the beginning of the civil wars in Iran and China, which meant that the only sort of political solution available was a coalition (as Hurley and Marshall attempted in China), or an alliance of the moderates and the armed forces (different versions of which were pursued by Ambassador Sullivan and the White House in Iran). Both were probably long shots. In Haiti, there was very little political organisation of any kind. This has proved to be a mixed blessing. In the short run, the Reagan administration could destabilise Duvalier without having to worry about bringing Marxists directly to power, but it also meant that there was no moderate civilian leadership ready to step in. The transitional government has since proved completely unsatisfactory and may be leading that unfortunate nation deeper into political trouble. In Cuba and Nicaragua, there was considerable moderate opposition at the outset, but the political solution failed anyway. It could be argued that the same thing might have happened in the Philippines if the election and its aftermath had not removed Marcos.

The presence of a robust and well-organised moderate opposition at the beginning of the mediation is important; it probably comes close to being a necessary condition for a successful political solution. It is not sufficient, however, because the strength of the various factions is not fixed but fluid. The balance between the moderates and radicals will probably change over time and there is good reason to think that it will not change for the better. For this reason, it is particularly important for the United States to act early enough, as the critics of past policy have urged, before the radicalisation of the revolution is too far advanced. If the political solution is to succeed, either power must be transferred to the moderates at a time when they (perhaps with the assistance of the armed forces) are still stronger than the extreme opposition, or the radicals must be drawn into a coalition before they have become powerful enough to overwhelm everyone else. In the past, American officials have often erred by waiting too long to apply pressure or state specifically what they actually want the government to do. What would happen if the effort were made sooner?

The answer, I believe, depends upon the second revolutionary trend, the balance of force between the government and the opposition as a whole. As we noted above, the strength, discipline and morale of the armed forces and police will decay as a successful revolution proceeds, though not at the same rate in every situation. If a leader is to be persuaded to step down or even to reduce his power substantially he must be convinced that his security forces cannot sustain him in office, at least at a cost in life and property that he deems acceptable. The sooner this realisation comes to him the better the chances will be for a moderate outcome. The problem for the US or any other mediator is that the earlier the dictator is asked to concede, the stronger the armed forces and police are likely to be, and hence the more confident the ruler will feel and the more resistant he will be to making concessions. An acceptable political solution can be achieved, then, only if the ruler begins to feel vulnerable at a time when the moderates are still ascendant in the opposition. Unfortunately, there is simply no guarantee that this will happen, even if the moderates have substantial support at the outset.

Reviewing these cases, one can see that the greatest difficulties have come when the government was optimistic about its ability to defeat the revolution and in fact had some reason to be. In three of the cases where the political solution failed, the remarkable thing in retrospect is how formidable the government's forces appeared to be early in the crisis. At the time of the Japanese surrender in September 1945, for example, the Chinese Nationalists held, according to official US estimates, a 5:1 advantage in combat troops and rifles and possessed 'a practical monopoly of heavy equipment, transport and an unopposed air arm'. In mid-1946 the Communists were thought to have 1 million men in arms, 400,000 of whom were not regular troops, to face the Government's host of 3 million.[88] The Nationalists had the best of the fighting in the spring, which left the KMT generals over-confident to the point of impatience. Chiang himself told Marshall during the June truce that he expected 'the ripe apple will fall into our laps . . . given time'. Marshall was later to attribute his failure in June to the KMT generals' belief that they could defeat the enemy in two months if given a free hand. By December the government's edge in numbers had diminished somewhat, to 2.6–1.1 million, but the government forces still had three or four times as many rifles as their opponents. Chiang believed at this time that the Communist army would be destroyed within eight to ten months. 'By the close of 1946', said the State Department White Paper on China, 'the Nationalists made impressive gains . . . [and] the superiority of the Government's forces was in most areas as yet unchallenged.'[89]

In Cuba, Castro was fighting an army he himself described as 'incomparable in numbers and in arms'. At the time of the summer offensive, Castro had no more than 800 followers, and probably closer to 300, in the Sierra Maestra. They may have possessed as few as 200 rifles in good condition. Batista sent 17 battalions (6–7000 men) to pursue them, and had another 33,000 men in reserve. A tank company was assigned to each battalion and there was also air and naval support.[90] The army's morale was questionable, but there were few desertions during the offensive, which came within an ace of defeating the guerrillas. In late June, the 18th battalion, advancing from the south, nearly overran Castro's headquarters on Pico Turquino. The attack was supposed to receive support from naval units offshore and a second column in the north, but the attacks were poorly co-ordinated and the rebels were able to cut off the 18th battalion.[91] If Batista's officers had displayed even a modest degree of military professionalism in this campaign, Castro would never have emerged from the Sierra Maestra.

The Nicaraguan National Guard defeated the Sandinista guerrillas easily in the first round of fighting in 1978, which was not surprising in view of their advantages in numbers and equipment. While the FSLN was relying on hunting rifles, pistols and home-made bombs, the Guard had at its disposal automatic weapons, tanks and planes. Obviously, the Guardsmen were not reluctant to utilise their firepower either. After the first round, the National Guard outnumbered the Sandinistas by approximately 10:1. Over the next few months, Somoza recruited heavily and increased the size of his army from 7500 to 11,000. At the same time, Venezuela, Costa Rica and Panama were reported to be cutting back their support for the rebels. American intelligence predicted before the second round that the Guard would be able to stop 'any feasible FSLN offensive'. What both Somoza and the US failed to anticipate was the rapid expansion of the guerrilla forces, which grew from under 1000 in early 1978 to 5000 in July 1979, reducing the Guard's edge in numbers to 1.8:1.[92]

In each of these cases, the government held impressive advantages in the quantity and quality of military force in the first stages of the revolution and enjoyed considerable success in battle in the early fighting. In light of this, it is not difficult to understand why the United States was unable to persuade the men in power to make concessions to the opposition. Indeed, under these circumstances it is hard to imagine what American officials could have said or done that would have convinced them. Few leaders are likely to concede to opponents they expect to defeat.

Interestingly, the situation was not that much different in this respect in the Philippines. When Senator Laxalt visited Marcos in October 1985, he found the dictator 'positive and optimistic—as it developed, unrealistically so'. Marcos reportedly asked the Senator if he had an 'image problem' in the US. Perhaps he ought to 'hire a public relations firm?'[93] Oddly enough, this over-confidence may have worked to the advantage of the US, and ultimately the opposition, at this point in that it led Marcos to think that he could quiet the US protests by staging a successfully managed election. Later, though, the effects of this could have been tragic.

At the beginning of the mutiny by Enrile and Ramos, the forces arrayed against them were overwhelming. When the two announced their rebellion, there were about 2–300 men with them at Camp Crame, with very little firepower, facing 10,000 troops in Manilla possessing armoured personnel carriers, heavy artillery, helicopters and F-5 fighter-bombers. It was also estimated that the number of those committed to RAM (the anti-Marcos reformist movement in the armed forces) totalled no more than 2000 of the 13,000-man officer corps at the beginning and none of the 230,000 enlisted men.[94] Why, then, did the rebellion succeed?

When General Ver called Enrile on 22 February 1986, Enrile asked him to delay any attacks until the morning. Erring far on the side of caution, Ver agreed and asked that the rebels reciprocate by not attacking Malacanang Palace (which was inconceivable at this time).

If Ver had acted immediately, it is hard to see how Enrile and Ramos could have extricated themselves. Instead, Ver hesitated and gave the Filipinos time to answer Cardinal Sin's call to protect the soldiers. By the time General Tadiar arrived the next afternoon with his forces, there were 40,000–50,000 people in the vicinity of Camp Crame and the Loyalists faced a more complex problem.[95]

At this point, it is still likely that the revolt could have been crushed if Tadiar had been willing to use force. In the view of a professional military man who witnessed much of what came to pass around Camp Crame, most of the troops were not won over by the civilians and would have been quite willing to follow orders to fire on them. The problem, he suggests, was not their fraternisation with the crowds but rather restraining them from attacking without orders. The troops were not trained for crowd control nor were they equipped with riot control gear, but the use of minimum force against civilians, perhaps just firing into the air, probably would have been sufficient to disperse the crowd. According to this view, it was General Tadiar's unwillingness, not the restraint of Marcos or the hesitation of the troops, that accounts for the victory of people power over the marines on 23 February.[96]

Even after the tide began to turn, Marcos still retained enough firepower to bring a swift, if sanguinary, halt to the military rebellion. Early on the morning of the 24th, marines under the command of Colonel Balbas removed some civilians from Camp Aquinaldo, directly across Camp Crame, and trained 105mm howitzers on the rebel stronghold. These artillery pieces were capable of killing Enrile, Ramos and everyone around them and there was nothing the mutineers could have done at that point to prevent it. Balbas was given the order to fire three times by Ver that morning. Each time he made some excuse and at one o'clock withdrew his unit, fearing he would face court-martial or worse.[97]

Marcos, in other words, collapsed at a time when the moderates were still strong in part because of the courage and determination of the moderate forces, but also because of General Ver's excessive caution and the scruples of two key commanders. None of these decisions could have been foreseen, and if any of them had not been made, the outcome might have been quite different.

The situation in Iran is more difficult to characterise. Unlike the other countries just mentioned, Iran did not experience a 'civil war', in the sense of two armies facing each other directly in battle, but the capabilities of the armed forces were still of great importance there.

The Iranian revolution was a test of their capacity to deter or contain demonstrations, strikes and riots, a test they ultimately failed. The most important factor in this situation was not numbers *per se*, but the morale and discipline of the troops. The Shah clearly had cause for concern on this point from the beginning. Half of his soldiers were recent recruits from the villages or campuses, paid just $1 a day; also, as noted in chapter 2, the troops were poorly equipped and trained for riot control. Still, the Shah and the American Ambassador were confident enough in July to go on extended vacations.[98] A *Washington Post* correspondent reported in mid-September that 'the army is under firm control' and showed 'flawless discipline in public places' in the last week. Although one mutiny had occurred, he found little evidence that the enlisted men were disloyal. In October, 'much of the opposition did not believe it possible to dethrone the Shah, excepting only after a full-scale bloody civil war', and when called upon to crush a particularly serious uprising in Amol at the end of that month, the army again performed well. In November, the US Military Advisory Group in Tehran reported that the army remained loyal to the Shah and retained 'the ability to act under stress'.[99] By December, journalists were beginning to report an increase in mutinies and desertions but soldiers continued to obey orders to fire on civilians and displayed 'remarkable discipline even beyond the point when they might have been expected to become demoralised'. At the time of Huyser's mission, desertions had increased to 500–1000 per day out of a force of 500,000. In the judgement of one observer, the army did not disintegrate altogether until after the Shah's departure.[100]

The problem for an 'iron fist' solution, however, was that the size of the crowds of protesters had grown steadily over the course of the revolution. By late December, according to one State Department official, it would have taken 100,000–300,000 deaths to clear the streets.[101] This occurred, as I have argued in an earlier chapter, because the Shah continually hesitated to use firm measures to curb the revolution, which suggests that another factor merits consideration and that is the character of the leader himself.

Most dictators are men who enjoy wielding power for its own sake and are extremely reluctant to give it up. As a well-placed Cuban told the State Department in late October 1958, Batista 'has a Napoleonic complex and considers that he is Cuba's legitimately-chosen leader and refuses to bow out until the end of his term . . . Batista has failed to realise the tragedy facing his country and to recognise the seriousness of the threat to his government'.[102] In addition, dictators, as a general rule, are not squeamish. Most of them have achieved power and held on to it because they have not been hesitant to spill blood when necessary to cow or eliminate their enemies. François Duvalier, whose cruelty was legendary, clearly fits this description; his son, according to some accounts, was a man of a different stamp. As an American journalist so aptly put it, Jean-Claude Duvalier lacked 'the passion for power' that animated most of the others mentioned here. Or, as a regime insider remarked at the time of his departure, 'Money was always more important for Jean-Claude than power. Money for his father was a way of keeping power. Power for Jean-Claude was a way of making money.'

This difference in personality may have been a significant factor in the relatively smooth transfer of power in Haiti. It was reported in early 1986 that after he had learned of the kidnapping of some nuns by the *Tontons Macoutes*, Baby Doc was so repelled at the measures his supporters were prepared to use to defeat the revolution that he simply lost his will to rule. Later, the US embassy spokesman explained the dictator's early departure by saying that Duvalier had concluded he could only prolong his rule through harsh repression and 'he was unwilling to do that', and in his parting statement Jean-Claude stressed his intention to minimise bloodshed and preserve his good name. On this view, then, some spark of humanity remained in the younger Duvalier which made him recoil at the thought of bloody repression and protracted civil war. It is hard to imagine his father, or many of the other rulers discussed here, behaving the same way.[103]

Mohammed Reza Pahlavi was also a more complex personality than may of these leaders. The Iranian monarch seems to have had a reasonably clear understanding of the balance of forces and the options available. As he told Ambassador Sullivan, there were three possibilities open to him: (1) drawing some moderates into the government; (2) bringing down the 'iron fist' on Khomeini's followers in the streets, probably with a considerable loss of life; or (3) abdication. The problem was that he refused to accept the implications of his own assessment and make a clear choice.[104] As noted above, he never conceded control of the army in his talks with the National Front; on the other hand, after the Jaleh Square incident he was reluctant to use harsh repression against the crowds. Facing death from cancer, the Shah did not want to be remembered as a brutal oppressor. As he himself explained later:

> A sovereign may not save his throne by shedding his countrymen's blood. . . . A sovereign is not a dictator. He cannot break the alliance that exists between him and his people. . . . A sovereign is given a crown and must bequeath it to the next generation.[105]

If the Shah had firmly committed himself to one course or the other, he might have had some chance either of accommodating or containing the revolutionary forces. But his prolonged indecision, perhaps aggravated by his illness and imminent death, made it possible for Khomeini to extend his influence over the urban proletariat to the point where he could not be denied a predominant voice in Iran's future government.[106]

To reiterate, revolutions can be thought of as an intersection of two trends, the radicalisation of the opposition and the decline in the strength and morale of the security forces. A solution acceptable to the United States can be achieved only if there is a favourable intersection of these trends, that is, if the security forces weaken at a time when the moderates are still strong enough to rule. The dictator's personality, however, may widen or narrow this zone of opportunity, as we have just noted. Many would argue that American policy can do so as well.

If the US intervenes when the government still has good reason to feel confident, there is not much chance of success. It is possible that US intervention might make all the difference, however, if it were to come at a time when the ruler was beginning to have doubts but was not quite willing to make concessions. Under such circumstances, the addition of US pressure might be enough to tip the leader in the direction of compromise before it is too late. Success would come, though, only if the United States were able and willing to mount effective pressure against the regime.

The United States may be unable to do so if leaders are successful in diversifying their sources of support when they anticipate US pressure. Given the number of countries supplying arms or assistance in the contemporary world, these efforts stand a good chance of succeeding. Early in 1978, Somoza decided to replace the American Garand M-1 rifle with the Israeli Galil assault rifle. Somoza also worked out a large arms deal with Argentina, so that by the time of the negotiations later in the year, those two countries, and not the United States, were his leading suppliers of arms. When US pressure put a stop to shipments from Israel later in 1978, Somoza was able to line up alternative sources elsewhere in central America.[107] Two decades before, Batista was able to arrange other sources of military supply after the United States embargoed arms to Cuba in March 1958, purchasing from the Dominican Republic, Nicaragua, Britain and Italy.[108] In Haiti, by contrast, the US was in a position to exert effective pressure. The Duvalier regime relied upon foreign assistance to provide one-third of its budget of $480 million. US aid, which amounted to $52 million for 1986, was a large percentage of the total, and Haiti's other major donors, France and Canada, were also demanding improvements in the observance of human rights.[109]

On other occasions, US threats to cut off support have not had the intended effect because they have lacked credibility. Chiang Kai-shek 'apparently thought that the United States would come to his aid sooner or later, notwithstanding his failure to co-operate with General Marshall and to reform his regime'.[110] In July 1978, Somoza was quoted as saying that Jimmy Carter 'would not have the nerve' to force him to resign.[111] Marcos, too, remained hopeful till the last that President Reagan's sympathy for him would lead him to disregard the advice of middle-level officials and the pressures from the US Congress. As he told an American correspondent, 'Your government is divided into bureaucratic factions. There is one faction there which closes its eyes to reality and has come out openly against my administration. There is another faction trying to help us. . . . The story in the diplomatic circles of course is that in Washington you need two ambassadors—one for Congress and another for the Executive Department.'[112] Ironically, all of these leaders were wrong. Washington was willing to cut off support for extended periods to all three, and dumped Somoza and Marcos altogether. Why do dictators underestimate Washington's determination?[113]

In chapter 1, it was noted that American statements of support may have the adverse side-effect of convincing an ally that the US cannot afford to see him fall. For example, the leader of the Laotian right became, in Arthur Schlesinger's words, a 'Frankenstein' after he concluded that the US was irrevocably committed to him, and the frequent statements of US support by the Reagan administration later proved to be an obstacle to their very sensible efforts to prod Marcos toward reform and eventual abdication.[114] If this is the only source of this sort of difficulty, it would be possible to increase US leverage by exercising more caution in making statements of support at the beginning. It is not, however. The process of radicalisation discussed above may lead the dictator to think that if he can survive the early part of the crisis the US will have no choice but to side with him to prevent the far left from coming to power. Some observers believe, for example, that Somoza negotiated with a view to driving the moderates and radicals together, and, in that respect at least, succeeded, though he miscalculated the American response.[115] Likewise, Chiang Kai-shek remained hopeful after the failure of the Marshall mission that the US would feel compelled to come to his assistance as relations with the USSR continued to deteriorate.[116]

Another source of difficulty is that the government of the United States seldom speaks with one voice and in most situations someone's voice can usually be heard telling the endangered ruler to stick to his guns regardless of what he is hearing from other American officials. Both Chiang Kai-shek and Anastasio Somoza had influential friends in the United States, outside the State Department and White House, who attempted to alter the policy set by the executive branch. In mid-1946, at a time when Marshall was trying to rein in Chiang and prevent the fighting in China from getting out of control, the House Foreign Affairs committee passed a large military assistance bill for China and Under Secretary Dean Acheson announced that $51.7 million of equipment still in the pipeline would be provided. At the same juncture, *Time* magazine and the Scripps-Howard newspaper chain were beginning their campaign to give the KMT all-out backing.[117] In 1978, Congressman Charles Wilson, an old friend of Somoza's, threatened to hold up the Panama Canal treaty in Congress if aid were not restored to Nicaragua. The administration tried to appease Wilson at that point by releasing $12 million in AID loans and $160,000 in military aid left over from 1976. Later in the year, Wilson visited Nicaragua and boasted to Somoza that he had the votes to block the Canal treaty. Another close friend of Somoza, John Murphy of New York, was chairman of the House committee with jurisdiction over the Canal treaty. Murphy met with President Carter in January 1979 and may have tried to link the two issues.[118]

Some of these difficulties are remediable, at least in principle. The United States could increase its leverage by being more careful about making commitments and attempting to reach consensus on policy so that the US government could speak with one voice. On the basis of the evidence available, though, it seems doubtful that US credibility or the lack of it was the crucial factor in the three situations where the regime's over-confidence defeated the political solution. Batista, after all, decided to continue to fight rather than concede after the US embargoed arms to him in March 1958. Ambassador Stuart reported from China in 1947 that while Chiang still hoped to receive American aid, 'he has made a point of telling Chinese who call upon him that China must stand on its own feet and face the future without American assistance'.[119] Finally, Somoza states in his memoirs that after he had had time to reflect on President Carter's letter in June, he concluded that he would fight on alone if necessary. The memoirs also make it clear that Carter did eventually get the message across and there was no doubt in Somoza's mind by December 1978 that the administration was seeking his resignation. Efforts to increase US leverage, then, even if successful, simply may not make that much difference.

In 1986, the Reagan administration and Congress combined to force out two dictators without delivering the countries they had ruled, or misruled, into the hands of a radical movement. Despite this, the historical record still shows that political solutions have failed more often than they have succeeded when undertaken under revolutionary conditions without the presence of US troops. Timing is important, especially with the moderate solution, because revolutions tend to radicalise as time passes; the longer the mediators delay, the weaker the moderates are likely to become. Past US efforts have failed, according to the critics, because American officials have waited too long to apply maximum leverage or specify what they want the leaders to do. A review of US policy in China, Cuba, Nicaragua and Iran demonstrates that the critics are at least partly right—frequently the United States has been 'too late'. In most cases, one can identify opportunities earlier in the course of the revolution that the United States missed because of poor intelligence, opposition from officials doubtful of the advisability of the political solution, or the reluctance of liberal officials to interfere in the politics of another country.

Viewed in the light of the factors discussed above, though, the effort could just as easily come 'too early' if American officials were to try to force out a leader still confident in his security forces or sceptical about US leverage. It is at least conceivable (though under present circumstances unlikely) that the various branches of the US government could co-ordinate policy to bring maximum pressure on a falling dictator. But even if this were accomplished, it is still going to be extremely difficult to force out a dictator optimistic about his chances of survival and determined to cling to power. The feasibility of the political solution, then, is heavily dependent on the conjunction of the two revolutionary trends. If attempted too soon, the dictator will probably feel too confident to heed US advice; if begun too late, the radicals will have become too strong or the military will be too disorganised. The moderate solution will be possible only at a moment when the government feels vulnerable enough to concede and the moderates are still dominant in the opposition. The problem is not just that this moment may be fleeting or difficult to anticipate. In some instances, it may never come at all.

If this analysis is correct, then the true lesson of the Philippine and Haitian revolutions may not be that political solutions are easily attainable if pursued forcefully and with expedition, but rather that they are even more dependent on favourable underlying circumstances, heroism and good fortune than we imagined before. Better policy may improve the past rate of success, but the safest conclusion at this point would seem to be that we cannot repose complete confidence in this method of dealing with political instability in friendly countries. The military revolt that produced the Philippine transition was, as Cardinal Sin exclaimed, 'a miracle . . . the answer to our prayers'. We can hope and pray that that miracle will be repeated elsewhere, but if the past is any indication, we can not rely on it.

III

Up to this point, the main concern has been whether a political solution, especially a moderate solution, can be put into place. Next, I would like to consider what happens once an inclusive solution, that is, one in which both the moderate and radical opposition are represented, is agreed upon. What are its chances for success, and what determines whether it will succeed or fail?

The United States has participated in the construction of these sorts of arrangements four times since 1945. One of these efforts, the mediation in China, has already been discussed. The other attempts occurred in Laos (1959–61), Vietnam (1972–75) and Zimbabwe–Rhodesia (1978–80). Let us take these up in turn.

The Geneva accords of 1954 had left two northeastern provinces of Laos in the hands of the Pathet Lao, a leftist group allied with the Vietminh. In 1959, the rightist government of Phoui Sananikone tried, with full American support, to reintegrate the military forces of the Pathet Lao into the national army while at the same time excluding them from representation in the cabinet. The effort failed and the Pathet Lao began fighting again in the summer. In August, centrists in the Royal Army overthrew the government and brought neutralist Souvanna Phouma to power. Souvanna invited the Pathet Lao to form a coalition in November and accepted aid from the Soviet Union. The rightists in the army then attacked the centrists, but the Pathet Lao and Vietminh came to the government's defence and the fighting was inconclusive. The negotiations that followed remained deadlocked through 1961 when the rightists held out for control of the Interior and Defence Ministries.[120]

According to one source, the rightists remained uncompromising because they assumed that their military position was so tenuous that the United States would not dare to put pressure on them. In 1962, however, American officials warned the rightists that the US would not intervene militarily and that aid might be cut off if they refused to give way. In May, just as the pressure was beginning to have some effect, the centrists and Pathet Lao attacked at Nam Tha and routed Phoui's army. The Kennedy administration responded by deploying 5000 American soldiers along the Thai side of the Mekong river and positioning an aircraft-carrier task force closer to Indochina. The Pathet Lao agreed shortly thereafter to enter into negotiations with the rightists.[121]

By 11 June 1962 the princes representing each faction had agreed on the composition of the cabinet. Souvanna was named prime minister and the two security ministries were given to centrists. The outside powers agreed to respect the territorial integrity of the country and withdraw all military personnel within 75 days, and Laos was to adopt a position of neutrality in the cold war.[122]

The coalition soon collapsed as a result of the efforts of the Pathet Lao to strengthen themselves at the centrists' expense by recruiting centrist officers susceptible to their overtures and assassinating those who were not. In February 1963, a centrist commander reacted to these provocations by killing the head of the Pathet Lao's network of agents. The Pathet Lao then launched an attack on the centrist's position on the Plain of Jars, and their representative in the coalition quit and rejoined his troops in the field.[123]

Although the political solution did not hold in Laos, the results were not damaging to American interests. Souvanna Phouma emerged as the leading political figure in Laos, but was driven into closer co-operation with the United States and the right, leaving the Johnson and Nixon administrations considerable freedom to conduct military operations in the country through the sixties.[124]

Calling Vietnam a 'failed political solution' may seem a cruel understatement, but is accurate even so. The agreement worked out between Le Duc Tho and Henry Kissinger in October 1972 was a ceasefire in place, meaning that the forces of the Vietcong and the North Vietnamese were permitted to hold their current positions in the South while the United States agreed to withdraw the small number of American troops remaining in the country within sixty days. The North was permitted to replace its soldiers in the South one for one, but was not allowed to augment its forces through infiltration. President Thieu was to continue in office, but a National Council of Reconciliation and Concord (NCRC), composed of representatives of the government, the Vietcong and neutralists, was to prepare the way for elections that were to end the struggle. In the interim, the territories of Laos and Cambodia would be out of bounds to both sides. Finally, the agreement was to be monitored by the International Commission of Control and Supervision (ICCS) and two Joint Military Commissions.[125]

Kissinger was unable to secure the approval of Thieu, however, and the North Vietnamese became suspicious. When the talks resumed, they revived their previous demand that Thieu be replaced immediately by a coalition government. President Nixon broke the deadlock by the controversial Christmas bombing and an agreement quite similar to the October draft was signed in Paris on 27 January 1973. Thieu's acquiescence had been obtained both by the threat of a separate peace and by Nixon's promise to come to his aid if the North Vietnamese staged another offensive.[126]

Soon after the signing of the agreement, Thieu offered to hold an election. The Vietcong refused, saying that they would not participate in elections until article 11, which guaranteed freedoms of speech, press and assembly, was implemented. Discussions began in March 1973 and produced nothing for about a year. In the meantime, land-grabbing operations were carried out by South Vietnam while the Communists remained more cautious. In March 1974, the South Vietnamese government suggested that the two sides begin working on an agreement to implement article 11, establish the NCRC and hold elections. But the South began boycotting the talks in the middle of April in protest against the military build-up being carried out by the Vietcong. The Vietcong then quit the negotiations as well, and the talks were never reconvened.[127]

Fighting had begun in earnest in late 1973. The next year, Congress cut the administration's aid requests for Vietnam drastically, with severe consequences for the morale of ARVN. At the same time, China and the USSR supplied North Vietnam very generously. In the spring of 1975, the North launched its fourth conventional offensive against South Vietnam. Lacking the support the United States had provided in the past, ARVN crumbled, and the Communists took Saigon, appropriately, on May Day.[128]

The sole success among these four cases took place in the former British colony of Rhodesia. In the first year of the Carter administration, negotiations between the white minority regime headed by Ian Smith and the black nationalist guerrillas opposing it broke down. Smith then turned to the black groups who had not taken up arms and put together an 'internal settlement' with them on 3 March 1978. Later in the month, three black leaders joined Smith on an Executive Council. Elections were held in April 1979 and the victor, Archbishop Abel Muzorewa, became his nation's first black prime minister on 1 June.

The Carter administration not only refused to recognise the internal settlement but also declined to lift US economic sanctions, even after Muzorewa had taken office. The administration held back, despite intense pressure from Congress, because they felt that the guerrillas were bound to win in the end and opposing them would offend much of black Africa and push the guerrillas toward the Soviets. Eventually, this isolation compelled Smith and Muzorewa to enter talks sponsored by the British at Lancaster House in London.

To the astonishment of many political observers, the negotiations produced a political solution to the Rhodesian conflict. The two sides drafted a new constitution at Lancaster House, then agreed to turn the country back temporarily to a British Resident-Commissioner who would manage the transition to elections. In the following months Lord Soames succeeded in reducing the level of violence enough to permit the voting to take place in March 1980. Robert Mugabe, the leader of one of the guerrilla factions, won the election and adopted a non-aligned foreign policy once in power.[129]

Thus, although the United States has successfully put inclusive solutions in place on four occasions, they eventually collapsed in every case but one. In thinking about why this has happened and what can be learned from it, it makes sense to begin by asking what made the sole success, Zimbabwe, different from the others.

The situation there differed in three respects from that elsewhere. First, the opposition was divided into at least three groups, which increased the leverage of the outside mediators. In the opinion of some observers, including the chief negotiator himself, one of the most important factors in the Zimbabwean success was the willingness of the British to consider a 'second-class solution' (that is, proceeding without Robert Mugabe), if Mugabe had not accepted their plan.[130] If he had refused to co-operate, Mrs Thatcher was apparently willing to give full support to an arrangement including Joshua Nkomo along with the parties to the internal settlement. Faced with this possibility, Mugabe (and more likely his sponsors, see below) came to see the proposed inclusive solution as the lesser risk. The British had this kind of leverage because of the unusual composition of the Zimbabwean opposition. Not only was there a split between moderates (those willing to co-operate in the internal settlement) and radicals (those who continued to fight), there was also a division (mostly ethnic) within the violent opposition between followers of Mugabe and Nkomo. The three-way political division in Laos did not lead to a lasting political solution, however, which suggests that there are other parts to the puzzle.

The attitude of the radicals' external allies was also different in Zimbabwe than everywhere else. Mozambique and Zambia were the most significant of the Front Line States, the key outside supporters of the Patriotic Front guerrillas. By the time of the Lancaster House conference, they were eager for a settlement because of the disruption the war was causing in their own societies. Mozambique was losing between $100 and $200 million per year in transit fees and commerce, but Zambia's situation was even worse. President Kaunda was faced with a huge debt, his country was nearly bankrupt and he was desperately short of foreign exchange. Zambia was also heavily reliant on Western loans, which made her vulnerable to outside pressure to end the war. At home, the Zambians were becoming impatient with the Zimbabwe African Peoples Movement (ZAPU) guerrillas, who were beginning to behave more like occupiers than allies. Finally, the Rhodesian army was still fully capable of punishing the Front Line States militarily. In September, the Rhodesians struck deep inside Zambia and Mozambique, attacking bridges and rice fields as well as the guerrilla camps. By October,

Zambia's links with the outside world had been severed completely.[131]

Mozambique and Zambia played an important role in getting the guerrillas to London in the first place, then applied pressure on their allies at two important junctures in the talks. In December, Mugabe flew to Dar es Salaam for consultations with his allies. He was determined to hold out at this time because of his concern over the 'Wall's Plan', under which the guerrillas were to gather in 15 assembly points in Zimbabwe's border regions. Mugabe feared that the assembly points would be vulnerable to air attack and that their location would suggest that the guerrillas had retreated. These concerns were not without foundation, but the Front Line statesmen, particularly Mozambique's Machel, prevailed upon Mugabe to sign despite his objections.[132]

In the other cases, the patrons of the leftist combatants failed to exercise restraint on their clients, if they did not actively work to undermine the accords. When George Marshall returned to the US in January 1947, he noted that the Chinese Communists 'did not appear irreconcilable last February', but that 'the course which [they have] pursued in recent months indicated an unwillingness to make a fair compromise'. This shift was almost certainly related to a change in Soviet policy. In June and July of 1946, the Soviets abandoned their previous restraint and began arming the Chinese Communists, transforming the Fourth Field Army from what one American observer had called 'little more than a collection of irregulars of the lowest order' in early summer to a formidably trained and equipped fighting force by January 1947. Among other things, the Soviets transferred 1226 artillery pieces and 369 tanks (mostly confiscated from the Japanese), reversing the Nationalist's superiority in firepower. The effect of this was to stiffen the bargaining position of the CCP at the very time (October 1946) when Marshall was beginning to have some success in reining in Chiang. The Soviet's build-up of the CCP's forces probably accounts, at least in part, for the increased obduracy of the Communists noted by Marshall in the later months of his mission, and certainly had much to do with the outcome of the civil war.[133]

In the first week of August 1962, US reconnaissance aircraft spotted a convoy of several hundred trucks moving North Vietnamese combat troops, tanks and artillery on to the Laotian Plain of Jars. By the end of the month, there were an estimated 10,000 Vietnamese soldiers in the country.[134] The Vietnamese also diverted some of the aid the USSR intended for the neutralists to the Pathet Lao, unbeknownst to the Soviets. In October 1962, the Soviets stopped their airlift to the neutralists, leaving them dependent on the Pathet Lao and North Vietnamese for supplies. When Hanoi began withholding oil, Kong Le turned to the US. In June 1963, Souvanna Phouma publicly condemned the large flow of *matériel* from the Vietnamese Communists to the Pathet Lao.[135] Although there is no firm evidence that Vietnamese joined the attack on Kong Le's forces in 1963, they certainly did nothing to hinder their Laotian clients and their presence must have given the Pathet Lao great confidence. As the authors of a Rand Corporation study put it, 'Souphanouvang's decision . . . to abandon his cabinet post in Vientiane and to resume the civil war could not have been taken without the consent and the cooperation of the Vietnamese Communists, on whom the Pathet Lao were dependent in all respects.'[136]

In the absence of co-operation from Hanoi, the US next tried to enlist the help of the Soviets. In April 1963, President Kennedy requested Khrushchev to press his Vietnamese allies to observe the agreement. By this time, the Sino-Soviet rift had developed and Khrushchev was vulnerable to Chinese charges of insufficient zeal in promoting wars of national liberation. The Soviet Chairman refused to lend his assistance and the settlement in Laos disintegrated.[137]

The problem in Vietnam is clear enough. There was not much willingness on either side to try to make the political solution work and the war was finally ended when the North simply invaded the South and conquered it. Critics of the Nixon administration say that this was quite predictable and that Kissinger's later attempts to shift the blame on to Congress for the fall of the South were disingenuous. But there is another side to the question. Nixon had promised Thieu that he would reintroduce American forces if the North launched an offensive. In 1972, the North had been beaten back when there were only 6000 American combat troops in Vietnam.[138] The difference then was American air power. In June 1973, Congress forbade the President, weakened politically by the spreading Watergate scandal, to undertake any further military operations in Vietnam after August. If Watergate had not happened and Nixon's hands had not been tied, would the North have risked an invasion of the South? And if Nixon could have deterred an invasion for a few years, would this have bought enough time for the South to build a society and an army strong enough to repel aggression from the North without American help? We cannot be certain, of course, but the opportunity was lost when Congress failed to match the assistance the larger Communist powers poured into Hanoi between 1973 and 1975 and reduced the risks the North would face in invading the South by prohibiting the use of American air power to punish or restrain the North.

The second condition necessary for an inclusive political solution to work, then, is co-operation from the patrons of the left. When their assistance is not forthcoming voluntarily, it is possible that the United States or some other power might be able to compel them. But even if the outside powers can be convinced to go along, an inclusive political solution will still face some enormous obstacles.

If the inclusive solution is to succeed, an arrangement must be put in place that will keep the two sides from fighting until elections can be held. In addition, the armies of the two sides will have to be merged at some point. If the transitional government is a coalition, the most intractable issue that must be faced is who is to be entrusted with the portfolios for defence and internal security. When the Communists were given control of the Interior Ministry in Czechoslovakia in the forties, they turned the police into their own private army and used it to seize power in 1948. The Laotian negotiations were stalled for months over this issue, which was finally resolved when the centrists were given the security ministries. The availability of a neutral third group made this problem somewhat more manageable, but despite the relatively favourable circumstances, the Laotian coalition still broke down within a year. In China and Vietnam, negotiations were begun to form coalitions, but the parties never reached agreement. As in many other respects, Zimbabwe was unique. Although it was an inclusive solution (in that the radicals were brought in along with the moderates and the right), the transition government was not a coalition, so the problems inherent in such arrangements did not arise.

Reintegration of the armed forces of the two sides has also proved to be extremely difficult. This can be accomplished only after the rebels have some assurance that they will not become the victims of retaliation, as befell the Greek left after the Varkiza agreement of 1945. This confidence is not likely to come soon in the absence of an overwhelming threat from the outside, and it did not come even then in China. The reintegration agreements reached in Laos and China were never implemented.

For these to succeed, and for the proper climate for elections to be maintained, the effective maintenance of law and order is a necessity, but this too has been exceedingly difficult to achieve. The machinery established to monitor and enforce the cease fire has failed time and again. The bodies created to monitor the settlements in Laos and Vietnam, to be honest about it, were designed not to work, but this may be exactly what one would expect when the Communists are strong enough to demand inclusion. The International Control Commission set up to monitor the agreement in Laos was not allowed to keep inspection teams in the countryside and was authorised to act only with the concurrence of the government of Laos (over which the Pathet Lao had a veto). Further, it was permitted to adopt conclusions and make recommendations only by a unanimous vote of the Indian, Canadian and Polish delegates who composed it. These provisions allowed the Polish delegate to obstruct investigations when fighting broke out on the Plain of Jars in 1961.[139]

The control machinery was also deeply flawed in Vietnam. The ICCS was composed of representatives from Canada, Indonesia, Poland and Hungary, and again was empowered to act only after a unanimous vote. Predictably, the Poles and Hungarians used their veto power to block investigations of violations by the North Vietnamese. The most serious impediment, however, was the out-right refusal of the North and the Vietcong to co-operate. Their interference made it impossible to determine who held contested territory or to verify the neutrality and resupply provisions of the treaty. The inspectors finally gave up after an unarmed American representative was shot looking for MIAs at an air-crash site and some Canadian observers were captured and held prisoner for several days. As a result, the North Vietnamese still had free run of Laos and Cambodia and were able to introduce men and *matériel* into the South much faster than the 1:1 replacement ratio permitted by the treaty. By the fall of 1974, there were more North Vietnamese soldiers in the South than there had been for ten years.[140]

The truce supervising teams in China were composed of three members, one each from the KMT and the CCP, along with one representative of the United States. Under the original terms of the ceasefire, the teams were permitted to act only when in unanimous agreement. The mechanism seemed to work well enough at first, but by March both sides were using this provision to block investigations. In May, when the Communists held the military initiative, their members hamstrung the teams by absenting themselves altogether. When their fortunes reversed the next month, the CCP agreed to permit the American member of the teams to cast the deciding vote, a measure the KMT had supported earlier. For the reasons already discussed, this modification was not enough to save the situation.[141]

Again, Zimbabwe was unusual, and perhaps *sui generis*. Power was placed in the hands of an outsider, who did not hesitate to take controversial steps to create a proper climate for elections. When the guerrillas were slow to reach the camps where they and the Rhodesian government forces were to assemble, Lord Soames refused to extend the deadline for the guerrillas' movement into the camps, and when the actions of Mugabe's forces endangered the ceasefire, he used the Rhodesian army and Muzorewa's auxiliaries to establish order. Later, Lord Soames threatened to ban parties that intimidated voters from campaigning or postpone the elections in areas where heavy intimidation had occurred.[142]

Finally, if elections can be held, the loser must accept the verdict. In China, Laos and Vietnam, the inclusive solution broke down before this stage, so we do not know for certain what would have happened if elections had been held. Realistically, though, one must ask how often parties who have been shooting at each other for years will allow the other side to take control of the government and obediently assume the role of loyal opposition. In the sole success, Zimbabwe, Robert Mugabe won a decisive victory in the elections. What would have happened if, as many observers expected, he had won only a plurality and Muzorewa, Ian Smith and Joshua Nkomo, the leader of the other Patriotic Front faction, had formed a coalition and excluded him from power?[143]

To conclude, the chances for the inclusive solution are enhanced if the radical/violent opposition is divided, if the moderate/middle forces have some military power, if the outside sponsors of the leftist forces are willing to restrain their clients and if the transitional government is based on something more workable than the usual combination of a domestic coalition and an international committee with divided authority and representation of all shades of opinion. Three out of these four conditions held in Zimbabwe: the transition was not handled by a coalition assisted by some sort of unwieldy multinational monitoring body but by an outsider acceptable to both parties; the Front Line States were anxious for an agreement; and the violent opposition was divided, allowing the British mediators to put greater pressure on the more obstinate revolutionaries. But the Rhodesian situation was unusual in all three respects and perhaps unique in the first. How often will third world countries accept a neo-colonial solution of that sort in the future?

The conditions that made success possible in Zimbabwe, then, are not likely to be present very frequently. For this reason, the moderate solution will usually be a more practical alternative. As we have seen, however, it too is highly dependent on factors beyond the control of outside mediators, and, contrary to critics of past US policy, timely intervention by the US will by no means guarantee its success.

Notes

1. Warren Cohen, *America's Response to China* (New York: Wiley, 1980), pp. 175–7; Paul Varg, *The Closing of the Door* (East Lansing: Michigan State University Press, 1973), pp. 156, 168; Richard Thornton, *China: The Struggle for Power* (Bloomington: Indiana University Press, 1973), pp. 156–7, provides an alternative account.
2. Cohen, *America's Response to China*, pp. 182–3.
3. Thornton, *Struggle for Power*, pp. 166, 179–80, 191. Control of the local governments was critical because it would determine the relative strength of the parties in the national govenment after the formation of the coalition.
4. Tang Tsou, *America's Failure in China* (Chicago: University of Chicago Press, 1963), pp. 317–23; Cohen, *America's Response to China*, p. 185.
5. Cohen, *America's Response to China*, pp. 185–6.
6. Varg, *Closing of Door*, pp. 245–7; Tsou, *America's Failure*, pp. 407–11; Thornton, *Struggle for Power*, p. 189.
7. Cohen, *America's Response to China*, p. 190; Thornton, *Struggle for Power*, pp. 198–9; Varg, *Closing of Door*, p. 271.
8. Thornton, *Struggle for Power*, pp. 200, 204; Tsou, *America's Failure*, pp. 434–6; Cohen, *America's Response to China*, p. 192; Varg, *Closing of Door*, pp. 274–5.
9. Quoted in Tsou, *America's Failure*, p. 438.
10. Earl E. T. Smith, *The Fourth Floor* (New York: Random House, 1962), pp. 20–1; Hugh Thomas, *Cuba: Or the Pursuit of Freedom* (London: Eyre & Spottiswoode, 1971), p. 946; Philip Bonsal, *Cuba, Castro, and the United States* (Pittsburgh: University of Pittsburgh Press, 1971), pp. 17–21; Ramon Bonachea and Ramon San Martin, *The Cuban Insurrection* (New Brunswick, New Jersey: Transaction Books, 1974), pp. 174–5.
11. *Draft White Paper on Cuba*, May 1962, pp. 44–7 (Declassified under the Freedom of Information Act, as are the documents that follow on Cuba. Box 13798, 78D287); also Deptel 384, 22 January 1958.
12. Deptel 442, 21 February 1958.
13. *Draft White Paper on Cuba*, pp. 48–9; Earl Smith, *Fourth Floor*, p. 66; Embtel 490, 26 February 1958.
14. Earl Smith, *Fourth Floor*, pp. 69–75; Wayne Smith, *The Closest of Enemies* (New York: Norton and Co., 1987), pp. 21–3; 'Memo of Conversation', 8 March 1958; Deptel 479, 5 March 1958, quotes Rubottom's expression of this before the Senate Foreign Relations Committee.

15. *Draft White Paper on Cuba*, pp. 49–51; Earl Smith, *Fourth Floor*, p. 73; Deptel 479, 8 March 1958; Embtel 503, 3 April 1958.

16. Earl Smith, *Fourth Floor*, p. 69; 'Memo of Conversation', 8 March 1958, appears to substantiate this.

17. Wayne Smith, *Closest of Enemies*, pp. 18–23, 27, 35–7.

18. Embtel 503, 4 March 1958.

19. Embtel 525, 12 March 1958.

20. 'Memorandum for Mr Snow', written by William Wieland, 7 March 1958.

21. Embtel 536, 14 March 1958; Earl Smith, *Fourth Floor*, p. 82.

22. Deptel 484, 6 November 1958. The first explicit call for Batista's replacement I found in the documents available was on 24 April 1958. In a memorandum to Mr Snow, H. A. Hoyt suggests that 'there are not very many who are going to believe that there will really be free elections unless Batista gives assurances and proof that he will retire from the scene (best thing would be for him to leave Cuba) and not remain a strong man behind a Batista-elected candidate'. Hoyt recommended that the US ignore Castro and make an 'appeal to Batista on the basis of patriotism' ('Thoughts on the Cuban Situation', 24 April 1958).

23. Wayne Smith, *Closest of Enemies*, pp. 23–6; Earl Smith, *Fourth Floor*, pp. 86–7.

24. US Congress, Senate, Subcommittee on Internal Security of the Senate Judiciary Committee, State Department Security: *The William Wieland Case*, 86th Congress, 1st Session, 1961, pp. 542–4; also 'Conversation with Nunez Portuondo', 1 April 1958. In 'Memorandum of Conversation', 8 March 1958, Smith asked for permission to make 'some noncommittal statement' in support of the National Harmony Commission (NHC) initiative 'along the lines that we have not intervened in the affairs of Cuba and that we do not intend to intervene' but that 'the people of the US earnestly desire and hope for a peaceful solution to this problem'. Rubottom agreed, but added that it ought to be made only after something had already taken place. On 1 April, two middle-level State Department officials met with Nunez Portuondo. The former Prime Minister asked them if the US could announce that it would refuse to recognise any Cuban government that did not come to power through proper elections. Nunez was told 'while it was an ingenious suggestion, it ran counter to basic elements of US foreign policy toward Latin America in general and Cuba in particular'. 'We reminded him', they recall, 'of our commitment, especially since 1934, not to intervene.' (Memo of Conversation, 1 April 1958) Finally, the Draft White Paper concludes with the observation that the 'policy which the US has followed in Cuban internal affairs has been widely recognised and approved of throughout the Western Hemisphere and within Cuba itself. In spite of many problems, provocations and pressures the US did not intervene, and an internal Cuban conflict has been resolved by the Cubans themselves. It has also enhanced its stature within the inter-American community' (p. 115).

25. Bonachea and San Martin, *Cuban Insurrection*, pp. 232–3, 262; Theodore Draper, *Castro's Revolution: Myths and Realities* (New York: Praeger, 1962), p. 14; Thomas, *Cuba*, pp. 990–1, 996–8; *Draft White Paper on Cuba*, pp. 55–6; 'Cuban Army Push Reported Halted', *New York Times*, 10 July 1958; 'New Offensive Expected', *New York Times*, 20 July 1958; 'Army Repulsed, Castro Reports', *New York Times*, 20 August 1958.

26. Embtel 182, 'Policy Paper on Cuba' by Ambassador Smith, 8 August 1958.

27. 'Memorandum for Mr Snow', 29 August 1958, pp. 3, 5.

28. John Dorschner and Roberto Fabricio, *The Winds of December* (New York: Coward, McCann, and Geoghan, 1980), pp. 158–9; Mario Lazo, *Dagger in the Heart* (New York: Funk & Wagnalls, 1968), pp. 160–2.

29. Dorschner and Fabricio, *Winds of December*, pp. 158–9.

30. Lazo, *Dagger in the Heart*, p. 173.

31. Dorschner and Fabricio, *Winds of December*, pp. 57–9.

32. Earl Smith, *Fourth Floor*, pp. 169–71; Dorschner and Fabricio, *Winds of December*, pp. 245, 351.

33. Dorschner and Fabricio, *Winds of December*, pp. 169–72, 459–61, 447–9; Thomas, *Cuba*, pp. 1028–9.

34. Dorschner and Fabricio, *Winds of December*, p. 534; Bonachea and San Martin, *Cuban Insurrection* p. 322; Rufo Lopez-Fresquet, *My Fourteen Months with Castro* (Cleveland: World Publishing Co., 1966), pp. 34–5.

35. Bernard Diederich, *Somoza* (New York: E. P. Dutton, 1981), pp. 144, 197; Richard Fagen, 'The End of the Affair', *Foreign Policy*, 36 (Fall 1979), p. 183; Paul Sigmund and Mary Speck, 'Virtue's Reward', in US Congress, Senate Committee on Foreign Relations (Subcommittee on Western Hemispheric Affairs), *Latin America*, 95th Congress, 2nd Session, 4 October 1978, pp. 211, 213.

36. Fagen, 'End of the Affair', pp. 183–4; Diederich, *Somoza*, pp. 154–5; Shirley Christian, *Nicaragua: Revolution in the Family* (New York: Random House, 1985), pp. 47–9.

37. John Booth, *The End and the Beginning* (Boulder, Colorado: Westview Press, 1982), p. 158; Diederich, *Somoza*, pp. 159, 165, 170–1, 184, 188; Sigmund and Speck, 'Virtue's Reward', p. 211. See also President Carter's response to President Perez of Venezuela quoted below in section II.

38. William LeoGrande, 'The Revolution in Nicaragua: Another Cuba?', *Foreign Affairs*, 58 (Fall 1979), p. 33–4; Booth , *End and Beginning*, pp. 160–1; Diederich, *Somoza*, pp. 168, 172; Christian, *Nicaragua*, pp. 56–7.

39. Diederich, *Somoza*, pp. 198–202; Christian, *Nicaragua*, pp. 61–6; Robert Pastor, *Condemned to Repetition: The United States and Nicaragua* (Princeton: Princeton University Press, 1987), p. 93; *This Week* (1978), pp. 195, 200.

40. Booth, *End and Beginning*, p. 165; Christian, *Nicaragua*, p. 70; Pastor, *Condemned to Repetition*, p. 83.

41. Booth, *End and Beginning*, p. 165; Christian, *Nicaragua*, pp. 41–2,

59–60, 72–4; Pastor, *Condemned to Repetition*, pp. 94, 101–2.

42. Booth, *End and Beginning*, pp. 165–7; Diederich, *Somoza*, pp. 207–9; Christian, *Nicaragua*, pp. 75–7.
43. Booth, *End and Beginning*, p. 170; Diederich, *Somoza*, p. 229.
44. See, for example, LeoGrande, 'Revolution in Nicaragua', p. 35.
45. Anastasio Somoza Debayle, as told to Jack Cox, *Nicaragua Betrayed* (Belmont, Massachusetts: Western Islands Publishers, 1980), pp. 143–8, 219–20, 318; Diederich, *Somoza*, p. 208.
46. Diederich, *Somoza*, pp. 222–3; Christian, *Nicaragua*, pp. 80–1; Booth, *End and Beginning*, p. 167; Somoza, *Nicaragua Betrayed*, pp. 226–8, quotation on p. 329.
47. Barry Rubin, *Paved with Good Intentions* (New York: Oxford University Press, 1980), pp. 213, 216.
48. 'Reading Iran's Next Chapter', *New York Times*, 13 December 1978, p. 1; Gary Sick, *All Fall Down: American's Tragic Encounter with Iran* (New York: Penguin, 1986), pp. 109, 117, 129–30.
49. Sick, *All Fall Down*, pp. 68, 73.
50. Sick, *All Fall Down*, pp. 3–4, 74–80, 87–8; Zbigniew Brzezinski, *Power and Principle: Memoirs of a National Security Advisor 1977–81* (New York: Farrar, Straus, Giroux, 1983), p. 364.
51. Sick, *All Fall Down*, pp. 69–70, 109, 150. It was at this point, obviously very late in the day, that discussions of some sort of political solution began at the highest levels of the US government. Lower-level State Department officials had been advocating this for some time (Sick, pp. 81–3). There were also embassy contacts with the opposition on the question of a regency council in late October. These were vetoed by Khomeini. (Sick, pp. 117–18).
52. Brzezinski, *Power and Principle*, pp. 373–4; Sick, *All Fall Down*, pp. 137–8.
53. William Sullivan, *Mission to Iran* (New York: Norton, 1981), pp. 201–3, 224–5; Brzezinski, *Power and Principle*, pp. 380–10.
54. Brzezinski, *Power and Principle*, pp. 375–6; Sick, *All Fall Down*, pp. 147–8, 152–3.
55. Michael Ledeen and William Lewis, *Debacle: The American Failure in Iran* (New York: Alfred Knopf, 1981), pp. 178–80; Sullivan, *Mission to Iran*, pp. 235–6; Brzezinski, *Power and Principle*, pp. 383, 386–9, 396; Sullivan correctly anticipated Bakhtiar's fate, but would his own plan have worked any better? It seems unlikely that the Iranian armed forces would have been any more willing to defend Bazargan than Bakhtiar, and Bazargan later showed little of the fortitude one would have needed to stand up to the Ayatolloh.
56. Suggested by Sick, *All Fall Down*, pp. 140–1.
57. LeoGrande, 'The Revolution in Nicaragua', pp. 33–4.
58. 'Duvalier's Troubles Pose Challenge for US Policy', *Washington Post*, 2 February 1986.
59. Leslie Gelb, 'Marcos Reported to Lose Support in Administration', *New York Times*, 26 January 1986.
60. 'Schultz in Manila, Affirms Support of US for Marcos', *New York Times*, 26 June 1983.

61. 'Reagan Avows His Amity for Marcos', *New York Times*, 5 October 1983.
62. Raymond Bonner, *Waltzing with a Dictator* (New York: Times Books, 1987), pp. 61–2; Lewis Simons, *Worth Dying For* (New York: William Morrow and Co., 1987), pp. 114–15.
63. Gelb, 'Marcos Reported to Lose Support'; 'US Pressing for Democratic Succession in Philippines', *Washington Post*, 12 March 1985; 'US Thinks Ahead to Post-Marcos Era', *New York Times*, 7 October 1984; Bonner, *Waltzing with a Dictator*, pp. 362–9.
64. 'A Diplomatic Dilemma', *Washington Post*, 27 October 1985; Gelb, 'Marcos Reported to Lose Support'.
65. Bonner, *Waltzing with a Dictator*, pp. 382–3.
66. US officials worried that the opposition was not ready for an election this soon. Gelb, 'Marcos Reported to Lose Support'; 'US Sends Laxalt to Talk to Marcos', *New York Times*, 15 October 1985; Bonner, *Waltzing with a Dictator*, pp. 386–7.
67. Gelb, 'Marcos Reported to Lose Support'; 'US Vows Rise in Aid if Manila Changes Policy', *New York Times*, 31 January 1986; Leslie Gelb, 'A Winning Style: Reagan and the Philippines', *New York Times Magazine*, 30 March 1986, p. 64; Simons, *Worth Dying For*, pp. 208–10; 'A Diplomatic Dilemma', *Washington Post*, 27 October 1985; 'Going into the Streets', *Time*, 127 (24 February 1986), p. 32; 'Tough US Choice on Marcos Is Seen', *New York Times*, 10 February 1986. The administration failed here. Congress cut the administration's request for $100 million in military aid to $55 million on 19 December. (*Congressional Quarterly Almanac 1985*, p. 368.)
68. Marcos compounded this problem in January when he announced that Ver would be reinstated as chief-of-staff of the armed forces.
69. 'Philippine Opposition Works Out Agreement', *New York Times*, 12 December 1985; Simons, *Worth Dying For*, pp. 218, 237; Bonner, *Waltzing with a Dictator*, p. 391.
70. Bonner, *Waltzing with a Dictator*, p. 420–1.
71. Simons, *Worth Dying For*, p. 274.
72. Bonner, *Waltzing with a Dictator*, pp. 427–9.
73. Simons, *Worth Dying For*, p. 274; 'In Manila: And Now?', *New York Times*, 11 February 1986; 'Marcos Is Declared Victor', *New York Times*, 16 February 1986; 'Going into the Streets', *Time*, 127 (24 February 1986), pp. 30–2.
74. 'Habib Mission: US Aim Is Complex', *New York Times*, 19 February 1986.
75. Bryan Johnson, *The Four Days of Courage* (New York: Free Press, 1987), pp. 97–100, 241–2; 'Marcos Loses Support', *New York Times*, 23 February 1986; 'Going into the Streets', *Time*, 127 (24 February 1986), pp. 30–2; Bonner, *Waltzing with a Dictator*, p. 436.
76. Johnson, *Four Days of Courage*, p. 101, 143, 160–2; Simons, *Worth Dying For*, pp. 285–6; Bonner, *Waltzing with a Dictator*, p. 437.
77. Simons, *Worth Dying For*, pp. 290–1; Bonner, *Waltzing with a Dictator*, pp. 437–8.

78. 'US Says Staying on Is Futile', *New York Times*, 25 February 1986; Simons, *Worth Dying For*, pp. 290–1, 296; Bonner, *Waltzing with a Dictator*, p. 439.

79. Paul Laxalt, 'My Conversations with Ferdinand Marcos: A Lesson in Practical Diplomacy', *Policy Review*, 37 (Summer 1986), p. 5; Simons, *Worth Dying For*, pp. 298–9.

80. Pastor, *Condemned to Repetition*, pp. 64–5; Christian, *Nicaragua*, p. 77; Sick, *All Fall Down*, p. 136; for Cuba, see notes above. More evidence on the aversion of President Carter and some of his top officials to intervention is provided by Pastor, pp. 73–4, 77–8, 82, 99, 113.

81. Rubin, *Paved with Good Intentions*, pp. 220–2; 'Religious Violence Perils Iranian Dissidents', *Washington Post*, 28 May 1978; 'Iran: Situation is Out of Control', *Washington Post*, 29 October 1978; 'Sanjabi Embraces Hard Anti-Shah Line', *Washington Post*, 12 November 1978.

82. John R. Beal, *Marshall in China* (Garden City, New Jersey: Doubleday, 1970), pp. 25–6, 253–5, 264; Carsun Chang, *The Third Force in China* (New York: Bookman Associates, 1952), pp. 113–15, 184–7, 195, 224, 229, 235; *United States Relations with China* (Washington D.C.: Department of State, 1949), pp. 213–16, 234, 688; James Sheridan, *China in Disintegration: The Republican Era in Chinese History, 1917–49* (New York: Free Press, 1975), pp. 279–83.

83. 'Haitian Conflict Imperils US Aid', *Washington Post*, 22 December 1985; 'Haiti's Duvalier Imposes State of Seige', *Washington Post*, 1 February 1986; 'Opposition Grows Bold in Haiti', *Washington Post*, 4 February 1986; 'The Opposition in Haiti', *New York Times*, 1 February 1986; 'Haiti Town Turns Out in Protest', *New York Times*, 3 February 1986.

84. Alan Riding, 'Nicaraguan Dissidents Say US Does Not Appreciate Gravity of Crisis', *New York Times*, 5 March 1978; Alan Riding, 'Nicaragua's Opposition Begins a Quick Left March', *New York Times*, 14 May 1978; Diederich, *Somoza*, p. 230; Pastor, *Condemned to Repetition*, pp. 72, 77–8, 95.

85. Wayne Smith, *Closest of Enemies*, pp. 20, 27.

86. R. Hart Phillips, 'Foes of Batista Scan Vote Pledge', *New York Times*, 8 March 1958.

87. Simons, *Worth Dying For*, pp. 92–3, 103.

88. Edmund Clubb, *20th Century China* (New York: Columbia University Press, 1972), pp. 254–5; *US Relations with China*, p. 311, 313.

89. Beal, *Marshall in China*, pp. 66, 83–4, 88, 109, 339; *US Relations with China*, pp. 161, 212–14, 313–14; Tsou, *America's Failure*, p. 425.

90. Draper, *Castro's Revolution*, pp. 12–13, 41; Thomas, *Cuba*, p. 997.

91. Thomas, *Cuba*, pp. 997–8; Bonachea and San Martin, *Cuban Insurrection*, pp. 232–3, 262; 'Cuban Army Push Reported Halted', *New York Times*, 10 July 1958.

92. Booth, *End and Beginning*, pp. 150, 157, 167, 174; Christian, *Nicaragua*, pp. 92, 94, 99; Pastor, *Condemned to Repetition*, pp. 84, 116, 123–4, 130–3.

93. Laxalt, 'My Conversations with Ferdinand Marcos', p. 2; 'A Diplomatic Dilemma', *Washington Post*, 27 October 1985.
94. Johnson, *Four Days of Courage*, p. 44.
95. Johnson, *Four Days of Courage*, pp. 73–4, 102; Simons, *Worth Dying For*, pp. 284–5.
96. Johnson, *Four Days of Courage*, pp. 104–34; Simons, *Worth Dying For*, pp. 288–90.
97. Johnson, *Four Days of Courage*, pp. 147–9, 155–6, 191, 195, 199–203, 211–12.
98. Richard Preece, 'US Policy toward Iran' (Unpublished Manuscript), p. 108; Rubin, *Paved with Good Intentions*, p. 210.
99. 'A Troubled Iran Gauges Level of Shah's Control', *Washington Post*, 15 September 1978; Sick, *All Fall Down*, p. 103; Rubin, *Paved with Good Intentions*, p. 219; Fereydoun Hoveyda, *The Fall of the Shah* (New York: Wyndam Books, 1980), pp. 165–6.
100. Sharif Arani, 'Iran: from the Shah's Dictatorship to Khomeini's Demagogic Theocracy', *Dissent*, 27 (Winter 1980), p. 18; Sick, *All Fall Down*, pp. 98, 164.
101. Confidential interview with a US State Department official deeply involved in the 1978 crisis.
102. 'Memo of Conversation with Enrique Perez-Cisneros', 29 October 1958,
103. Keith Richburg, 'Our Haitian Meddling Worked', *Washington Post*, 23 February 1986; also 'Schultz's Words Heeded', *Washington Post*, 10 February 1986; 'Duvalier Flies into Exile', *Washington Post*, 8 February 1986. Against this, one could cite evidence that the army was refusing to continue to do the dirty work by early February and that the regime was left holding only the capital with the pre-Lenten carnival approaching, which would put large numbers of people in the streets. (James Ferguson, *Papa Doc, Baby Doc: Haiti and the Duvaliers* [Oxford: Basil Blackwell, 1987], pp. 112–17.) But although the army was not following orders, it was also not preventing the *Tontons Macoutes*, who were twice as numerous, from attacking the crowds, and the state of seige declared on 1 February did appear to be working. (Ferguson, *Papa Doc, Baby Doc*, p. 114.)
104. Sick, *All Fall Down*, pp. 130, 153.
105. Mohammad Reza Pahlavi, *Answer to History* (New York: Stein & Day, 1981), p. 167.
106. Sick, *All Fall Down*, pp. 130, 153.
107. Diederich, *Somoza*, p. 216; 'Unable to Force Somoza Out, US Lacks Clout with Foes', *New York Times*, 1 July 1979; Christian, *Nicaragua*, pp. 91–2.
108. *Draft White Paper on Cuba*, pp. 54–5.
109. 'Haitian Conflict Imperils US Aid', *Washington Post*, 22 December 1985.
110. Tsou, *America's Failure*, p. 437; *US Relations with China*, p. 192.
111. US Congress, House of Representatives Committee on Foreign Affairs, 96th Congress, 1st Session, *US Policy toward Nicaragua* (Testimony of Richard Millett) pp. 15–16; 'Somoza and His Foes Both Looking to US for Aid', *New York Times*, 26 July 1978.

112. Bonner, *Waltzing with a Dictator*, p. 381.
113. In the two recent successes, lack of credibility was not an obstacle, though for somewhat different reasons. Duvalier was so inclined to take the US at its word that George Schultz's statement in early February that the US would 'favor a government coming to power through democratic processes' was enough to convince him that he had lost American support. ('Schultz's Word Heeded', *Washington Post*, 10 February 1986) In the Philippines, on the other hand, there was a potential problem. Congress was not the source of it, since most legislators were more impatient with Marcos than the administration and eager to cut him off. The potential snag was Marcos's belief, which was not altogether unfounded, that President Reagan himself did not share the views of the middle-level State Department officials who had been making policy on a day to day basis and might yet be willing to come to his defence. The administration relied on Senator Laxalt to overcome this. Laxalt has said that the personal relationship he established with Marcos in October was invaluable in persuading him to leave later. As mentioned above, others think that Laxalt actually contributed to the problem. (Bonner, *Waltzing with a Dictator*, pp. 382–3)
114. Arthur Schlesinger, *The Bitter Heritage* (Boston: Houghton Mifflin, 1967), pp. 112–13.
115. Mark Falcoff, *Small Nations, Large Issues* (Washington D.C.: American Enterprise Institute, 1984), p. 62; LeoGrande, 'The Revolution in Nicaragua', pp. 34–5.
116. *US Relations with China*, p. 235.
117. Tsou, *America's Failure*, p. 437; Cohen, *America's Response to China*, p. 190; Varg, *Closing of Door*, p. 278.
118. Diederich, *Somoza*, p. 224–5; Christian, *Nicaragua*, pp. 87–8. Shirley Christian has suggested that Murphy may have extracted a quid pro quo from the White House in return for his support for the Panama Canal legislation. (The administration delayed taking action against Somoza for a few weeks.) However, Carter officials deny this and Somoza states in his memoirs that Murphy told him after this conversation that Carter's opposition to him was unyielding. Murphy 'simply could not get through to him'. (Somoza, *Nicaragua Betrayed*, p. 226.)
119. *US Relations with China*, p. 235.
120. Charles Stevenson, *The End of Nowhere*, (Boston: Beacon Press, 1972), pp. 40–5, 116–17; Martin Goldstein, *American Policy toward Laos* (Rutherford, New Jersey: Farleigh Dickinson University Press, 1973), pp. 142–3, 150–3, 158, 175–7, 209–11, 255–6; Arthur Dommen, *Conflict in Laos* (London: Pall Mall, 1964), pp. 127, 159–66, 170–81, 187, 206–8; Roger Hilsman, *To Move a Nation* (New York: Doubleday, 1964), p. 127.
121. Goldstein, *American Policy toward Laos*, pp. 255–6; David Hall, 'The Laotian War of 1962 and the Indo-Pakistani War of 1971', in Barry Blechman and Stephen Kaplan (eds), *Force without War* (Washington: Brookings Institution, 1978), pp. 145–6, 173; Stevenson, *End of Nowhere*, p. 150.

122. Dommen, *Conflict in Laos*, pp. 219–20; Stevenson, *End of Nowhere*, p. 178; Goldstein, *American Policy toward Laos*, pp. 263–5.
123. Goldstein, *American Policy toward Laos*, pp. 293–4; Stevenson, *End of Nowhere*, pp. 183, 188; Hilsman, *To Move a Nation*, p. 153.
124. Dommen, *Conflict in Laos*, p. 267; Stevenson, *End of Nowhere*, pp. 203, 218–20.
125. Sir Robert Thompson, *Peace Is Not at Hand* (New York: David McKay, 1974), pp. 125–6; George Herring, *America's Longest War* (New York: Wiley, 1979), p. 245; Allen Goodman, *The Lost Peace* (Stanford, California: Hoover Institution Press, 1978), p. 173.
126. Herring, *America's Longest War*, p. 249.
127. Goodman, *Lost Peace*, pp. 174–5; Thompson, *Peace Is Not at Hand*, pp. 153–4.
128. Herring, *America's Longest War*, pp. 253–61.
129. 'Instant Zimbabwe', *The Economist*, 272 (8 September 1979), pp. 18–19; 'Carrington's Gamble', *The Economist*, 272 (15 September 1979), pp. 15–16; 'Progress', *The Economist*, 272 (29 September 1979), p. 65; *Africa Today*, January–February 1980, March–April 1980.
130. Xan Smiley, 'Zimbabwe, Southern Africa, and the Rise of Robert Mugabe', *Foreign Affairs*, 58 (Summer 1980), pp. 1065–7. Lord Carrington stressed the importance of this in a conversation with the author at the Southern Center for International Studies, Atlanta Georgia, 3 April 1987. He also mentioned the pressure put upon Mugabe by the front line states, to be discussed shortly.
131. Richard Hill, 'Rhodesia and Her Neighbors', *Current History*, 73 (December 1977), pp. 133–4.
132. 'Back to Earth', *The Economist*, 273 (22 December 1979), p. 37; 'Rhodesia Parley Reaches Accord over Transition', *New York Times*, 16 November 1979; Smiley, 'Zimbabwe, Southern Africa, and the Rise of Robert Mugabe', pp. 1066–67. Lord Carrington's judgement is that Mugabe expected to win the war and really did not want a negotiated peace for that reason. Hence, the pressure of the front line states was crucial (conversation of 3 April 1987).
133. Thornton, *Struggle for Power*, pp. 204–7.
134. Dommen, *Conflict in Laos*, pp. 238–9. By way of comparison, Kong Le, the centrist, had about 10,000 men; Phoumi, the rightist, 48,000; and the Pathet Lao, 19,000 (Dommen, p. 242).
135. Dommen, *Conflict in Laos*, pp. 234–5, 253–3.
136. Paul Langer and Joseph Zasloff, *North Vietnam and the Pathet Lao*, (Cambridge, Massachusetts: Harvard University Press), p. 87.
137. Dommen, *Conflict in Laos*, p. 263.
138. Herring, *America's Longest War*, p. 240.
139. Dommen, *Conflict in Laos*, pp. 225–6, 249–53.
140. Goodman, *Lost Peace*, pp. 171–3; Thompson, *Peace Is Not at Hand*, pp. 139–40.
141. Varg, *Closing of Door*, pp. 244–5, 250–2, 264–5; Tsou, *America's Failure*, p. 422.
142. 'The Guerrillas Come in: Now for the Vote', *The Economist*, 274 (12 January 1980), pp. 44–6; 'Bullying for Votes', *The Economist*, 274

(9 February 1986), p. 65; 'Now, How Will the Soldiers Vote?', *The Economist*, 274 (1 March 1980), pp. 35–6.

143. Smiley, 'Zimbabwe, Southern Africa, and the Rise of Robert Mugabe', pp. 1069–70. According to Lord Carrington, Rhodesian and South African intelligence reported before the election that no one was likely to receive a majority of the votes. If Mugabe had lost and been excluded from a coalition, said Carrington, he would have resumed fighting (conversation of 3 April 1987).

4 Conciliation with Revolutionary Regimes

'We drove them to the Soviets!' This, too, is a notion that appears with great frequency in recent writings on American foreign policy. The argument, of course, is that revolutionary governments would be interested in good relations with the United States if only they were treated with more understanding or sympathy, but that the US has reacted to them time and again with mechanical hostility, giving them no choice but to turn to the USSR. This view may be accurate for individual cases, but it is demonstrably false as a generalisation. In point of fact, the United States has pursued conciliatory policies toward revolutionary governments on many occasions since 1945, and, as we shall see, has very little to show for it in many instances.[1]

The first of these cases chronologically, and one of the most important, is the brief attempt by Secretary of State Dean Acheson to drive a wedge between Chinese Communists and the USSR at the end of the Chinese civil war. The activities of the KMT's supporters in Congress prevented Acheson from implementing the wedge policy consistently, however, and by the end of 1950, the United States found itself at war with China. The Truman administration might have had difficulty fending off the China lobby in any event, but the actions of the CCP played an important role in destroying the credibility of Acheson's approach.

At the outset, there seemed to be some cause for optimism. On 28 June 1949, moderates in the Communist party contacted the US Ambassador in Nanking and suggested that he travel to Peking to discuss future relations between the two countries with Mao and Chou En-lai. The question was referred to Washington. Two days later, while the matter was under discussion in the State Department, Mao deliberately thwarted the attempt in his famous 'lean to one side' speech:

> the Chinese people must lean either to the side of imperialism or to that of socialism. There can be no exception. There can be no sitting on the fence; there is no third road.

155

Mao's speech had the desired effect. The State Department was convinced that the time was not propitious for an approach to the Communists, and the trip was cancelled.[2]

In August 1949, the Truman administration published the thousand-page White Paper to rebut the charge that it had 'lost' China and provide a rationale for disengagement. The next month, the China lobby threatened to cut or delay US assistance to Europe, compelling the administration to allocate $75 million in aid for 'the general area of China'.[3]

On the 1st of October, Mao announced the formation of the People's Republic and requested recognition as the legitimate government of China. The CCP's treatment of US personnel in China had made it politically difficult for the administration to recognise the regime immediately, so Acheson stated that the US would grant recognition when the PRC met a certain standard of behaviour. In July, the vice-consul in Shanghai had been arrested and beaten by the police. The consul-general in Mukden and four of his staff were held under house arrest for several months during 1949 and then thrown in jail on 24 October. President Truman gave consideration to a naval blockade after the second incident, but was persuaded to observe restraint by Acheson so as to avoid strengthening the hand of the CCP's pro-Moscow faction. On 12 December, the five were released and deported.[4]

The Nationalists fled from the mainland to Formosa in December. Pressure then began building in Congress to defend the island against invasion. President Truman firmly rejected the appeals from Chiang's backers on 5 January 1950, asserting that 'the US will not pursue a course which will lead to involvement in the civil conflict in China'. The President explicitly ruled out the use of American troops or expenditure of any of the $75 million in aid to purchase arms for Taiwan. A week later, the Secretary of State reaffirmed the administration's position in a speech at the National Press Club. Acheson excluded Taiwan from the US 'defense perimeter' in Asia and reiterated his view that Soviet cupidity would eventually antagonise China if the United States '[does not] deflect from the Russians to ourselves the wrath and the hatred of the Chinese people'.[5]

If Mao had had any interest in *rapprochement* with the United States at this time, these statements on a matter of the greatest concern to the Communists ought to have relieved tension at least to some degree and cleared the way for a more constructive dialogue. Instead, just two days after Acheson's speech, the Communists seized part of the US diplomatic compound in Peking. When the US consul-general tried to meet with Chou En-lai to discuss the incident, he was refused an audience.[6] The State Department then fulfilled an earlier threat and withdrew all official US personnel from China. Recognition of the People's Republic (PRC) would now have met furious opposition in Congress, but President Truman was in no mood for it in any case. 'I won't recognise a bunch of bandits', he is said to have remarked.[7]

The Korean War was still several months in the future, but any reasonable chance for better relations was now lost. US policy toward the PRC was not fully conciliatory in 1949 and early 1950—the China lobby prevented the administration from disengaging quickly and forced it to delay recognition. But it seems unlikely that the Communists would have been receptive even if Acheson's hands had not been tied. As Warren Cohen has said:

> it was apparent that the Chinese Communists and Chiang's friends in America had entered into a symbiotic relationship, feeding off each other's hate, adding to the misery of men of good will throughout the world. Every abuse by Mao's men provided ammunition for those who sought to stiffen American opposition to Mao's government. Every statement by the likes of Senators Knowland, Styles Bridges, and Kenneth Wherry facilitated Mao's anti-American campaign and led to new abuses. The cycle was still very much in existence . . . on June 25, 1950.[8]

The story was much the same in Cuba, the most widely discussed and probably the least understood of these cases. In July 1960, Congress voted to eliminate Cuba's sugar quota, forcing the Cubans to look elsewhere to market their major crop. Khrushchev then came to Castro's rescue and close relations between the two countries soon developed. Hence, it may appear that the United States left Castro no choice but to turn to the Soviets. But this change in American policy (which may or may not have been well advised), came after the Eisenhower administration had pursued a conciliatory policy towards Cuba for nearly eighteen months.

The United States recognised the new Cuban government, even before Castro had reached Havana, and withdrew the American military mission after the Cubans requested it. Earl Smith, who had announced that he doubted that the United States could work with Castro, was replaced by Phillip Bonsal, an advocate of *rapprochement*. Bonsal had represented the US in Bolivia in the first

year after the leftist Nationalist Revolutionary Movement (MNR)
took power there, and hoped to apply the same conciliatory approach
to Castro. As he explains:

> During my first weeks in Havana I endeavored through as many
> channels as possible to convey goodwill and readiness to enter
> into serious negotiation on any matters the regime might wish to
> raise. I took the unusual step of making publicised calls on each of
> the ministers in Castro's cabinet. I tried to develop with each one
> of them a relationship of cordial confidence and to instill in them
> a belief that the government of the United States was prepared
> to give most sympathetic and constructive consideration to any
> proposals of the new Cuban government in the field of relations
> between the two countries. . . . I made every effort to avoid the
> attitude of thinly disguised paternalism which these people had
> been taught to believe had characterized some of my predecessors.[9]

Despite this, Castro kept Bonsal waiting for three months before
seeing him, and then addressed him, as he later recalled, 'as to a
servant'. Bonsal was received on only one other occasion before his
departure in October 1960.[10]

Castro contacted Moscow as early as June 1959 and began working
out arrangements to increase trade with the eastern bloc in early
1960. The shift in American policy did not come until after the *La
Coubre* incident in March 1960, when Castro attempted to cast the
blame on the United States for an explosion in Havana harbour.
American policy toward Cuba was predominantly conciliatory up to
that point, and thus could not have been the reason Castro turned to
the Soviets.[11]

The mistaken notion that the United States drove Castro to
the Russians rests on three faulty arguments. First, it is alleged
that the US reaction to Castro's domestic reforms, particularly the
Agrarian Reform Law of May 1959, convinced Castro of American
hostility and that the US would have emasculated his programme in
order to protect American property. The United States responded
to the Agrarian Reform Law with a note that accepted Cuba's
right to expropriate American properties, but asked that there be
'prompt, adequate, and effective' compensation. The *New York
Times* described the note as 'courteous and within the legitimate
bounds of a friendly relationship', and conservative critics thought it
polite to the point of timidity, but Castro rejected it irascibly, saying
that the US could take the 21 year bonds at the 4.5 per cent he

promised or leave them. In the end, no compensation of any sort was ever paid.[12]

American officials tried to negotiate with the Cubans on this matter and did not, as Castro later claimed, demand immediate payment at a value determined by the US. The United States received compromise proposals from moderate Cuban representatives in the early fall of 1959, but the agreement fell through after those officials were forced out of the government in November. Nonetheless, Bonsal again stressed his acceptance of the reform and willingness to negotiate in a futile public statement of US policy in January 1960.[13] One last effort was made to break the deadlock in March 1960, when the Argentine Ambassador, Julio Amoedo, was called upon to mediate. According to Amoedo, the United States was prepared to 'assist in the financing of the agrarian reform, as well as other economic and social matters', if Castro would stop insulting the US and begin negotiations again with Bonsal. The State Department, however, denies that the offer was made.[14]

Second, it is alleged that the United States condoned or at least did not make a serious effort to curtail attacks against Cuba carried out by airplanes based in Florida. These attacks burned a few cane mills in fall 1959 but did not pose a serious threat to Castro, though he made much of them. In October and November, the US took steps to tighten enforcement and was partially, but not completely successful. Castro was not able to control his own borders, either, but he continued to rail at the United States when the efforts were less than perfect.[15] According to one report, a legal council of the American embassy approached the Cuban government in March 1960 with a proposal that the United States would apologise about the flights and offer Cuba new planes and technological assistance to stop them. The offer was made privately because the United States did not want to be embarrassed by a public refusal. The Cubans considered the proposal briefly, then rejected it.[16]

Finally, it is suggested that the United States did not offer sufficient financial support to Cuba in the first year of the revolution. According to revisionist historian, William A. Williams, American officials hoped that Cuba's difficult economic situation would force Castro to accept an IMF stabilisation plan that would prevent him from moving too far to the left. Williams also asks why the United States did not respond to Castro's call at Buenos Aires in May for $30 billion in aid to Latin America. The inadequate American response, Williams argues, left Castro no choice but to look elsewhere.[17]

The problem with Williams's argument is that the Cuban leadership showed no hesitation about the terms on which aid was offered in the first months. On 20 March 1959, Castro was quoted as saying that capital for industrial development 'could come from the United States, from England, from France, from Germany . . .. It would seem that there is abundant capital in the world at this time because we have received many offers of loans and investments.'[18] The Cubans were encouraged by their preliminary discussions with American officials and Castro planned to take an economic delegation with him on his visit to the US in April 1959.

Rufo Lopez-Fresquet, who was then serving as Minister of Finance, accompanied Castro to Washington. On 17 April, he met with Treasury Secretary Robert Anderson. On orders from Castro, Lopez-Fresquet turned evasive when Anderson brought up the subject of financial aid. The next day, Assistant Secretary Roy Rubottom repeated the offer to help Cuba carry out her economic plans, and again the Cuban Minister avoided any sort of commitment to accept US assistance.[19]

The trip to the United States forced Castro to decide what course his revolution would follow. His decision can be inferred from the pattern of developments in the spring of 1959 and after. Prior to his departure for the US, Castro cancelled the elections and after his return to the island, the moderates began leaving the government. Those who remained were purged in the summer and fall.[20] To reiterate, Castro was not forced to do this by American policy, he chose it as the best way of meeting his objectives, for reasons we will discuss below.

More recently, Washington has had the same experience with Castro's protégées, the Sandinistas. The victors in the struggle against Somoza inherited a country ravaged by civil war: the fighting had left no less than a million people hungry, 250,000 without shelter, 45,000 dead, 40,000 orphaned and 160,000 wounded. In late July 1979, within ten days of the FSLN's assumption of power, the Carter administration undertook an ambitious relief effort in Nicaragua, shipping over 1700 metric tons of food and 9600 pounds of medical supplies in a period of two weeks. The US also made available $8 million in emergency financial assistance to relieve the Nicaraguan Central Bank of a dire shortage of hard currency.[21] Daniel Ortega, the Sandinista leader, was invited to the White House on 24 September 1979. President Carter stressed his desire for friendship and willingness to assist the new government during the meeting, but added that the regime's alignment, observance of human rights and relations with its neighbours were a serious concern for Washington. Ortega, for his part, expressed keen interest in US aid and assured Carter that 'Nicaragua is not a factor in the radicalisation of El Salvador—now, in the past, and it will not be in the future.' Later, he recalled that the US President had 'left us with the sense that it was possible to overcome the problems which we had with the United States over 100 years of history.'[22] By the time of their meeting, the US had already allocated $47 million in assistance to Nicaragua. In November, the administration presented Congress with a request for an additional $75 million in aid, most of which was to be directed to the private sector. After a delay of several months, the legislation was passed, but with the proviso that the President would have to certify that Nicaragua was not abetting foreign revolutionaries. Despite the delay, the Sandinistas still received $110 million from the United States during the Carter administration—more than any other source in their first two years in power, and five times as much as Somoza had been granted from Washington in his last two years.[23]

As in Cuba, the US was represented by an ambassador who favoured reconciliation and was willing to labour long and hard to achieve it. As an American journalist said of Lawrence Pezzullo, one year after the revolution: 'Despite having suffered a year of Sandinista Yankee-baiting, he felt that the United States might still be able to influence and moderate the path of Nicaragua. He continued to believe that most Sandinista leaders wanted to do the best thing for their country and to hope they would eventually outgrow their rhetoric and propaganda.' Pezzullo played a more active role than Bonsal, however, at least for a time. Among other things, he helped arrange the compromise of spring 1980 through which COSEP (Superior Council of Private Enterprise, formerly COSIP until summer 1979) was persuaded to send delegates to the Council of State by the FSLN's promise to announce a timetable for elections by 19 July, a promise they did not keep.[24]

Judging from the Sandinistas' rhetoric and diplomatic positions, the tolerance and generosity of the Carter administration seemed to have little effect. At the non-aligned conference in Havana in early September 1979, Ortega presented an extended indictment of US policy in Nicaragua since 1855, laced with Marxist phraseology, and was one of the few delegates willing to recognise the Vietnamese puppet regime in Cambodia. On 28 September, only four days after his meeting with Carter, Ortega declared to the United Nations that Nicaragua was still 'a target for imperialist policy'. 'The most aggressive circles of the United States and of Central America', he continued, 'dream of restoring Somozaism to our country. A macabre alliance . . . is trying to develop the idea that Sandinoism is a threat to the government of El Salvador.' Unlike Cuba and Grenada, Nicaragua abstained (and refused to support the Soviets openly) in the UN on the first vote on Afghanistan, but in March 1980, four top Sandinista leaders travelled to Moscow and signed a communique expressing their support for Soviet foreign policy on matters such as South Africa and the intermediate-range nuclear force deployments in Western Europe. Among other things, the communique contained a passage blaming events in Afghanistan on 'imperialist and reactionary forces aimed at subverting the inalienable rights of the people of the Democratic Republic of Afghanistan and of other peoples . . . to follow the path of progressive transformation'.[25]

On the most important issue, though, Washington was more successful in curbing the Sandinista's radicalism, at least for a time. The FSLN leadership continued to debate the matter internally, but provided no assistance to the Salvadoran rebels until late summer 1980, largely out of concern for the US reaction. Humberto Ortega promised to provide the FMLN with arms and ammunition at the time of the first anniversary of the revolution, but deliveries on a limited scale did not begin until September, just as Jimmy Carter was facing the decision whether to certify Nicaragua. The intelligence available at that moment was considered ambiguous by the President's advisors, so, despite the public pressure and political risks, Carter decided to continue the aid programme but repeat his warnings to the Sandinistas through the Ambassador and the Deputy Assistant Secretary. The Sandinistas halted their assistance to the Salvadorans temporarily, but reversed the decision in early November and agreed to give all-out backing to the FMLN's 'final offensive'. According to captured documents, Ronald Reagan's imminent victory at the polls was not a factor in their decision: 'the United States elections no longer pose any problems; the results do not matter'. This time, the size of the shipments—109 tons in the month of November—left no room for doubt, and the Carter administration had no choice but to cancel the remaining $15 million of the $75 million aid package in January 1981.[26]

But that did not end American attempts at conciliation. Though the Reagan administration announced the termination of the aid programme on 1 April 1981, $6.9 million of aid still in the pipeline was disbursed to Nicaragua between January and August, and in November the administration requested another $33 million from Congress in 1982. Beginning on 12 August, Assistant Secretary Thomas Enders met five times with Sandinista officials before late October. In these discussions he offered to renew economic aid to Nicaragua and deny US assistance to the anti-Sandinista exile groups if the Sandinistas would cut off their arms shipments to El Salvador, halt their military build-up, keep their promises of political and economic pluralism at home and loosen their association with Cuba and the USSR. It was only after the Sandinista leadership failed to make any constructive response to Enders' proposals that the supposedly reflexive hardliners in the Reagan administration turned toward a more confrontational posture.[27]

American attempts at conciliation with radical governments in the middle-east have been equally frustrating. Consider the results of US policy toward the military junta headed by General Kassem, which overthrew the pro-Western government of Nuri as Said in July 1958. The United States recognised the new regime on 2 August and restored partial arms shipments on the 20th. Troubleshooter Robert Murphy pledged that the US would not interfere in Iraq during his visit the same month, and in December Assistant Secretary Rountree braved stoning by Iraqi mobs to carry on talks with the leadership.[28]

Kassem declared that his foreign policy would be one of 'positive neutralism', but his neutralism appeared to tilt increasingly to the Soviet side in the first months after the coup. A Soviet representative arrived in Baghdad in August with an offer of technical and economic aid and a $137 million agreement was arranged by the following spring. Iraq also began receiving Soviet arms in December and in June 1959 concluded a $100 million arms deal with the USSR. In March, Kassem pulled his country out of the Baghdad Pact and closed two air bases to the West. Great Britain and the United States continued to supply Iraq with arms throughout those months in a vain effort to maintain their influence, but Kassem cancelled Iraq's military assistance agreement with the US despite this and announced in late May that he would no longer accept American aid of any sort.[29] On 14 June 1960, minister Ibraham Kubbah told his hosts in East Berlin that 'Iraq belongs to the same camp as East Germany—the camp of peace, independence, and freedom.'[30]

The American attempt at conciliation with Colonel Qaddaffi after his 1969 takeover in Libya was equally futile. The policy was implemented by Ambassador John Palmer, who initially viewed the colonel as a deeply religious and intensely nationalistic man who would remain firmly anti-Soviet unless the United States gave him some reason to change his mind. On Palmer's recommendation, the US recognised the new regime quickly. In early December 1969, US intelligence warned Qaddaffi of an impending coup, allowing him to arrest and imprison the pro-Western officers leading the conspiracy. According to some sources, the US also helped to block two other coup attempts later. In 1970, again on advice from the Ambassador, Washington vacated Wheelus air force base and offered to sell weapons to Libya. Major Jalloud, the second-ranking member of the new regime, had led Palmer to think that Libya would be willing to deal constructively with the US if the facility were abandoned. As soon as the withdrawal was completed, Palmer was informed that good relations between the two countries were impossible as long as the United States continued to support Israel, and top Libyan officials were told to have nothing to do with the American embassy in Tripoli. After two more years of frustration, Palmer requested his own recall and left in 1972.[31]

In the years that followed, Qaddaffi embarked on a menacing and sometimes bizarre course of action that adversely affected American interests in a number of ways. Libya became a leading member of the Steadfastness and Rejection Front (the group of radical Arab states whose purpose was to block American peace initiatives in the region), as well as a generous supplier of the most intransigent factions of the Palestinian movement. In the mid-seventies Qaddaffi made attempts to undermine or overthrow several governments of the area friendly to the United States, including Tunisia, Egypt, Sudan and Morocco. Prior to 1974, US officials could console themselves by noting Qaddaffi's resistance to Soviet blandishments and willingness to take steps damaging to the interests of the USSR as well as the West. But in that year, Jalloud visited Moscow and signed a communique expressing 'the identity or closeness of the positions of the Soviet Union and the Libyan Arab Republic on the most important international problems'. Over the next four years, the Soviets shipped some $3.4 billion in arms to Libya.[32]

American conciliation fared no better with the Shah's successors in Iran. The Carter administration first recalled William Sullivan, whom the Iranians might have considered tainted by his association with the Shah. The State Department made an effort to blunt the edge of a Senate resolution deploring the brutality of Khomeini's government by praise of the revolution's objectives and by speaking softly about the regime's executions. In August, the Iranian army was supplied with spare parts, which were then used by Khomeini's forces to attack the Kurds, a group the US had aided up until 1975. The administration also sold heating oil to Iran to tide them over the shortages caused by the oil strikes. Most notably, the Shah was denied sanctuary in the United States, at least until President Carter changed his mind in October 1979. To the critics, that 'refusal . . . to provide its old friend and ally a haven in his hour of need . . . was . . . a greater blow to American prestige than even the fall of the Shah'. The futility of the policy became obvious with the taking of the American embassy by the Iranian 'students' in November 1979.[33]

The Eisenhower administration's approach to Nasser is a more ambiguous case. American policy toward the military junta that over-threw King Farouk in 1952 was, admittedly, not fully conciliatory. The administration withheld military assistance from Nasser until after he received arms from the Soviet Union, first at the request of the British, and after in order to persuade Nasser to join the proposed Middle-East Defence Organisation. Later, of course, Secretary of State Dulles withdrew a previous American offer to finance the construction of the Aswan Dam, provoking Nasser's seizure of the Suez Canal and giving the USSR another opening.

It is worth recalling, however, the circumstances surrounding the famous renege. One factor influencing Dulles's decision to cancel the offer was the mood in Congress. A few weeks before Dulles's talk with the Egyptian ambassador, the Senate Finance Committee had voted unanimously to proscribe any use of funds for the dam in the fiscal year of 1957. The reasons for this were complex, including the potential damage the dam might do to cotton producers in the United States. But the vote was undoubtedly influenced by some of the actions taken by Nasser in the previous months. Radio Cairo had beamed subversive broadcasts at the Palestinian population of Jordan; these Great Britain blamed for the dismissal of the British commander of the Arab Legion. Tensions continued to mount on the border between Egypt and Israel, but Nasser refused to restrain the *fedayeen* operating out of Egyptian territory. Worst of all from the US perspective, Nasser had recognised the Communist regime in China in May, Egypt has becoming the first nation to do so since the Korean war. For these reasons, even if Dulles had been willing to reward Nasser's neutralism, the Egyptian leader's recent foreign policy would have made it difficult for the administration to convince Congress to appropriate the funds.[34]

Perhaps, then, the lesson of Suez was that the United States must show more patience with the newly independent countries of the third world. The Kennedy administration attempted to do so in Ghana, and the results were equally disappointing. Previously, Eisenhower officials had described the country as 'moving toward the Soviet bloc' under the leadership of Kwame Nkrumah, but President Kennedy was encouraged by his personal interview with the Ghanaian in March 1961 and promised in July to fund a large-scale dam project on the Volta river. At about the same time, Nkrumah went on a tour of the Communist countries. The communique he signed in Moscow was one of the most detailed the Soviets had signed with an African leader. Washington was distressed to learn that Nkrumah had sided with the Soviet Union on every international issue discussed, including Berlin.[35]

Undaunted, Kennedy made the final decision to fund the Volta dam in November and signed a $40 million agreement with Ghana in January of 1962. The President apparently felt that his policy of *rapprochement* with the nonaligned countries would be damaged if he pulled back, and also that Nkrumah's nationalist sentiments would eventually prove stronger than his Marxist leanings if the US could retain some sort of presence in Ghana. Once again, the bet was proved wrong. Nkrumah turned violently against the West thereafter and relied increasingly on the Soviet Union until his fall in 1966.[36]

Washington's policies toward the radical regime set up in Ethiopia after the fall of Haile Selassie were no more successful than in Ghana. In 1974, lower-grade officers from the Ethiopian armed forces gradually displaced the ageing Haile Selassie in a kind of creeping coup. It was not obvious at the outset what direction the ruling junta, the *Dergue*, would take, though the State Department was initially somewhat optimistic. The *Dergue's* chairman, General Aman, was considered moderate, friendly to the United States and conciliatory toward the Eritrean rebels. To consolidate American influence, the US agreed in the early summer to make available $100 million in military sales and assistance to Ethiopia in 1974 and 1975, a substantial increase over the $10 million received in recent years by Haile Selassie.[37]

On 22 November 1974, Aman was assassinated, almost certainly on orders from Mengistu Haile Mariam, the future strongman. A month later, the *Dergue* issued a ten-point programme calling for sweeping nationalisation and the creation of a revolutionary political party. Radical economic changes were introduced at a rapid pace in the next few months. The US response to this was restrained. In June 1975, the Assistant Secretary for African Affairs told the *Dergue*'s representative that the US 'was in no way unhappy with the Ethiopian government's efforts to improve the welfare of the Ethiopian people' and would raise no objection to the nationalisations provided that compensation was given to American citizens, as required by international law. This message was reiterated by the Carter administration.[38]

In February 1975, the *Dergue* sent the army into the province of Eritrea to crush a separatist movement there, and shortly afterward requested an emergency shipment of $30 million in ammunition. The Ford administration temporised for a month, then agreed to sell $7 million in ammunition while expressing the hope that the government would negotiate with the rebels.[39] The *Dergue* was bitterly disappointed in the level of assistance provided by the United States. Over the next few months, the government-controlled media stepped up their attacks on the United States and the regime became increasingly repressive. Despite this, the Ford administration made one last attempt to regain influence in the spring of 1976 by offering to provide two squadrons of F-5E fighter-bombers and to consider a request for an additional $100 million in other military supplies.[40] The break between, Ethiopia and the US finally came in the spring of 1977 when the *Dergue* told American military personnel to leave on short notice, and sought help from the USSR.[41]

It is true that the US did not give the *Dergue* everything they wanted when they wanted it. The Ford administration's reluctance over their first request has already been mentioned. In addition, Kissinger coupled the US offer of the F-5Es with a warning to the regime to call off the planned invasion of Eritrea by a 'peasant army', and the Carter administration finally cut off military grants (though not sales) in late February 1977 because of the regime's human rights violations. Nevertheless, the amount of American arms sent to Ethiopia, even if less than the *Dergue* desired and later than they would have preferred, was still quite large by historical standards. From 1974 to 1977, the United States provided Ethiopia with $180 in arms, one and a half times as much as Haile Selassie received in his entire reign. Moreover, the Soviets were even more hesitant to assist Ethiopia than the United States were until late 1977; they had invested too much in Somalia to cast it aside casually. Pro-Soviet members of the *Dergue* contacted the Soviets as early as September 1974. They were told that the Soviet Union 'would understand' if they kept their tie with the United States.[42] Late in 1975, the Soviets made an offer so inadequate for the *Dergue's* needs as to be insulting.[43] During the summer of 1976, impatient leftist officers at Debre Zeit Air Force Base demanded to know why the *Dergue* was still relying on the United States for arms. Mengistu is said to have responded by asking them 'what else can we do, the Soviets will not provide them?'[44] The Soviet's hesitation continued after the *Dergue* dramatically broke ties with the US in April 1977 and even after Somalia invaded the Ogaden region and put the regime in grave danger. Despite this, the leftist officers still threw in their lot with the Soviets in spring 1977. The *Dergue*, David Korn concludes, 'wanted ties with the Soviet Union, and . . . courted the Soviets with such determination that finally they had no choice but to yield and put their investment in Somalia at risk'.[45]

American relations with Vietnam after the fall of Saigon are somewhat more complicated but fit into the same general pattern. Shortly after their victory over the south, the leadership in Hanoi seemed to be keeping the Soviets at arms length and pursuing *rapprochement* with the West. The Soviets pressed the Vietnamese to sign the usual 'treaty of friendship and cooperation', join COMECON and grant them military bases, but Hanoi refused them all three. Reports suggested that the moderates, led by Pham Van Dong, remained in control at this time. They wanted Vietnam to receive half of her aid from non-Communist sources and were particularly interested in American oil technology. They also drew up a foreign investment code that included tax concessions for foreign investors and recognised the right to repatriate profits.[46] By 1980, however, Vietnam had granted the Russians use of the naval facilities at Cam Ranh Bay and the air base at Da Nang and was receiving $3 million per day in economic support.[47] What had happened in the interim?

Within two months of his inauguration, President Carter sent a delegation to Hanoi headed by labour leader Leonard Woodcock. The timing and composition of the group—most had been vocal opponents of the war—were intended to convince Hanoi of US sincerity. Woodcock bent over backwards to please his hosts, asserting that the US ought to provide reconstruction aid to Vietnam 'as a matter of honor'. Under pressure from the US representatives, the Vietnamese agreed at this time to set up a bureau to investigate American MIAs, leading Carter to pronounce the trip 'a superb success'.[48] Negotiations resumed in Paris in May 1977 between Richard Holbrooke, the Assistant Secretary of State for East Asia, and Phan

Hien. Holbrooke immediately offered to normalise relations with Hanoi, lift the US trade embargo and support the admission of Vietnam to the United Nations regardless of the outcome of the negotiations. Much to the surprise of the American representative, Phan Hien brusquely rejected the proposal and repeated the Vietnamese's previous demand for a large commitment of US aid as a precondition to normalisation. When Holbrooke refused, the Vietnamese released to the press a letter from former President Nixon pledging $3.25 billion in economic assistance. This tactic so incensed Congress that legislation was quickly passed forbidding US negotiators from even discussing the subject of aid with Vietnam. Despite this, the Carter administration kept its promise and voted in favour of Vietnam's admission to the UN in the fall.[49]

The stalemate continued until July 1978. At this point, Vietnam approached the US and offered to normalise relations without preconditions. For a number of reasons, the Carter administration chose to postpone action on this initiative until after the Congressional elections in November. The Vietnamese grew tired of waiting, however, and announced on 3 November the signing of a treaty of friendship with the Soviet Union. By this time, there was also persuasive evidence that the boat people were fleeing the country as a result of government policy. The US then cancelled the talks with Vietnam. With the invasion of Cambodia on Christmas Day and the Chinese reprisal the next year, the pattern of alignments in the region hardened and Vietnam moved into close association with the USSR for the foreseeable future.[50]

Some observers seem to suggest that the Carter administration missed an opportunity to achieve better relations with Vietnam and forestall the consolidation of Soviet influence in the summer of 1978. Blame in these accounts is usually laid at the feet of national security advisor Zbigniew Brzezinski, who was eager to promote closer cooperation with China and did not want the issue of Vietnam to come between the US and the PRC.[51] This argument is not convincing. US intelligence was predicting a Vietnamese attack on Cambodia as early as May 1978.[52] Once Vietnam had made the decision to settle accounts with the Khmer Rouge, it became imperative for them to neutralise Pol Pot's ally on their northern border. Their anxiety about China quickened their interest in accommodation with the United States, but strengthened the Soviets' hand even more. In June 1978, Vietnam granted the Soviets the privileges they had previously withheld (most importantly the use of airfields and ports) in return for a commitment in the treaty of friendship to take 'effective measures' to repel any attack on Vietnam by China. It is important to bear in mind that this understanding was reached one month *before* the Vietnamese contacted the United States.[53] Hence, it does not appear that the US could have headed off Vietnam's alliance with the Soviet Union, even if the Carter administration had chosen to endanger the developing relationship with China and set aside its own human rights policy by dealing with Vietnam in the fall of 1978. Here, as in the other cases above, the charge that the United States 'drove them to the Russians' can not stand up to closer scrutiny.

In the face of the evidence presented above, it is difficult to maintain that the United States has reacted with Pavlovian hostility to revolutionary governments. In every case but one discussed thus far (Egypt is a partial exception) American policy was predominantly conciliatory, giving the new leadership ample incentive to deal with Washington if they had been so inclined. Yet in every instance the United States and the revolutionary government ended up in a state of hostility or tension. Why has this happened so frequently?

Four general factors are involved. The first, and the most important, is the attitude of the new leadership. Two sorts of ideas can make those that possess them (or in some cases, those possessed by them) unreceptive to conciliation by the United States. A commitment to Marxism, particularly if it is seen as obliging one to maintain loyalty to the world Communist movement, is the first of these. The supposed 'lost opportunity in China' is an excellent example.

The failure of Acheson's 'wedge policy' in China would not have come as a surprise to those who were acquainted with Mao's past thoughts on foreign relations and the CCP's foreign policy line throughout its history. As early as 1926, Mao had believed in the notion of 'two camps' enunciated above. In the article 'Analysis of the Classes in Chinese Society', he asserted that 'the present world situation is one in which two big forces, revolution and counter-revolution, are engaged in the final struggle. . . . There is no room for anyone to remain "independent".'[54] At the onset of the

Second World War, Mao had written in his best known work, *On New Democracy*:

> As the conflict between the socialist Soviet Union and the imperialist Great Britain and the United States becomes further intensified, it is inevitable that China must stand either on one side or on the other. Is it possible to incline to neither side? No, this is an illusion. All the countries of the world will be swept into one or the other of these two camps, and in the world today 'neutrality' is becoming merely a deceptive phrase.[55]

The American Ambassador in China before the war found the CCP leaders 'extremely intelligent' but inclined to 'see that world—especially the US—largely through a murky haze of their own self-indoctrination'. When Edgar Snow visited Mao in the late thirties, his host asked him when he expected revolution in the United States.[56] After the war, Mao's perspective was still the same. In 1947, he suggested that the 'United States imperialists [have drawn up] a plan for enslaving the world, [and will] run amuck like wild beasts in Europe, Asia, and other parts of the world.'[57]

The picture is the same for the CCP as a whole. One study of CCP writings from 1922–33 found 'little hope that a Communist–controlled China might be friendly to the United States'.[58] Another scholar has suggested that the idea of alignment with the Soviet Union 'had been central to the CCP's world view since its founding' and that 'the CCP had openly stated that . . . China would be aligned with the Soviet Union . . . for more than a decade'.[59]

Moreover, the CCP had supported Soviet policy faithfully in the past, even when the policies were unpopular in China and damaging to their domestic political position. At a time when Chinese intellectuals hoped for an alliance of the democracies and the USSR to check fascism, the CCP voiced their approval of Stalin's pact with Hitler and the subsequent invasion of Poland, and characterised the outbreak of fighting in Europe as 'a robber war, with justice on neither side'. (Then, like all the other Communist parties, the CCP switched to an 'anti-fascist united front line' after Soviet Russia was invaded.) The CCP also defended the Soviet-Japanese Neutrality Pact of 1941, even though the agreement hinted at recognition of the Japanese puppet state of Manchoukou and contradicted the 1924 treaty with China recognising Chinese sovereignty over Outer Mongolia.[60]

The Communists' statements during the Second World War sometimes suggested that co-operation with capitalist states might be possible after the war, but such co-operation was predicated upon a continuation of the alliance between the US and the Soviet Union. When the Soviets announced their return to the two camps doctrine in September 1947, the Chinese Communists seconded them emphatically, and continued to stress their adherence to it over the next two years. The party also gave full support to Stalin in his campaign against Tito. Thus, Mao's 'lean to one side' speech was not a new departure for the CCP, but a reiteration of what they had been saying for years.[61]

President Kennedy's failure with Kwame Nkrumah illustrates another way in which ideology can impede American efforts at conciliation. To repeat, Nkrumah overlooked Kennedy's generosity and aligned Ghana with the Soviet Union. In so doing, he seems to have been motivated less by hostility toward the United States than by his admiration for the Soviet Union. On his trip to the USSR in 1961, Nkrumah effusively praised the 'glorious achievements of the Communist revolution'. One might suspect that a bit of flattery was being used here to loosen the Soviets' purse strings, but Ghanaian sources later indicated that much of what Nkrumah had said was entirely sincere. Nkrumah was so taken with the Soviet Union that he not only remodelled the Convention People's Party (by then Ghana's sole political organisation) on democratic centralist principles and drew up plans to introduce collectivised agriculture in his country, but also outfitted his Presidential Guard Regiment in Russian jackboots and had them taught to goose-step like the troops he had seen in the USSR.[62]

Many will grant that loyalty to world Communism may have been an important influence in the late forties, or even the early sixties, but after Tito's break with Stalin, the Sino-Soviet split, Eurocommunism and so on, can we really expect ideological enthusiasm and loyalty to the Communist cause to exercise much influence on foreign policy today?

Consider the evidence presented on Nicaragua by Miguel Bolanos Hunter, who worked as a counter-intelligence officer for the Sandinistas until his defection in May 1983. Bolanos reports that the head of the Nicaraguan intelligence service was formerly a colonel in the Cuban intelligence organisation who has been working with the Sandinistas for 15 years. He estimates that there were 70 Russians involved in Nicaraguan State Security, along with 400 Cubans, 40–50 East Germans and 20–25 Bulgarians. By the time of his departure, the Sandinistas had supplied the Salvadoran guerrillas to the point where they had five times as many arms as the Sandinistas possessed when they overthrew Somoza. Not just the FMLN, but also the Argentine Montoneros, the Guatemalan Geurrilla Army of the Poor and the M-19 of Columbia had their bases of operation in Managua. The Cinchoneros, the Honduran guerrillas, were trained in Nicaragua in 1980–81, and the Sandinistas were working covertly to infiltrate Costa Rican unions in the hope of provoking a political crisis there in the future.[63] As Bolanos concludes:

> The Sandinistas have been fighting for twenty years to implant Communism. It is totally illogical to think that they would have friendly relations with the United States when they believe that it is their historic mission to export Communism to the rest of Latin America. Those Americans who naively think that negotiations will solve problems don't know the Sandinistas.[64]

Bolanos's account is corroborated by the evidence presented by journalist Shirley Christian. After the Sandinista Assembly convened in September 1979, a 36-page report was printed summarising the mood of the delegates. The report was secret, but it circulated privately and Miss Christian was able to obtain a copy. In it, the Sandinistas referred to their co-operation with non-Marxist forces as an 'alliance of convenience' necessary to bring down Somoza, prevent US intervention and attract financial assistance from Western countries. The report also suggested that relative moderation in policy and co-operation with 'bourgeois' parties ought to continue during an 'intermediate' stage for the same reasons.[65] She also reports that on 23 June 1981, Humberto Ortega spoke, assuming it was off the record, to a group of Sandinista military officers. (Copies of the speech were later made public, but with some important deletions.) Ortega repeated the statement of the earlier report that the FSLN's co-operation with the Nicaraguan moderates was merely a tactical manoeuvre. The non-Marxists were now frankly viewed as enemies of the revolution. Ortega expounded the ideological inspiration of his party as follows:

> our revolution had a profoundly anti-imperialist character, profoundly revolutionary, profoundly classist; we are anti-Yankee, we against the bourgeoisie, we are inspired by the historic traditions of our people, we are inspired by *sandinismo*, which is the most beautiful tradition of this people, developed by Carlos Fonseca, we are guided by the scientific doctrine of the revolution, by Marxism-Leninism. We are saying that Marxism-Leninism is the scientific

doctrine that guides our revolution, the instrument of analysis of our Vanguard for understanding [the revolution's] historic process and for carrying out the revolution.[66]

Later, Bayardo Arce, one of the top Sandinista leaders, explained why the Sandinistas had decided to hold elections:

It is convenient to be able to call elections now and remove one of the US policy justifications for aggression against Nicaragua, because the others are impossible for us to concede. Imperialism asks three things of us: to abandon our internationalism (aid to the Salvadoran guerrillas), abandon our strategic links with the Soviet Union and the socialist community, and democracy. We cannot stop being internationalists unless we also stop being revolutionaries. We cannot abandon our strategic links unless we also stop being revolutionaries. This is not subject to any consideration. But the superstructure, the democracy, as they call it, the bourgeois democracy, is indeed an element where we can make some positive headway in the construction of Socialism in Nicaragua.[67]

Arce was known to be one of the hardliners in the FSLN, but in Miss Christian's judgement, 'more than five years of Sandinista rule had demonstrated that the adherents of this view held at the very least a veto on public policy in Nicaragua and more probably reflected what most of the *comandantes* wanted for their country'.[68]

Hatred of the United States or the Western world as a whole has also frustrated US efforts at accommodation. Fidel Castro is probably the best illustration of this. It has been noted many times that Castro was probably not a Communist at the time he took power in 1959. Later, he converted to Communism as a means of attracting the support of a somewhat hesitant Soviet Union. In other words, Castro's foreign policy was not initially derived from a commitment to Communism, but rather his Communism was an outgrowth of his foreign policy. Careless observers sometimes refer to Castro as a nationalist who sought to free his country from foreign interference, but in the end his foreign policy has left Cuba more dependent on the Soviet Union than it ever was on the United States. Fidel Castro was not interested in removing foreign influence from Cuba, but *United States* influence.

According to Rufo Lopez-Fresquet, the former Minister of Finance, 'Castro has always been motivated by hate. . . . He has a psychopathic suspicion of everything American. . . . Nothing that the

United States could have done, not the highest degree of cooperation, understanding, or sympathy, could have caused Castro to remain a friend.'[69] This raw emotion was expressed spontaneously often enough to convince one that Lopez is correct. In January 1959, before Castro had decided to break with the United States, someone asked him about the criticism of his executions of Batistianos by American commentators. 'If the Americans don't like what is happening in Cuba,' he blurted out, 'they can land the Marines and then there will be 200,000 gringos dead.'[70] In 1958, Castro reacted to the bombing of a peasant's home with ammunition acquired from the US by writing to a friend that 'when I saw the rockets fired at Mario's house, I swore to myself that the Americans were going to pay dearly for what they were doing. When the war is over, a much wider and bigger war will begin for me. The war I am going to launch against them.'[71]

Radical nationalists in the middle-east have seldom shown much interest in accommodation with the United States, and again their attitudes seem to be the most obvious explanation. According to Shaul Bakhash, the Ayatollah Khomeini assumed that the Western powers intended to 'dominate and plunder' the Islamic world. To do so required the destruction of Islam; Israel was seen as the West's means of accomplishing this. Rulers friendly to the West were, by definition, agents of the great powers. Khomeini believed Iran to be a 'prisoner' of America, and felt that only through clerical rule could his country achieve independence. These views were of long standing. Mobilising his followers for the campaign against the White Revolution in 1963, Khomeini declared that 'in the interests of Jews, America, and Israel, we must be jailed and killed; we must be sacrificed to the evil intentions of foreigners'. During the same period, Khomeini explained that the Iranian army had attacked a seminary because 'Israel does not want the Koran to survive in this country. Israel, through its black agents, crushed the Faiziyyeh. It crushes us . . . .' Later, while in exile, the Ayatollah encouraged representatives of the Palestine Liberation Organisation to 'uproot this germ of corruption' (that is, Israel) and referred to the leadership of Israel as 'a gang of Jews'. On economic matters, the same extremist tone was evident after the visit of some American investors in 1970: 'the Shah will place the agriculture, economy, forests, even food distribution and tourism throughout the country in their (foreign) hands; and for the Iranian nation nothing will remain except hardship and toil for the capitalist, humiliation and poverty.'[72]

Readers of Colonel Qaddaffi's Green Book have found it filled
with the same sorts of xenophobic outpourings. According to Edward
Haley, author of a valuable full-length study of Qaddaffi's regime, the
colonel's aims are simple: 'to achieve a wider role for Libya . . . in the
middle east, Africa, and the Islamic countries . . . and to weaken the
West and, if possible, Israel. In a sense, these are the opposite sides
of the same coin: by weakening the West the possibility of a wider
role for Libya is enhanced.' But what is remarkable about Qaddaffi
is not his intentions, but the lengths to which he has been willing
to go in pursuit of them. To quote again from Haley, 'no terrorist
acts have been too odious, no boundaries too sacred, no projects
too vast or dangerous—the "Islamic bomb"—to be denied Libyan
participation'.[73]

Specifically, Qaddaffi became in the seventies the leading sponsor
of international terrorism. Early in the decade, Qaddaffi provided the
funds, arms and training for the massacre perpetrated at the Olympic
games in Munich. In 1973, the Italy–Libya Association was founded
by a man considered too extreme by the neo-fascist party in Italy.
Qaddaffi's aim in that case was to pay right-wing terrorists to kill
Jews.[74] In 1979, a group of journalists were allowed to see Qaddaffi's
training camps for guerrillas and terrorists. They witnessed as many
as 20,000 trainees from 20 European countries and both ends of the
political spectrum drilling under the tutelage of Syrians, Palestinians,
Cubans and East Germans, all well supplied with sophisticated and
deadly small arms. David Newsome, an Undersecretary of State
during the Carter administration, reports that 'the Libyans have
provided money, training, and in some cases arms for virtually every
group in the world with revolutionary credentials'.[75] The interesting
point, again, is that Qaddaffi displayed no particular ideological
preference in these expenditures. Anyone who was willing to
pack a gun and shoot at Western politicians and businessmen
was eligible. This suggests that the Colonel has been motivated
less by the aim of attacking capitalism or establishing a particular
form of government than simply the desire to sow disorder among
those whom he considers his enemies. The lengths to which he has
been willing to go demonstrate the depth of his hostility to the
West.

What is the origin of Qaddaffi's views? A full investigation of this
would probably lead us out of the realm of politics and into that of
psychotherapy. (And by 1972, according to some reports, Qaddaffi
had already suffered three nervous breakdowns.[76]) Suffice it to say

that men such as the Ayatollah Khomeini and Colonel Qaddaffi are not likely candidates for a successful policy of conciliation. It is also important to note that their antipathy toward the US is not based on a commitment to Marxism.

The basic point is simple, but still bears repeating: where the new leadership has been strongly committed to Marxism, violently anti-American, or both, American conciliation has usually fallen on deaf ears. This is probably the most basic and important reason for the failure of these attempts at *rapprochement*, but it is not the only one; domestic politics may also stand in the way. Revolutionary regimes that seek to eliminate their political competitors may find that enemies abroad are too useful to be dispensed with. For this reason, American enmity may seem more desirable to the new leadership than American friendship. Or, as Jean-Paul Sartre quipped about Cuba, 'if the United States had not existed, Castro would have had to invent it'.[77]

Castro cancelled elections in April 1959, apparently deciding at that time in favour of the radical path. A purge of the moderates followed. In July, Manuel Urrutia, the President, made the mistake of condemning the Cuban Communists and was ousted, though Castro's histrionics on television failed to elicit the expected degree of enthusiasm from the Cuban public. In October, a more serious threat developed in the person of Hubert Matos, the rebel army commander in Camaguey province. Matos had been expressing his concern about Communist penetration of the government for several months. On the 20th, he resigned his post and took several supporters with him. Unlike Urrutia, Matos had enough of a following to make him a formidable obstacle to Castro's plans for the consolidation of dictatorial power. Castro put Matos on trial in December, delivering a seven-hour tirade himself in the court room, and Matos and his compatriots were sent to jail, where they were to spend the next twenty years of their lives (some of it, according to Matos, in a space little larger than a coffin).[78]

Providentially for Castro, the former head of the rebel air force offered a diversion from these events the day after Matos's resignation. On 21 October, Pedro Diaz Lanz flew an airplane from somewhere in Florida to drop anti-Castro leaflets over Havana. He was fired on by Cuban air force planes and anti-aircraft guns, and some of the loose shells killed innocent bystanders. Five days later, Castro took to the podium to exercise his considerable demagogic skills. The American Ambassador describes the scene as follows:

> Castro addressed a vast throng of his fellow citizens. He described the Diaz Lanz flight as an attempt to bomb the Cuban Revolution into submission. He said he had a report that other planes were even then on their way from Florida to bomb Havana (none appeared). He shook his fist, roared defiance at the northern sky, foamed at the mouth, and in every way comported himself in a manner reminiscent of Hitler at his most hysterical and most odious. There was the same blatant disregard for truth, the same pathological extremes of expression, gesticulation, and movement. Castro seemed indeed to have taken leave of his senses. . . . He asked the crowd if it wished the revolutionary tribunals restored for the expeditious trial of traitors. The answer was a roared affirmative mingled with shouts of '*¡Paredon! ¡Paredon!*' ('To the execution wall with them!') It was a repulsive spectacle of mass hatred inspired by the man wholly and knowingly responsible for the lies used to arouse mob passions.[79]

With the crowd whipped into this frenzy, the *lider maximo* declared that Matos was linked with Diaz Lanz and that the foreign threat necessitated the creation of a popular militia. Not coincidentally, the existence of a militia would reduce Castro's dependence on the rebel army, where support for Matos was growing.[80]

Rapprochement with the Iranian revolutionaries would have been difficult in any case for reasons noted above, but revolutionary politics created an additional barrier. American officials had hoped that once the Shah was gone the Iranians would realise that the Soviet Union was much closer to Iran than was the United States, and that whatever injustices the Iranians imagined that they had suffered from the United States, their geopolitical interests would be best served by some sort of co-operation with the US. Indeed, Mehdi Bazargan, the head of Iran's provisional government, was concerned about the Soviets' intentions toward his country and had discussed with American officials the possibility of an exchange of intelligence on the USSR as well as the sale of spare military parts to Iran.[81]

But, not for the first time, national interests were set aside by those concerned about their immediate future in the country's internal power struggles. It may not have been sensible foreign policy to antagonise a powerful country, but provocation of the United States served the domestic political aims of the radical clerics very effectively. Just three days after Bazargan met with Zbigniew Brzezinski in Algiers, the American embassy was taken in Teheran. In the aftermath, the moderate Bazargan was forced to resign. The embassy seizure proved to be the turning-point in the Iranian revolution. After Bazargan was ousted, the radicals were able to blackmail or discredit large numbers of moderate politicians by releasing or threatening to release embassy documents recounting their discussions with American officials, discussions in which they had usually suggested that better relations between the two countries would be desirable. These tactics later prevented another relative moderate, President Bani-Sadr, from consolidating power. Eventually, Bani-Sadr was impeached and forced to flee Iran surreptitiously.[82]

Another concern of the supporters of the hostage-taking was the passage of the new constitution drawn up by Khomeini's followers. The constitution faced opposition from many quarters, so the seizure of the Americans, in the words of Michael Fischer, 'must have seemed like a godsend to silence criticism of the new constitution and to smooth [its] passage.'[83]

Finally, the hostages helped the radical clerics hold on to power at a time when opposition was building in many quarters. The month before the taking of the hostages had seen demonstrations over the 30 per cent rate of unemployment, clashes between fishermen angry over the government's revocation of their right to fish caviar (which left 10 or more dead) and unrest among the ethnic minorities in Baluchistan, Kurdistan and Khuzistan. A member of the Iranian government assessed the situation in this way:

> In order to rally the masses, this kind of thing [i.e., the kidnapping] should continue. If this campaign against the Americans ends just by a trial of these Americans and their deportation, it will be a disaster. It has to go further. We have to divert this to the reconstruction of the country. When the masses are completely mobilised against the Americans, it is easier to tell them to go to the fields and do this or that.[84]

Thus, the provocative, or to put it bluntly, criminal, foreign policy of the radical clerics and their 'student' supporters did make sense from an internal perspective, even if it put their country in the wrong in the eyes of the rest of the world.

Domestic politics may also have played a role in the evolution of foreign policy in Ethiopia. The critical juncture for the United States in Ethiopia was in the spring of 1977, when the *Dergue* demanded that the American presence in their country come to an abrupt end. The timing of this can be explained by the outcome of the power struggle in Addis Ababa. In early February a pro-Soviet candidate, Mengistu Haile Mariam, emerged as top dog in the *Dergue* after another round of intramural bloodletting. Mengistu met with the Soviet Ambassador within 24 hours of his victory, and announced one week later that 'in the future Ethiopia will look to the socialist countries for arms.'[85] Mengistu's immediate purpose is quite clear. The Soviets had given him to understand that they would extend full support to the *Dergue* only if he acted decisively to eliminate US influence.[86] What is less obvious is why the brutal former major was so determined to attract Soviet support, particularly in view of their past hesitation.

According to one source, Mengistu was not an ideologue, nor even well read in the Marxist literature, but was aware of the advantages of seeming 'revolutionary' in the political atmosphere in which he found himself.[87] After the execution of the notables and the implementation of the land reform, the most dangerous political opposition to the *Dergue* was a civilian Marxist party, the EPRP. Shortly after his seizure of power in February 1977, Mengistu began arming urban militia squads to destroy the EPRP at the neighbourhood level in Addis Ababa. The EPRP responded by staging mass demonstrations by its student supporters. On 29 April, just five days after the expulsion of most of the Americans, Mengistu's toughs shot between 500 and 1500 of these youths, leaving the corpses in the streets of the capital to be consumed by roving hyenas.[88]

In these grim circumstances, the connection with the United States was probably seen as a serious liability to the regime, even though the USSR had been reluctant and proved to be unreliable in the following months. Continuing ties with the United States would make the *Dergue* susceptible to the leftists' charges of not being sufficiently revolutionary; alignment with the Soviet Union gave Mengistu the revolutionary cachet he needed to strengthen his hold on power.

International security threats are the third factor shaping the foreign policies of revolutionary governments. Frequently in history, foreign dangers have compelled nations to set aside their ideological preferences, as when republican France allied with Tsarist Russia in 1891. But in Ethiopia and Vietnam the security concerns of the regimes reinforced, rather than crosscut, their ideological proclivities. With the death of General Aman, the *Dergue* committed itself to a military solution of the Eritrean conflict. To achieve this, they needed a much bigger army than they had inherited from Haile Selassie. The US was clearly uncomfortable with their policy on Eritrea; only the Soviets, they thought, could give them the tools to finish off the Eritrean rebels.[89] Later, in July 1977, after the *Dergue* had broken with the United States, Somalia attacked the Ogaden desert region of Ethiopia. The Soviets had not yet decided to give Ethiopia all-out support against their ally Somalia and the *Dergue* turned back to the United States for help. President Carter demurred, and the Russians eventually overcame their hesitation and intervened in support of the Ethiopians, winning a stunning victory through the airlift of Cuban proxies.[90]

As aforementioned, the Vietnamese initially had some interest in extracting aid from the United States and keeping their distance from the Russians, but this policy had to be jettisoned once the Vietnamese foresaw the need for some sort of protection against Pol Pot's allies in Peking. Having antagonised the Chinese by their invasion of Cambodia and their persecution of the Chinese ethnic minority in Vietnam, they could hardly expect the United States to take their part against China.

Thus, where the United States is unwilling or unable to offer protection to revolutionary governments, they may be forced to rely more heavily on the Soviet Union than they would otherwise prefer. This might well have been the case in Mozambique as well, as will become evident below.

The last factor to take into account is the policy of the United States in other places and at other times. As we have seen, the United States has pursued conciliatory policies toward revolutionary regimes on many occasions. But in most cases that conciliation has been bilateral only. At the same time, American policy in other regions of the globe or parts of the same region has been deeply objectionable to some of these governments. This is especially true in the middle-east, where support for Israel is obviously a severe handicap to the United States in its dealings with radical nationalists. To cite only one example, some believe that Qaddaffi's decision in 1974 to seek closer relations with the Soviet bloc was precipitated by the disengagement agreement between Egypt and Israel brokered by Henry Kissinger, which convinced him that Sadat was 'handing over Egypt to American imperialism'.[91] In this case, as in many others, it was simply not possible for the United States to alter global or regional policies to suit the new government.

Further, even though American policy has frequently been conciliatory, it has not always been so. The occasions where the United
States has attempted to destabilise a revolutionary government may
create suspicion that makes other leftists unreceptive to a conciliatory
policy. One such case may have been Iraq, where the efforts to
improve relations with the new government were hindered by the US
intervention in Lebanon. According to some reports, the Ayatollah's
followers did not believe that the Shah was ill and thought that he
had been readmitted to the United States in order to promote a plot
to restore the Shah to power.[92]

Again, Cuba is a useful example. It has been suggested that the
American destabilisation of the Arbenz regime in Guatemala in 1954
became a crucial determinant in the policy of Castro in 1959. A number
of scholars have concluded that the events in Guatemala convinced
Castro that American hostility was inevitable, leading him to think
that he had no choice but to find foreign support if his revolution were
to survive.[93] This notion is corroborated by Lopez-Fresquet, who says
that 'the bearded leader thought that he would not be long in power.
He believed that after he began his intended aggressions on American
property, the US would surely use its colossal strength to bring about
his overthrow.'[94]

But one ought not to leap to the conclusion that things would
have been much different if the Eisenhower administration had not
intervened against Arbenz. The Cuban revolutionaries were also
aware of the more conciliatory policy Washington had pursued in
Bolivia (more on this below), but were no more anxious to repeat
that experience than that of Guatemala. In their view, the American
tie had ultimately restrained the left wing of the Nationalist Revolutionary Movement, preventing them from achieving a truly radical
restructuring of their country.[95] Also, as we noted above, the hostility
of the United States was useful to Castro in his effort to eliminate
his political opponents. To quote again from Lopez-Fresquet, 'it was
never Castro's intention to ask [the US] for aid. If the US had helped
Cuba, he could never have presented the American as the enemy of
the revolution'.[96]

These, then, are the reasons why American attempts at conciliation
with revolutionary regimes have ended in failure so often. But some

may object at this point that ideological animosity to the United States is to be expected as long as the US supports the enemies of revolutionary movements and treats the revolutionaries with great suspicion as long as they are in opposition. Those who make this argument usually suggest that if the United States stopped attempting to block the revolutionaries' path to power, they would be more receptive to US overtures if and when they succeeded in overthrowing the government.

It is impossible to answer this line of argument entirely convincingly since we cannot replay history, but we can weigh its persuasiveness in an indirect way by looking at three particular cases. The first is Nicaragua. As the critics have said, the United States first tried to prevent the Sandinistas from taking power and then tried to limit their share of power. What would have happened if the US had not stood in their way?

Costa Rica, a country similar to the United States in its domestic structure and ideology, supported the Sandinista's revolution against Somoza. They allowed the rebels to operate out of their territory in 1978 and 1979 and supplied them military assistance even earlier than Cuba did. But later, when Castro asked Nicaragua to compete with Costa Rica for a seat on the UN Security Council to deny Costa Rica the seat, the Sandinistas co-operated. Despite their considerable debt to Costa Rica, the Sandinistas felt a stronger allegiance to Cuba, where many of them had lived at one time or another.[97] More recently, according to Bolanos, the Sandinistas have been working to destabilise Costa Rica despite their past friendship.

It is also revealing to consider a country in which the United States, in effect, has no past. India, a former British colony where the US role was minimal prior to independence, is such a case. By the early fifties, the United States was already the largest donor of aid. Despite this, India's 'non-aligned' foreign policy seemed to American officials to tilt in a pro-Soviet direction. India supported the Soviet and Chinese positions on the Korean war in the United Nations, but refused to denounce China's conquest of Tibet or the Russian's invasion of Hungary. At the same time Indian leaders routinely blamed the United States for the intensification of the cold war. What accounts for this?[98]

The Congress Party granted Nehru considerable autonomy in making foreign policy, so an understanding of his views is particularly important in understanding Indian foreign policy in this period. In 1927, Nehru returned from a meeting of the 'International Congress against Imperialism' in Brussels to speak to a gathering of Congress officials. Nehru told them how his discussions with Latin American delegates had opened his eyes toward 'the rising imperialism of the United States', and had led him to the conclusion that 'the great problem of the future will be American imperialism, even more than British imperialism'. Nehru's travels had convinced him that 'the only key to the solution of the world's problems and of India's problems lies in socialism' and that 'if the future is full of hope it is largely because of Soviet Russia and what it has done'. Nehru also firmly believed that 'modern imperialism is an outgrowth of capitalism and cannot be separated from it'. It would be neither fair nor accurate to portray Nehru as a doctrinaire leftist or an uncritical admirer of the USSR, but he was, unquestionably, strongly influenced by Marxism. The Indian case suggests that a new leadership may turn against the United States even if it is generous to the country and has not attempted to keep them out of power or abetted their oppressors.[99]

The last case of interest here is Venezuela. The Eisenhower administration had supported a corrupt and degenerate dictator, Marcos Perez Jimenez, through the fifties, even pinning a medal of honour on him in 1954. Shortly after Perez Jimenez was toppled in 1958, Vice-President Nixon and Mrs Nixon were sent to Caracas to repair the damage. The Nixon's car was set upon by an angry mob in what appeared to be an orchestrated attack. The windows of the car were smashed with rocks and sticks and the Nixons were covered from head to foot with, as the Vice President put it, 'a liquid that was not rain'.[100]

Obviously, anti-American feelings were running high in Venezuela in 1958. Yet, three years later, Venezuela was pursuing a foreign policy that has been described as 'generally friendly, but not subservient to the United States'.[101] Partly, this can be credited to the Kennedy administration's Alliance for Progress, which won the American President great popularity in the region, but the most important factor was the coming to power of the reformist but solidly anti-Communist *Accion Democratica* party led by Romulo Betancourt. In other words, past American support of an unpopular dictator was no bar to good relations when the moderate forces came to power later.

The Venezuelan pattern was repeated in three other cases listed as successes in the table on page p.192. In Portugal, the policy of the United States was barely conciliatory at all, as Secretary Kissinger credited overly pessimistic reports on the strength of the Communists, leading him to refuse to send aid to the country for several months and later to consider expelling Portugal from NATO. Ultimately, the moderates won the power struggle, eliminated the Communists from the government and remained in NATO.[102]

The Dominican Republic has been discussed extensively already. The Eisenhower and Kennedy administrations helped to precipitate the end of the Trujillo regime there by imposing economic sanctions and providing arms to a group of conspirators who later assassinated the tyrant. Then, when members of the Trujillo family manoeuvred to retake control, the US positioned a naval task force group three miles off shore from Santo Domingo, convincing the late dictator's brothers to leave the country. This updated version of gunboat diplomacy was popular on the island but the short-term success there was also possible because moderate forces were around to pick up the pieces after Trujillo's death.

In Bolivia, the Marxist-influenced MNR took power through a revolution in 1952 and immediately nationalised the tin mines. But the Bolivian Ambassador in Washington made every effort to reassure the Eisenhower administration that the MNR was not hostile to private property in general and that the tin interests, which were 10 per cent American, would be compensated fairly. The administration responded by making Bolivia one of only three governments in Latin America to receive outright grants of aid in the fifties. The results proved to be quite satisfactory from the US standpoint. Bolivia voted with Secretary Dulles's 1954 Caracas resolution condemning Communism, supported the US in the Cuban missile crisis and eventually broke relations with Castro in 1964. The MNR also rejected a Soviet offer to build a tin smelter in 1960 and never bothered to exchange ambassadors with Moscow.[103]

Bolivia's economic woes at the time of the revolution may have been an important influence on her foreign policy. A fall in world tin prices had lead to a steep decline in the country's foreign exchange earnings and since one quarter of the country's food was imported, exports were essential to feed the population. Negotiations on a tin agreement with the United States had stalled in 1951 and Bolivian tin would continue to sit on the docks as the talks remained at an *impasse*. The low-grade ore could not be processed in European smelters and the Soviets showed no interest at this time in coming to Bolivia's assistance. The MNR, in other words, needed a tin agreement with the United States in the worst way, and this may account at least in part for their willingness to accommodate the United States.[104]

As we have seen, American policies of conciliation are most likely to meet with success when moderate political forces assume control after the overthrow of the old regime. In cases such as Bolivia, moderation may be encouraged or reinforced by a high degree of economic dependence, but as the history of Cuba shows, dependency is no guarantee of an outcome favourable to the United States. Conversely, when radical nationalists or Marxists have seized power, policies of conciliation have usually failed. The pattern is mostly attributable, it seems, not primarily to differences in American policy or the strength of economic ties but in the reactions of the new leadership to similar policies, reactions that seem to be strongly influenced by the ideological bent of the regime. Conciliation with radicals has not failed in every case, however. An examination of three of these instances may be instructive.

Chronologically, the first is Yugoslavia. Here the United States invested $1.2 billion between 1949 and 1955 to preserve Tito's independence and deny his country's 33 divisions and strategic position on the Adriatic to the Warsaw Pact. If the effort was successful, it was not because of any initial lack of zeal on Tito's part for the Communist cause. In the first years after the Second World War, the Yugoslav leader promoted international Communism as enthusiastically as Stalin, shooting down American planes that entered Yugoslav airspace, pressing territorial demands on Carinthia and Trieste and abetting the Greek Communist insurgents. Even after his expulsion from the Communist movement, Tito still affirmed his 'faithfulness and solidarity' to the Soviet Union in a speech to the Yugoslav Communist party in July 1948.[105] As John Campbell explains:

> the decision to defy the Soviet Union and Stalin was one of tremendous psychological difficulty for the Yugoslav Communists. Tito himself had fought for Communism in the Russian civil war. He had been a Communist agent for years. The 'movement', with its center in Moscow, had been his life.[106]

Tito sought aid from the United States only after Stalin openly attempted to overthrow him in the summer of 1948. The Soviet dictator boasted that he would 'shake his little finger and then there will be no more Tito', then applied an economic boycott to Yugoslavia, formed a government in exile, and abrogated the alliances between Yugoslavia and the other satellites. Within a few months, the United States and Yugoslavia were cautiously edging toward each other and the first American assistance arrived later in 1949. Tito expressed his gratitude by closing the border with Greece in July 1949, tilting the balance toward the government in the Greek civil war.[107]

The second exceptional case is Guinea, a former French colony which received its independence in 1960. Guinea's leader, Sekou Toure, demanded complete independence and refused to participate in the French Community, bringing down on his head the wrath of President De Gaulle, who withdrew all French technicians and halted budgetary support. The General also requested that the United States co-operate in the isolation of Guinea. When the Eisenhower administration complied, Toure looked for help from the Russians. By the end of 1961, when Leonid Brezhnev visited Conakry, the Soviets were supplying 75 per cent of Guinea's imports and had 1500 advisors in the country. Toure was subsequently granted the Lenin Peace Prize and after his support for Castro during the Bay of Pigs, most observers in the West were conceding Guinea to the east bloc.[108]

But John Kennedy had met Sekou Toure previously in, of all places, Disneyland, and had come away convinced that his nationalist leanings were stronger than his sympathy for Communism. On the recommendation of Ambassador William Attwood, Kennedy gave his approval to a $25 million aid package in the middle of 1961. Later in the same year, the Guineans began complaining about the Soviet aid programme. Soviet aid came behind schedule, and when it finally arrived, the objects of Soviet generosity found the food rotting, the grain fermenting and some of the farm machinery equipped with snow ploughs.[109]

In the late fall, Soviet Ambassador Daniel Solod was caught instigating student protests against the government and a secret Communist organisation was uncovered in the town of Labe. Toure began to suspect that the Russians were trying to foment a revolt and declared Solod *persona non grata* in December. Only a few days afterwards, Guinea began moving back toward the West. Soviet technicians remained, but the Russians were denied landing rights for planes headed for the Caribbean during the Cuban missile crisis and trade between the USSR and Guinea fell sharply over the next few years. After Toure's second meeting with Kennedy, personal relations between the two men remained very cordial.[110] Summing up the episode, Arthur Schlesinger notes that the Soviet's blunders created the opportunity for the United States in Guinea, but adds that 'if Washington had persisted in its conviction that Guinea was irreclaimable, [we] would not have been in a position to take advantage'.[111]

The last of the three exceptions is Mozambique, which won its independence from Portugal in 1975. The policy of the United States in the first years after the revolution was conciliatory. President Ford promised the regime early recognition immediately after his inauguration and supplied $10 million in aid in 1976. The policy was continued by the Carter administration and by spring 1978 the United States had provided Mozambique with $25 million in assistance. Despite this, the early indications were not encouraging. The ruling Frelimo party closed the US consulate and did not invite the United States to its independence ceremonies.[112] The new leadership's pronouncements on foreign policy also sounded unpromising: promotion of national liberation movements was seen as 'an international duty' and the eastern bloc nations were viewed as 'natural allies' whose assistance would be 'an important strategic factor for dissuasion of the aggressive plans of imperialism'. President Samora Machel visited Moscow in 1976 and in the following year signed a treaty of friendship and co-operation with the USSR. Frelimo also adopted a rigidly Marxist economic plan in 1977 and placed an estimated 12,000 opponents in 're-education' camps.[113]

Frelimo's commitment to world revolution stopped short of slavish adherence to Soviet demands, however. Mozambique declared itself to be a non-aligned country, though government spokesmen added that they did not interpret that to mean equidistance between the superpowers. More significantly, they refused to grant the Russians the prize they coveted most, a naval base on the Indian ocean littoral. (Soviet vessels were permitted to use Mozambique's ports, however.)[114] It has been suggested that the Soviets' subsequent reluctance to support Mozambique at the same level as Ethiopia and Angola may have stemmed from this. Mozambique relied almost exclusively on the USSR as an arms supplier until 1982 and received $300 million in arms in that period. But Frelimo was disappointed both with the cost and quality of the weapons, many of which were earlier models than those sent to the other African clients of the USSR. The levels of economic assistance were also unimpressive. Through 1978, the eastern bloc as a whole had granted $25 million, with the Soviet Union contributing only $5 million of the total.[115]

In 1978, President Samora Machel met Jimmy Carter and is said to have told him that he would 'wipe the slate clean' with the United States. Two Western observers sympathetic to Frelimo attributed this to 'the realisation that the socialist countries were either unable or unwilling to provide capital and advanced technology on the scale required to achieve its ambitious billion dollar development projects'. Ironically, Congress was losing patience with Frelimo just as Machel was becoming more responsive, and prohibited Mozambique from receiving US assistance in the 1978 foreign aid bill.[116]

In 1979–80, the pattern of Mozambique's foreign policy was somewhat inconsistent. Machel co-operated with the efforts of Britain and the United States to bring about a political settlement in Rhodesia but seemed to be leaning to the Soviet side on most other issues. Frelimo voiced support for the Sandinistas and other revolutionary groups, gave some assistance to the African National Congress (ANC), and was one of the few African states to support the Soviet invasion of Afghanistan and the Vietnamese occupation of Cambodia. One explanation for the latter positions is that the Frelimo leadership was worried about aggression from South Africa and wanted to avoid antagonising the Russians in the event that their protection might be needed. South Africa had attacked the suburbs of Maputo in January 1979 and began to assist the MNR guerrillas, who were becoming a serious threat to Frelimo. Two days after the South African incursion, the Soviets sent two warships to Maputo and warned that they would stage reprisals if there were further attacks. The Russians also promised in May of the next year to increase the quality and quantity of arms they were providing to Mozambique.

At that time it appeared that security needs might drive Frelimo closer to the USSR than they would have initially preferred, repeating the pattern in Vietnam.[117] But when the Soviets were presented with a clear opportunity to consolidate their influence, they passed it over. In 1980, Frelimo asked for admission to COMECON and was turned down, perhaps because Frelimo's economic plans were already going awry and the Soviets were not eager to take another expensive commitment after the invasion of Afghanistan, the rebellion in Poland and their existing projects in Africa.[118]

In 1984, Mozambique turned sharply back toward the West. In March, the government signed the Nkomati Accord with South Africa, which obliged each country to prevent guerrillas from using its territory to stage attacks on the other. The United States played a key intermediary role in this agreement and the Soviet Union, a supporter of the ANC, was left on the outside as it had been earlier at Camp David. Later, in September, Mozambique bowed to pressure from her Western creditors and joined the IMF and World Bank.

By 1983 Frelimo was in deep trouble, both economically and militarily. Because of drought, the widening guerrilla conflict and the regime's own half-baked economic schemes agricultural production had fallen 50 per cent, leading to the death by starvation of approximately 100,000 people in 1983. The regime's economic failure also provided an opportunity for the Mozambique National Resistance (MNR). Established by the Rhodesian government in the seventies to harass Mozambique, the MNR was assumed to be dying out after the defeat of Ian Smith's white minority government. But support from South Africa and the collapse of Mozambique's agriculture revived the guerrillas, who numbered some 10,000 by 1984 and were posing an acute threat to the government.[119] The Soviet response in this situation was disappointing, even disillusioning, to the government. The Soviets provided very little disaster relief during the famine in 1983 and the cynicism of Soviet policy was not lost on the African Marxists. A senior government official told journalist David Lamb that the USSR seemed to be more interested in destabilising South Africa then assisting the Africans with their economic and security problems. 'The Russians would just as soon see the region burning' he commented bitterly.[120] Moreover, Soviet military advisors had trained and equipped Mozambique's army for conventional war rather than guerrilla engagements and Frelimo found these tactics ineffective against the MNR. According to Allen Isaacman, 'by 1983 Frelimo concluded that the USSR was unwilling or unable to provide the military assistance that they had been led to expect', and they had begun to look for alternatives.[121]

Specifically, Frelimo had decided, in the words of one government official, that 'we can't afford in this region not to have relations with the United States'. If the Soviet naval presence could not deter the MNR and Soviet arms and advice were not providing effective defence against them, the only alternative was to deal directly with their patron, and only the United States was in a position to influence Pretoria.[122] Of course, nothing would have come of this had Washington remained unresponsive. Chester Crocker, the administration's chief diplomat for southern Africa, had said publicly in 1981 that Marxism would not be 'the litmus test for the choice of regional partners' for the United States.[123] After some initial misunderstandings, the administration lifted restrictions on aid in 1982 and provided $22 million in emergency assistance to Mozambique in 1984, more than to any other country in Africa that year. Regular economic assistance was also increased, reaching a level of $30 million in fiscal year 1986.[124]

Mozambique has not broken all ties with the USSR and has certainly not become an uncritical admirer of the United States. But the 'non-alignment' since the Nkomati Accord seems to be much more genuine than the policy of the mid-seventies.[125] It may be that although the leaders of Frelimo were sincere Marxists, their desire for independence and (paradoxically) the extreme dependence of their economy on South Africa and the West would naturally have led them to keep their distance from the USSR. But the Soviets contributed to their own difficulties in maintaining Mozambique's loyalty by cutting back support when they did not achieve their maximum goal quickly. Even so, it appeared in the early eighties as if Mozambique's leaders might be drawn into a much closer relationship with the Soviet Union than they desired by the dreadful circumstances obtaining at that time. But the Soviets were either unable or uninterested in taking advantage of the opportunity afforded by Mozambique's war and famine. As Crocker has noted, it was only after 'the failure of Marxist economics and the conspicuous inability of the Soviet Union to assist Mozambique with security and political problems' became apparent that Frelimo sought improved relations with the United States.[126]

The United States, then, has pursued policies of conciliation with the governments established after the fall of pro-Western regimes more often than the critics seem to realise. When the successors have been moderate, these policies have almost always succeeded; when radicals have come to power, the attempts at conciliation have usually met with frustration. The ideologically based hostility of Marxists and radical nationalists toward the United States is the most obvious and convincing explanation for this, though revolutionary domestic politics, the need for protection against external threats and some aspects of American global or regional policy may also be involved. There have been at least three exceptions to this pattern, but it is important to consider why these exceptions occurred. In Mozambique, as previously in Yugoslavia and Guinea, constructive relations were achieved with radical regimes only after they had become disillusioned with the quantity or quality of Soviet assistance or alarmed at the prospect of Soviet interference. The United States has not, as a general rule, driven radical governments to the Soviets; on occasion, however, the Soviets have driven regimes initially well disposed to them back toward the United States. It would surely be preferable, though, if the defence of the interests of the United States and her allies in the third world rested on something more reliable than the clumsiness of their chief adversary. It is now time to consider what, if anything, that might be.

TABLE: Ideological complexion of leadership:

Outcome:	Moderate	Radical
Success	Venezuela	Yugoslavia
	Dominican Republic	Guinea
	Bolivia	Mozambique
	Portugal	
Failure	India?	China
		Cuba
		Iraq
		Ghana
		Libya
		Ethiopia
		Vietnam
		Iran
		Nicaragua

Notes

1. I will define 'conciliatory' as sufficient to give the new leadership incentive to work with the United States. In some of these cases, American policy will not be *purely* conciliatory; that is, the US may be unresponsive on some issues and the regime may not get everything it would like. But it will not be misleading to call such a policy 'conciliatory' if it is much more conciliatory than confrontational, or if the US is offering more than the Russians or other major powers. Implicit or explicit in the discussion that follows will be judgments about the success or failure of these conciliatory policies. I will define 'success' as a situation in which the new regime (1) enters into normal trading relations with the US, and does not reorient its trade toward the eastern bloc; (2) remains non-aligned, in the true, not the Cuban, sense, (3) does not take actions seriously damaging to US interests. Note that this definition does not require that a regime become a Soviet client in order to be considered a 'failure'. 'Revolutionary government', as used here, will mean, naturally, governments coming to power through the violent overthrow of their predecessors. It will also be used for governments of a leftist disposition coming to power through other means, including coups and decolonisation. The definition was

broadened in this way to expand the range of analogous cases available. In so doing, I have tried not to stack the deck in favour of the thesis I will develop, as a review of the table above will show.)

2. Tang Tsou, *America's Failure in China* (Chicago: University of Chicago Press, 1963), p. 505; Stephen Goldstein, 'Chinese Communist Policy toward the US', pp. 274–5; Michael Hunt, 'Mao Tse-tung and the Issue of Accommodation with the United States', pp. 206–8, both in Waldo Heinrichs and Dorothy Borg (eds), *Uncertain Years* (New York: Columbia University Press, 1980).

3. Warren Cohen, *America's Response to China* (New York: Wiley, 1971), p. 199; David Mayers, *Cracking the Monolith: US Policy Against the Sino–Soviet Alliance, 1949–55* (Baton Rouge, Louisiana: Louisiana State University Press, 1986), p. 54; Tsou, *America's Failure*, p. 512.

4. Tsou, *America's Failure*, pp. 515–17; Mayers, *Cracking the Monolith*, p. 58.

5. Tsou, *America's Failure*, pp. 520, 531, 534–5.

6. Mayers, *Cracking the Monolith*, pp. 72–3.

7. Mayers, *Cracking the Monolith*, p. 73.

8. Cohen, *America's Response to China*, pp. 201–2.

9. Philip Bonsal, *Cuba, Castro, and the United States* (Pittsburgh: University of Pittsburgh Press, 1971), p. 51.

10. Mario Lazo, *Dagger in the Heart* (New York: Funk & Wagnalls, 1968), p. 178; Theodore Draper, *Castro's Revolution: Myths and Realities* (New York: Praeger, 1962), pp. 163–4; John B. Martin, *US Policy in the Caribbean* (Boulder, Colorado: Westview, 1978), p. 40; Rufo Lopez-Fresquet, *My Fourteen Months with Castro* (Cleveland: World Publishing Co., 1966), p. 167.

11. Bonsal, *Cuba, Castro, and the United States*, pp. 149–51. US policy was not fully conciliatory, however. After Castro's seizure of power, the arms embargo continued. The US refused to sell arms to Cuba, and at one point also intervened to dissuade the British. When word of this leaked, it did damage relations with Cuba. The action was taken, most likely, in reaction to the invasions Castro undertook in June 1959 of Haiti and the Dominican Republic. Both efforts failed miserably, but suggested that Castro's aims were not defensive, as he protested. (Andres Suarez, *Cuba: Castroism and Communism 1959–66* [Cambridge: MIT Press, 1967], p. 72; Bonsal, *Cuba, Castro, and the United States*, pp. 76–7, 98–9.)

12. Ruby Hart Phillips, *The Cuban Dilemma* (New York: Oblensky, 1963), pp. 84–5; Cole Blasier, 'The Elimination of US Influence' in *Revolutionary Change in Cuba*, Carmelo Mesa-Lago (ed.)(Pittsburgh: University of Pittsburgh Press, 1971), p. 63.

13. Blasier, 'The Elimination of US Influence', p. 63; Bonsal, *Cuba, Castro, and the United States*, pp. 122–3.

14. Suarez, *Cuba*, pp. 85–6.

15. Bonsal, *Cuba, Castro, and the United States*, pp. 98, 114.

16. Lopez-Fresquet, *My Fourteen Months with Castro*, pp. 174–5.

17. William A. Williams, *The United States, Castro, and Cuba* (Ann Arbor, Michigan: University Microfilms International, 1979), pp. 111–12, 120.

18. Jorge Dominguez, *Cuba: Order and Revolution* (Cambridge, Massachusetts: Belknap Press, 1978), p. 144.
19. Lopez-Fresquet, *My Fourteen Months with Castro*, p. 108.
20. On the turn of the revolution to the left, see Dominguez, *Cuba*, pp. 144–6; Lopez-Fresquet, *My Fourteen Months with Castro*, p. 106, and Cole Blasier, *The Hovering Giant* (Pittsburgh: University of Pittsburgh Press, 1976), p. 181.
21. Shirley Christian, *Nicaragua: Revolution in the Family* (New York: Random House, 1985), pp. 142, 194; Robert Pastor, *Condemned to Repetition: The United States and Nicaragua* (Princeton, New Jersey: Princeton University Press, 1987), pp. 187, 195–6.
22. 'Sandinistas Asserts War Has Taken 12,000 Lives', *New York Times*, 18 July 1985, p. 7; Pastor, *Condemned to Repetition*, pp. 206–7.
23. Pastor, *Condemned to Repetition*, pp. 207, 209–10, 217, 229; Paul Sigmund, 'Latin America: Change or Continuity?' in *Foreign Affairs*, 60 (America and the World 1981), pp. 639; George Will, 'If We Spurn Contras, Who Will Believe in America?', *Atlanta Journal–Constitution*, 21 April 1985, p. 3M. US aid, however, was not a huge percentage of the total, just $62 out of a total of $580 in the first year according to Shirley Christian, *Nicaragua*, p. 165.
24. Christian, *Nicaragua*, pp. 165–7, 154–60; Pastor, *Condemned to Repetition*, pp. 195, 211–12, 215, 221.
25. Jeane Kirkpatrick, 'US Security and Latin America', reprinted in *Dictatorships and Double Standards* (New York: Simon & Schuster, 1982) pp. 78–9; Christian, *Nicaragua*, p. 142; Pastor, *Condemned to Repetition*, p. 201, 207, 211.
26. Pastor, *Condemned to Repetition*, pp. 216–27; Christian, *Nicaragua*, p. 168.
27. Paul Sigmund, pp. 638–41; Christian, p. 199; Arturo Cruz, 'Nicaragua's Imperiled Revolution', *Foreign Affairs*, 61 (Summer 1983), pp. 1041ff; Pastor, *Condemned to Repetition*, pp. 233–4. Pastor attributes Enders' failure partly to the administration's decisions to stage military manoeuvres in the region and reduce economic aid. On the issue of whether the administration ought to have terminated aid in April, see Pastor, *Condemned to Repetition*, p. 231 and Christian, *Nicaragua*, pp. 194–7.
28. 'Iraq Is Recognized by US', *New York Times*, 3 August 1958; 'Murphy Hopeful on Course of Arabs' Movement', *New York Times*, 11 August 1958; 'US Arms Vessel Arrives in Iraq', *New York Times*, 21 August 1958; 'US Said to Test Iraq', *New York Times*, 21 August 1958; 'US Assistant Secretary Rountree in Baghdad for Talks', *New York Times*, December 16, 1958.
29. Alex Smolansky, *The Soviet Union and the Arab East under Khrushchev* (Lewisburg, Pennsylvania: Bucknell University Press, 1974), pp. 117–20, 157–9; Dana Schmidt, 'Macmillan Would Aid Iraq', *New York Times*, 24 March 1959; 'Iraq Said to Call for End to US Aid', *New York Times*, 30 May 1959; Richard Nyrop, *et al.*, *Area Handbook for Iraq* (Washington: US Government Printing Office, 1971), p. 214.
30. Smolansky, *Soviet Union and the Arab East*, pp. 157–8.

31. Edward Haley, *Qaddaffi and the US since 1969* (New York: Praeger, 1984), pp. 4–5, 21; John Cooley, *Libyan Sandstorm* (New York: Holt, Rinehart, and Winston, 1982), pp. 13–14, 84, 86–94.

32. 'In a Ring of Enemies', *The Economist*, 260 (14 August 1976), pp. 47–8; 'Libyans Arm and Train World Terrorists', *New York Times*, 16 July 1976; Haley, *Qaddaffi and the US*, pp. 7, 59; Cooley, *Libyan Sandstorm*, pp. 85–6, 245–6.

33. Michael Ledeen and William Lewis, *Debacle* (New York: Alfred Knopf, 1981), pp. 217–25; Barry Rubin, *Paved with Good Intentions* (New York: Oxford University Press, 1980), p. 287.

34. Gail Meyer, *Egypt and the United States: The Formative Years* (Rutherford, New Jersey: Farleigh Dickinson University Press, 1980), pp. 139–41.

35. Arthur Schlesinger, *A Thousand Days* (Boston: Houghton Mifflin, 1965), pp. 570–3; Robert Legvold, *Soviet Policy in West Africa* (Cambridge, Massachusetts: Harvard University Press, 1970) pp. 137–8.

36. Schlesinger, *A Thousand Days*, p. 573.

37. David Korn, *Ethiopia, The United States and the Soviet Union* (Carbondale, Illinois: Southern Illinois University Press, 1986, pp. 7–8, 15.

38. Korn, *Ethiopia*, pp. 11–13.

39. Korn, *Ethiopia*, p. 14.

40. Korn, *Ethiopia*, pp. 15–16.

41. 'Soviet Ethiopian Gain Could Be Short-lived', *Christian Science Monitor*, 25 April 1977, p. 1; 'Ethiopian Leader to Visit Moscow', *New York Times*, 1 May 1977; p. 3; Steven David, 'The Realignment of Third World Regimes from One Superpower to Another' (PhD. Dissertation, Harvard University, October 1980), pp. 95, 113–19, 130.

42. Korn, *Ethiopia*, pp. 27, 21, 17.

43. David, 'Realignment', pp. 115–16, 119–20, 123.

44. Korn, *Ethiopia*, p 17; Marina and David Ottaway, *Ethiopia: Empire in Revolution* (New York: Holmes & Meier, 1978), p. 167.

45. Korn, *Ethiopia*, p. 45.

46. Derek Davies, 'Carter's Neglect, Moscow's Victory', *Far Eastern Economic Review*, 103 (2 February 1979), p. 17; Gareth Porter, 'The Great Power Triangle in SE Asia', *Current History*, 79 (December 1980), p. 163.

47. Carlyle Thayer, 'Vietnam: Beleaguered Outpost of Socialism', *Current History*, 79 (December 1980), p. 169.

48. Elizabeth Becker, *When the War Was Over* (New York: Simon & Schuster, 1986), pp. 385–9; 'US Mission to Hanoi Begins Talks', *New York Times*, 17 March 1977.

49. Becker, *When the War Was Over*, pp. 390–2.

50. Becker, *When the War Was Over*, pp. 399–402.

51. Becker, *When the War Was Over*, pp. 401–2; Porter, 'The Great Power Triangle in SE Asia', pp. 195–6.

52. Becker, *When the War Was Over*, pp. 396.

53. Porter, 'The Great Power Triangle in SE Asia', p. 164.

54. Tsou, *America's Failure in China*, p. 209.
55. Tsou, *America's Failure in China*, p. 210.
56. Hunt, 'Mao Tse–tung and the Issue of Accommodation', pp. 228, 230, 227.
57. Hunt 'Mao Tse–tung and the Issue of Accommodation', pp. 228, 230, 227.
58. Warren Cohen, 'The Development of Chinese Communist Policy toward the US, 1934–45', *Orbis II*, (Summer 1967), pp. 236–7.
59. Goldstein, 'Chinese Communist Policy', p. 236.
60. Tsou, *America's Failure in China*, pp. 211–13.
61. Goldstein, 'Chinese Communist Policy', pp. 253, 256, 271–2.
62. Legvold, *Soviet Policy in West Africa*, pp. 130–6.
63. Miguel Bolanos Hunter, 'Nicaragua: A View from Within', in Mark Falcoff and Robert Royal (eds), *Crisis and Opportunity: US Policy in Central America and the Caribbean* (Washington: Ethics and Public Policy Center, 1984), pp. 393–5.
64. Bolanos, 'Nicaragua: A View from Within', p. 397.
65. Christian, *Nicaragua*, p. 129.
66. Christian, *Nicaragua*, p. 191.
67. Christian, *Nicaragua*, p. 298–9.
68. Christian, *Nicaragua*, pp. 299, 306–7.
69. Lopez-Fresquet, *My Fourteen Months with Castro*, pp. 165–7.
70. Phillips, *The Cuban Dilemma*, p. 28.
71. Herbert Matthews, *Castro: A Political Autobiography* (London: Allen Lane, 1969), p. 107.
72. Shaul Bakhash, *The Reign of the Ayatollahs* (New York: Basic Books, 1984), pp. 34, 36–7, 28.
73. Haley, *Qaddaffi and the US*, p. 11.
74. Haley, *Qaddaffi and the US*, p. 39.
75. Claire Sterling, *The Terror Network* (New York: Holt, Rinehart, and Winston, 1981), pp. 259–63.
76. Edward Sheehan, 'Colonel Qaddaffi: Libya's Mystical Revolutionary', *New York Times Magazine*, 6 February, 1972, p. 58; Sterling, *The Terror Network*, p. 259; Cooley, *Libyan Sandstorm*, p. 136.
77. Matthews, *Castro*, p. 50.
78. Suarez, *Cuba*, pp. 43, 64, 69–70.
79. Bonsal, *Cuba, Castro, and the United States*, pp. 106–7.
80. Phillips, *The Cuban Dilemma*, p. 112; Bonsal, *Cuba, Castro, and the United States*, p. 106.
81. Bakhash, *Reign of the Ayatollahs*, pp. 69–70.
82. Bakhash, *Reign of the Ayatollahs*, p. 217; John Kifner, 'Iran: Obsessesed with Martyrdom', *New York Times Magazine*, 16 December 1984, p. 52.
83. Michael M. J. Fischer, *Iran: From Religious Dispute to Revolution* (Cambridge, Massachusetts: Harvard University Press, 1980), pp. 233–6.
84. Ibraham Yazdi was the speaker. Fischer, *Iran*, pp. 238. The information in the paragraph above from Fischer, p. 233.
85. David, 'Realignment', pp. 127–8; Korn, *Ethiopia*, pp. 17–18.

86.   Ottaways, *Ethiopia*, pp. 78, 167–18.
87.   David, 'Realignment', pp. 92, 96, 102–3, 121–2; Korn, *Ethiopia*, pp. 17–18.
88.   Korn, *Ethiopia*, p. 26; David and Marina Ottaway, *AfroCommunism* (New York: Holmes & Meier, 1986), p. 153.
89.   Korn, *Ethiopia*, p. 18.
90.   David, 'Realignment', p. 79; 'US Is Shifting to Neutral Role on Africa's Horn', *New York Times*, 3 October 1977; 'Carter Signs Aid Bill', *New York Times*, 2 November 1977.
91.   Cooley, *Libyan Sandstorm*, p. 247.
92.   Fischer, *Iran*, p. 233.
93.   Herbert Dinerstein, *The Making of a Missile Crisis* (Baltimore: Johns Hopkins University Press, 1976), pp. 1, 16–18, 19–20, 22; Blasier, *The Hovering Giant*, p. 57.
94.   Lopez-Fresquet, *My Fourteen Months with Castro*, p. 177, also 165, 167; Bonsal, *Cuba, Castro, and the United States*, pp. 66–7 agrees.
95.   Dominguez, *Cuba*, p. 145.
96.   Lopez-Fresquet, *My Fourteen Months with Castro*, p. 106.
97.   Jack Anderson, 'When Cuba Overplayed Its Hand', *Washington Post*, 23 November 1980, p. c7.
98.   S. M. Burke, *Mainsprings of Indian and Pakistani Foreign Policies* (Minneapolis: University of Minnesota Press, 1974), pp. 128–31; G. W. Choudhurry, *India, Pakistan, and the Great Powers* (New York: Praeger, 1972), p. 15; Norman Palmer, *South Asia and US Policy* (Boston: Houghton Mifflin, 1966), p. 16; Robert Trumball, 'Nehru Acts to Win Popularity in US', *New York Times*, 23 October 1950. For example, the Indian ambassador to China blamed the cold war on 'the opportunistic policies of the United States'; Vice President Radhakrishnan accused the Western powers of trying to 'crush Russia'; and Krishna Menon suggested that the US wished to create a vacuum in India which she herself would fill.
99.   Burke, *Mainsprings of Indian and Pakistani Foreign Policies*, pp. 99–101; William Barnds, *India, Pakistan, and the Great Powers* (New York: Praeger, 1972), p. 46.
100. 'US Flies Troops to Caribbean as Mobs Attack Nixon in Caracas', *New York Times*, 14 May 1958, p. 1.
101. Robert Alexander, *The Venezuelan Democratic Revolution* (New Brunswick NJ: Rutgers University Press, 1964), p. 18.
102. Tad Szulc, 'Behind Portugal's Revolution', *Foreign Policy*, 21 (Winter 1975–6), *passim*.
103. Cole Blasier, 'The United States and the Revolution', in James Malloy (ed.), *Beyond the Revolution: Bolivia since 1952* (Pittsburgh: University of Pittsburgh Press, 1971), pp. 65–76, 91–2.
104. Blasier, 'The United States and the Revolution', pp. 62–3, 70–1, 99–100.
105. John Campbell, *Tito's Separate Road* (New York: Harper & Row, 1967), pp. 11, 18–19, 28–9; Adam Ulam, *Expansion and Coexistence* (New York: Praeger, 1974), p. 469; Phillip Windsor, 'Yugoslavia 1951 and Czechoslovakia 1968', in Barry Blechman and Stephen Kaplan

(eds), *Force Without War* (Washington: Brookings Institution, 1978), pp. 443–4.
106. Campbell, *Tito's Separate Road*, p. 13.
107. Windsor, 'Yugoslavia 1951 and Czechoslovakia 1968', pp. 448–50; Campbell, *Tito's Separate Road*, p. 16.
108. Joan Nelson, *Aid, Influence, and Foreign Policy* (New York: Macmillan, 1968), p. 114; Schlesinger, *A Thousand Days*, pp. 567–8; Legvold, *Soviet Policy in West Africa* p. 120.
109. Fritz Schatten, *Communism in Africa* (New York: Praeger, 1966), p. 140; Legvold, *Soviet Policy in West Africa*, pp. 122, 125–6; Schlesinger, *A Thousand Days*, pp. 568–9.
110. Legvold, *Soviet Policy in West Africa*, pp. 125–7; Schlesinger, *A Thousand Days*, pp. 569–70.
111. Schlesinger, *A Thousand Days*, p. 570.
112. Harold Nelson, *et. al.*, *Mozambique: A Country Study* (Washington, DC: US Government Printing Office, 1985), p. 234; *Africa Confidential*, 14 April 1978, pp. 2–4; *Africa Report*, March–April 1978, p. 36; 'Marxist State Tilts Profitably to the West', *Business Week*, 10 December, 1979, p. 47.
113. Robert Henderson, 'Principles and Practice in Mozambique's Foreign Policy', *World Today*, 34 (July 1978), pp. 277, 280–1; 'US Extends Recognition', *New York Times*, 26 June 1975, p. 3; 'Reversal of Alliances', *The Economist*, 259 (22 May 1976), pp. 57–8; Ottaways, *AfroCommunism*, p. 179; Norman Macqueen, 'Mozambique's Widening Foreign Policy', *World Today*, 40 (January 1984), p. 23; Allen and Barbara Isaacman, *Mozambique: From Colonialism to Revolution 1900–82* (Boulder, Colorado: Westview: 1983), pp. 184–5; David Lamb, *The Africans* (New York: Random House, 1983), p. 181.
114. Keith Somerville, 'The USSR and Southern Africa', *Journal of Modern African Studies*, 22, 1 (1984), p. 86; Ottaways, *AfroCommunism*, pp. 178–9; Nelson, *Mozambique: A Country Study*, p. 274; Isaacmans, *Mozambique: From Colonialism to Revolution*, p. 183.
115. Isaacmans, *Mozambique: From Colonialism to Revolution*, p. 181; Ottaways, *AfroCommunism*, p. 171. Somerville ('The USSR and Southern Africa'), says that $25 million was disbursed by 1983, though more than that had been promised.
116. Isaacmans, *Mozambique: From Colonialism to Revolution*, p. 53. *Congressional Quarterly Almanac*, 1978, pp. 123–4, 130, 403, 420–1. The prohibition was waived in December 1980 by the Carter administration to reward Frelimo for their co-operation on the Rhodesian issue. (Nelson, *Mozambique: A Country Study*, pp. 234–5.)
117. Isaacmans, *Mozambique: From Colonialism to Revolution*, p. 50; 'Spreading Trouble', *The Economist*, 286 (26 March 1983), p. 45.
118. Macqueen, 'Mozambique's Widening Foreign Policy', p. 23.
119. Allen Isaacman, 'Mozambique and the Regional Conflict in Southern Africa', *Current History*, 86 (May 1987), p. 232; 'A War and Drought Extend the Famine in Mozambique', *New York Times*, 9 November 1986, p. IV3; David Lamb, 'Mozambique's Move away from Communism', *Reader's Digest*, 126 (April 1985), pp. 94, 98.

120. Macqueen, 'Mozambique's Widening Foreign Policy', p. 23; Lamb, 'Mozambique's Move', pp. 94, 99; Isaacman, 'Mozambique and the Regional Conflict', p. 233.

121. 'Mozambique's Marxists Turn toward the West', *US News and World Report*, 98 (25 February, 1985), pp. 37–8; Isaacman, 'Mozambique and the Regional Conflict', p. 232; Nelson, *Mozambique: A Country Study*, p. 276; Macqueen, 'Mozambique's Widening Foreign Policy', pp. 23–7.

122. Macqueen, 'Mozambique's Widening Foreign Policy', pp. 23, 28; Glenn Frankel, 'Long-Hostile Mozambique Supports US Policy', *Washington Post*, 5 February 1984.

123. Herbert Howe, 'US Policy in Southern Africa', *Current History*, 85 (May 1986), p. 206.

124. 'Mozambique's Marxists', p. 38; Lamb, 'Mozambique's Move', p. 98; Isaacman, 'Mozambique and the Regional Conflict', p. 233. The 1987 figures were $75 million in food aid and $10 million in economic aid. ('Commonwealth Offers to Aid Mozambique against Rebels', *New York Times*, 8 November 1987.)

125. Mozambique votes with the US only about 10 per cent of the time in the United Nations. (Nelson, *Mozambique: A Country Study*, p. 223; Lamb, 'Mozambique's Move', p. 99.) Mozambique's representative at the United Nations was absent at the most recent vote on the Soviet occupation of Afghanistan; Ethiopia and Angola voted against the resolution. 'How General Assembly Voted', *New York Times*, 11 November 1987.

126. Nelson, *Mozambique: A Country Study*, p. 235; also Lamb, 'Mozambique's Move', p. 98 on their disillusionment with the USSR.

Conclusion

This study began by rejecting the sixties vintage caricature of American foreign policy toward regime change. According to that view, the United States invariably backs repressive dictatorships to the hilt and mechanically opposes any group seeking radical change. As we have seen, American support of existing governments has often been combined with pressure on them to adopt moderate reform or liberalisation; the United States has frequently abandoned governments whose authority was decaying and attempted to replace them with moderate elements of the opposition or a coalition government; and conciliation with regimes that have unseated former friends of the US has been attempted on many occasions.

Unfortunately, these policies have not been extraordinarily successful. US officials have usually been able to convince the leaders of countries highly dependent on American assistance to appoint reformers or adopt a reform programme, but the reforms have faced determined opposition from conservative forces and it has been difficult, for a number of reasons, to break this resistance. Liberalisation has proved to be a hazardous undertaking that has exploded in the faces of the well-meaning leaders who have tried to encourage it from the outside. Political solutions, both of the moderate and inclusive type, have failed in every case but two or three examined here, a record that can be attributed more to the difficulty of the task than to the ineptness of US officials. Lastly, attempts at conciliation have succeeded, but this has usually occurred when moderates have won the power struggle or the Soviets have driven the new leadership to the West. Efforts to reach an accommodation with radical regimes have usually met with frustration.

What are the implications of these findings for future policy? Let us begin with the subject of chapter 4, conciliation with revolutionary regimes. The poor results of past attempts at conciliation with radical governments would seem at first glance to damage severely the case of the non-interventionists. But they would respond with two arguments.

The first, and by now familiar, objection is that efforts at conciliation fail largely because the United States's past hostility toward the radicals has left them too distrustful to be responsive later. Several instances were mentioned in chapters 2 and 3 where the United States provided indirect assistance to revolutionaries by convincing the government to lift restrictions on opposition activity (Cuba, Iran, Nicaragua), stopped supporting the government outright (Nicaragua, Cuba) or allowed friends of the revolution to operate out of American territory without much hindrance (Cuba). There are some signs that this was appreciated by members of the moderate opposition, but the extreme opponents who eventually took power in many of these instances have shown few signs of gratitude. ('When this war ends, a wider one will begin', and so on.)

The second, and weightier, argument has been presented best by Richard Feinberg.[1] Feinberg argues that radical governments will gravitate to the West if they are given no reason not to because they are interested primarily in the economic development of their countries, an objective to which the West can contribute much more than the Soviet Union. Feinberg would not be discouraged by the results of chapter 4 since his emphasis is on the long run. If we are patient, he thinks, they will eventually find that their interests are best served by a constructive relationship with the West and act accordingly.

Feinberg presents his case well but it is not totally convincing, at least to this observer. First, even if radical states do abandon the Soviets eventually, they can do a great deal of harm in the meantime. Egypt and China are certainly among the Soviet's most frustrating episodes, but before they deserted Moscow, the Chinese fought the US in Korea, provoked two dangerous crises over the Taiwan straits and created enough anxiety in the mind of Lyndon Johnson with the rhetoric about wars of national liberation to draw him into Vietnam. Egypt launched two wars in the middle-east with Soviet weapons, each of which inflamed the Arab world against the West, raised the danger of East–West confrontation and damaged the world economy.[2]

Second, Feinberg errs in assuming that economic development, as understood by American liberals, is necessarily the highest priority of radical third world governments. Kwame Nkrumah, for example, was admonished by his Hungarian economic advisor that Ghana could not hope to industrialise without assistance from the West. Despite this, Nkrumah declared his belief in 'scientific socialism', thereby frightening away European and American investors. Two years later, foreign investment was only one-tenth as large as Ghana's economic plan had envisioned.[3] In Vietnam, food production declined for five straight years after the fall of Saigon to a point well below that during the war. By 1979, the regime's 'target' for food consumption per capita was 1300 calories a day, 300 less than subsistence level. Reflecting on the damage the Hanoi politburo was wreaking on the Vietnamese economy, Douglas Pike concluded, in a brutal understatement, that 'the Vietnamese leadership does not now behave in an economically rational manner'. In Pike's view, the desperate economic condition of Vietnam by the late seventies was as important a factor in their decision to align with the USSR as the security concerns mentioned in chapter 4.[4]

Richard Lowenthal has noted that Marxist movements are typically divided into utopian and modernising factions.[5] The latter are those who, as Feinberg says, give first priority to economic development; the former place higher value on ideological goals, or mistakenly believe that modernisation is not incompatible with their attainment. In China the modernisers appear to have won, at least for now, but this took place only after 20 years of struggle and several disastrous egalitarian improvisations by Mao Tse-tung. China's change of course and Gorbachev's attempts to revive the Soviet economy may convince third world states to avoid such ideological excesses. For the sake of those people who fall under Communist rule in the future, one hopes so. But Maoist or Stalinist practices have been repeated with disquieting frequency by Marxist governments and this trend has continued through the recent past with no apparent signs of changing. Marxist utopians do not seem to learn from the errors of their predecessors elsewhere but keep repeating the same mistakes and crimes again and again, most recently in places like Cambodia, Vietnam, Ethiopia and Mozambique.

Finally, many third world countries can afford to strike a posture of non-alignment because there is a rough balance of power in the world between the West and the Soviet bloc that allows the third world to play off the two superpowers. If the United States were to retreat into isolation, that balance would no longer exist and it would become more difficult for weaker countries to resist Moscow's pressure.

All of this is not to say that the United States ought to ignore or attempt to destabilise every radical regime that comes to power. It may be that it is usually best to exhaust all friendly means, even if the chances of success are slight. It may also be that if we were to examine the hardline policies as thoroughly as the conciliatory ones, their track record would not look much better. But that question is best left for another time. The one thing we can say with some confidence is that if the future resembles the past, conciliation with radical governments will usually fail. Hence, it would be foolishly optimistic to assume that the United States can stand aside and let friendly governments fall, as the non-interventionists suggest, and then patch things up with whomever comes to power. Regardless of how much restraint the United States observes, even at earlier stages in the process, some regimes will simply not respond to gestures of conciliation. In effect, there is no backstop. If policy fails earlier, the country will probably be 'lost' to the West at least for several years.

If this is so, it then becomes more important to achieve an acceptable outcome at the earlier stages. Notwithstanding the hopeful signs in 1986, political solutions have failed much more often than they have succeeded in the past and even those recent successes now appear somewhat problematical. Realistic proponents of the political solution, such as Charles Krauthammer, have suggested that it ought to be attempted only when the moderate opposition is relatively strong.[6] But as we have seen, the moderate solution can fail even when this condition obtains if the dictator remains intransigent and loses his strength slowly, producing a radicalisation of the revolution. Protracted crisis eventually weakened the moderates in Cuba and Nicaragua and might have done so in the Philippines had it not been for the providential alliance of Enrile's opportunism and the nun's idealism. Considering these difficulties, ought the United States to continue to try?

In Laos and Yemen, American interests were furthered by the attempts to impose a political solution even though the solutions came apart. The short-lived Yemen settlement, which was not discussed in chapter 3, prevented Egypt from posing a threat to Saudi Arabia and the Laotian centrists ended up on much better terms with the United States after the Pathet Lao double-crossed them. The political situation in both Haiti and the Philippines remains unsettled at the time of this writing and it is quite conceivable that neither country will look very much like a 'success' in a few years. Still, it is hard to imagine what other policy would have served the interests of the United States and the peoples of those islands more effectively than the political solutions applied by the United States. Marcos and Duvalier were not the only problems those societies faced by 1986, but their removal was almost certainly a precondition for addressing the others. A moderate solution may not be sufficient in and of itself to pull a nation out of danger, but it can still be useful and necessary where the ruler himself has become the focus of resentment.

In three other instances, however, American efforts not only failed to produce a political solution but also weakened the existing government, which was eventually overthrown by forces hostile to the United States. In July 1946, General Marshall refused to fill a large order placed by the Chinese Nationalists for ammunition and spare parts in an attempt to press them into negotiations. The Nationalists received no further shipments from the United States until late 1948. The embargo did not produce a political solution, however, though it did force Chiang to alter what appeared at the time to be a winning strategy and may have weakened the Nationalists decisively. Likewise, the State Department embargoed arms to Batista in March 1958 in an attempt to convince the dictator to move toward a political solution. Batista refused, but the embargo itself was a serious blow to the morale of the Cuban army and a clear message to everyone in Cuba that the United States no longer supported the government. The pattern was also repeated in Nicaragua. After the negotiations failed in late 1978, the Carter administration broke off all economic and military aid to Somoza, carrying out the threat made earlier.

In all three cases, the sanctions weakened the government without convincing it to adopt the solution US officials were proposing. Each of the three governments then fell and was replaced by a regime hostile to the United States. Did the pursuit of a political solution, as Jeane Kirkpatrick has alleged, lead to the overthrow of friendly governments in China, Cuba and Nicaragua?

This is a difficult issue to settle. Let us begin with Richard Thornton's description of the course of the Chinese civil war in the summer of 1946:

> From early July, Nationalist armies moved onto the offensive, clearing the north China plain area. In the course of the next two and a half months, success followed success as Chiang's troops defeated the Communists in encounter after encounter. By mid-September, Chiang had gained control of the major rail links in the north China area and had bottled Communist forces up in the mountainous areas of central Shantung and Shansi. Two further advances were under way in west Shantung and in north Kiangsu when they were suddenly halted. What had happened?[7]

Marshall had applied the embargo. When Washington refused to meet his request for ammunition and spare parts, Chiang called a halt to most offensive manoeuvres in order to conserve supplies. Chiang concluded that it was no longer possible to defeat the enemy and that the best he could hope for was to hold what he had taken and eventually to build up his stocks out of domestic production. Hence, in the winter of 1946, Nationalist troops constructed pill boxes and barbed-wire barriers around the towns they held and assumed a purely defensive posture. Later, in the spring of 1948, shortages of ammunition were the critical factor in the KMT's defeat at Weihsien, which cut off the Nationalists in Manchuria from resupply in north China. Without the embargo, could Chiang have continued the offensive and finished off his opponents in 1947 or survived their counterthrust in 1948?[8]

Mao fought the civil war with mobile tactics, avoiding positional battles and abandoning territory (even his home base of Yenan) to conserve his forces. He remained confident in the summer of 1946, despite the reverses suffered by his forces, because of the Nationalists' lack of popular support, the low morale of their troops and the severe difficulties facing the Chinese economy.[9] Chiang, on the other hand, was intent on seizing territory. As a result, his troops were eventually strung out along the railroads to protect lines of supply from central China. Confined to garrison duty, the Nationalist soldiers lost their offensive spirit. It may well be that over-extension would have compelled Chiang to switch to a defensive strategy even without the embargo. Thornton also fails to mention the American intelligence reports that found that corruption, defections and tactical blunders, not the lack of supplies, were the source of the Nationalists' difficulties later. In some cases, entire divisions went over to the Communists, who were also able to convert large numbers of prisoners of war after only one day in their re-education camps. In the China White Paper, General David Barr states emphatically that 'no battle has been lost since my arrival due to lack of ammunition or equipment.'[10]

The Draft White Paper on Cuba written by State Department officials in the early sixties is similar in intent to the earlier tome concerning China. As before, American officials defended themselves against the charge that they put the Communists in power by pointing out the weaknesses in the dictator's army, in this case a prototypical 'political army' of the sort described by Douglas Blaufarb:

The efforts of the Army to suppress the rebels had usually been relatively halfhearted and ineffectual from the start. After the expanded recruitment of March, 1958, numbers of green troops . . . appeared in Oriente Province. They were lacking in training and will to fight and were not inspired by their commanding officers, who failed to lead them in combat and were reportedly more interested in the opportunities for graft which the situation presented. Numerous reports were received of rebel supplies being permitted to pass through army lines for a fee, while a steady trickle of army weapons moved to the rebels in return for cash. Earlier purges of many of the better trained (usually in the US) officers, perhaps 500 in total, were undoubtedly reflected in the poor state of command which existed in the Cuban Army.[11]

In response to the charge that the US arms embargo led to Batista's overthrow, the White Paper points out, quite correctly, that Batista received arms from many other sources. On 7 April 1958, a few weeks after the embargo had been reinstated, the US Army Attache in Havana described the Cuban army forces as 'fully capable (in numbers and equipment) [of] eliminating Castro except [that they lack the] . . . tactical brains or will to close decisively with [the] rebels.'[12] Against this, we can set the judgement of many observers of diverse ideological perspectives that the embargo, though perhaps not decisive in a direct material sense, was nonetheless 'the most critical decision of the war.'[13] According to the American Ambassador, 'the action on the part of the United States in suspending the shipment of arms had a devastating psychological effect on the government of Cuba—and the reverse, it gave a great psychological uplift to the revolutionaries. The action was interpreted by the people of Cuba as a withdrawal of support for Batista, as in fact it was.'[14]

The Nicaraguan National Guard was also a political army, and a small one at that, even for a country of only a few million.[15] The Carter administration reduced the average annual economic assistance to 75 per cent in real terms in 1977–8, and military aid to 43 per cent. This reduction in assistance produced both tangible and intangible effects. Tangibly, it diminished the resources available to the National Guard, forcing Somoza to turn to 'increasingly desperate international borrowing and internal fiscal measures' to pay for weapons and men. But as in Cuba, the intangible effects may have been even more important. The change in American policy shook the resolve of many of the regime's former supporters, who began to drift toward accommodation with the opposition as instability continued, and emboldened the Sandinistas, who began to lose their fear of having to face US Marines if they defeated the Guard.[16] Somoza himself stated that most of his countrymen believed that 'it is in Washington where the decision is being made about the survival or disappearance of Somocismo or of Somoza himself'. As John Booth, author of a study of the Nicaraguan revolution sympathetic to the Sandinistas, concludes, 'although the United States did not defeat Somoza, US policy gradually eroded the regime's coercive strength and its support'.[17]

Thus, it is difficult to say whether these regimes could have survived if American efforts to promote political solutions had not weakened them. But even if Chiang, Batista and Somoza could have survived with continued American support, ought it to have been provided? The publics in Cuba and Nicaragua, and probably China as well, were eager to be rid of their dictators. An American effort to prop them up against the will of many of their subjects, even if successful, would have been costly, controversial and morally problematical.

If the political solution cannot be made to work in such situations, the United States will be left with a choice between intervention in support of a discredited dictator or non-intervention that leaves the way open for the anti-American left. Is the US then caught in a dilemma with no satisfactory solution? Perhaps not. The scruples of American officials regarding intervention in other countries have been a fatal handicap in the efforts to replace falling dictators with the moderate opposition. Mauricio Solaun, the Ambassador in Nicaragua during the revolution, has blamed the failure on the Carter administration's 'unwillingness to go all the way' against Somoza. As he explains, 'because we were not willing to use overt or covert force, we were not able to change the government of Nicaragua.'[18] The same could probably be said of Batista and Cuba. This difficulty would not have deterred Henry Kissinger, who remarked later that 'if we were prepared to move against Somoza, I think we should have also been prepared simultaneously to put in his place a moderate alternative'.[19] In an administration committed to non-intervention, this may have been ruled out from the start, but it may have been the only way of avoiding the intractable situation Carter was faced with by the spring of 1979.

The alternative is to approach these situations with the same ruthlessness the CIA and the Kennedy administration demonstrated in the Dominican Republic. These officials used some of the same means against Trujillo which had been used before against crumbling dictators, but when they did not produce immediate results they associated themselves with a plot to assassinate Rafael Trujillo.[20] Intervention of this sort is controversial, to say the least. But consider the other options available. Is it better to pursue a political solution with means too gentle to remove the dictator before the revolution turns radical and anti-Western? Is it better to offer full backing to an unpopular dictator to keep the radicals out of power? Is it better to assume that a Castro or a Khomeini can be won over with a few smiles from the US Ambassador or millions of dollars of aid? The morality of an action can be judged only in light of the alternatives, and all these alternatives are bad.

The hazards of liberalisation were made all too apparent in chapter 2. It is obviously difficult to interpret the record there as justification for an aggressive human rights policy of the sort practised by the Carter administration. But the United States need not and probably ought not to abandon all efforts at encouraging friendly dictators to permit their subjects greater freedom. The US need not because the two disastrous cases of chapter 2, Iran and Hungary, were brought about in large part, though certainly not entirely, by tactical mistakes, some of which were imposed on the leaders from the outside. Liberalisation was transformed into revolution in Iran and Hungary only after the governments or their foreign allies caused the people to lose both their hope and their fear. If the United States were to pursue liberalisation with a greater understanding of the dangers a bad government faces as it tries to change its ways, the chances of disaster would be reduced. In particular, one must bear in mind that concessions that appear to be made from weakness are more likely to be destabilising and that successful liberalisation may proceed in fits and starts, as did Brazil's.

The United States ought not to abandon some sort of human rights policy altogether because there are often greater risks in continually turning a blind eye toward abuses of power by US allies than in trying to rectify them. Specifically, the risk of a policy of indifference or even sincere but 'quiet and friendly' persuasion is that the people of that country will interpret public silence as approval and come to associate the US too closely with the government and its abuses. This is especially true in countries where the opposition is predominantly moderate and not anti-American. If US silence is interpreted as complicity, it may unintentionally radicalise the opposition. Human rights criticism of the regime is one way of protecting the United States against this.

It makes sense to run the risks of outspoken criticism of the government, then, in countries where the opposition is strong and moderate and American interests would not be damaged by a change of regime (as in the Philippines recently, or the Colonels' Greece). Where the opposition is strong and anti-American, more caution is called for. Where the opposition is weak, the main consideration ought to be about means, that is, which strategy will be most likely to bring beneficial changes? In most cases, quiet persuasion needs to be supplemented with some public criticism if it is to have any credibility.

If only by process of elimination, reformist intervention now seems the most promising avenue open to American policy-makers in dealing with third world instability. It appeared in chapter 1 that US efforts to support or impose reform played a key role in the survival of pro-Western governments in Greece, the Philippines, Iran, Venezuela and probably now El Salvador. The only unqualified success was in Venezuela, however, where the US role was less significant. Elsewhere, part of the programme was either ignored at the outset or subverted later. In some cases, this was or may yet prove to be fatal to the regime.

The first requirement of this strategy, that of placing reformers in power or persuading the existing leadership to accept reform, has not always been easily attained, but is probably not the most difficult aspect of the problem. Typically, the hardest part has been overcoming the resistance of opponents of reform in the armed forces or upper classes, especially when they have been able to exploit democratic institutions to block changes that would endanger their privileges, or when the existence of a serious threat from the far left has led them to assume that they are indispensable to the United States. How ought American officials to deal with this dilemma?

Democratic government is not only an ideal to which the public of the United States is deeply attached, it is also a valuable diplomatic asset not to be discarded casually. One has only to consider, for example, the contribution of the honest election in the Philippines in 1951 to the defeat of the Huks to understand this. Moreover, recent US efforts to combine democracy and reform in El Salvador have not been altogether unsuccessful. The Christian Democratic leader, Jose Napoleon Duarte, won the Presidency in 1984, and in March of the next year his party confounded the sceptics and won control of the Salvadoran legislature. (The leading party of the right, D'Aubuisson's ARENA, claimed that the second election was fraudulent and demanded its nullification, but the army rejected their plea for support and the result proved irreversible.) At the time of this writing, there are said to be plans to resubmit phase II of the original programme to the legislature, though it is not clear that Duarte has enough influence to enact it.[21]

Despite this, western publics and officials must realise that democracy is likely to survive in the long run only when the underlying socio-economic conditions are conducive to its operation.[22] Where the distance between rich and poor is immense, some redistribution usually has to take place before the democratic alternation between government and loyal opposition becomes possible, and this may never come about if democratic institutions are dominated by the privileged classes. Hence, in cases where there is a trade-off between reform and democracy, it will usually be sensible to give first priority to reform in the short run to create the conditions under which democracy can flourish in the long run.

The right's over-confidence in American backing is also likely to remain a serious obstacle in the future. Reactionaries in an embattled country will usually understand, if they are not fools, that the American President does not want to cut off his nose to spite his face, and so the more important a country is to the US, the more difficult it will be to make believable threats to discipline them. But in the past, American officials have tended to look at the problem of 'credibility' from one side only. They have worried about impressing the immediate enemy, the Chinese or the Russians, or American allies inside and outside the country with their determination to stand by the friends of the United States. In some respects, they have succeeded too well. Over-confidence in American support has not only impeded reformist intervention in places like El Salvador and Vietnam, it has also made it much more difficult to achieve political solutions, as noted in chapter 3. In the future, public declarations of support ought to be extended more cautiously, preferably only after the leaders allied to the US have made equally firm commitments to reform measures that will win them greater legitimacy. US officials must also be prepared to make good on threats to withhold support at least occasionally if they expect to be taken seriously. The danger of this is obvious, especially for Democratic administrations: it may lead to the familiar charges of having 'lost' the country if the withdrawal of US assistance is followed by the regime's collapse. But increases in American aid without serious demands for reform only put more resources in the hands of the government and make it even less necessary for them to attend to the demands and needs of their publics;[23] and those who see unreformed militaries as a 'safety net' for the United States in the third world would do well to ponder the ineffectiveness of the armies of Chiang and Batista against their far less numerous opponents. Political armies of that sort are no safety net, but a snare.

This is undeniably a difficult problem, but the record of the past should not lead us to accept a counsel of despair.[24] The United States did successfully promote reform of the Greek and Philippine armies, and might have done a good deal more in China if Roosevelt had used a different sort of approach. Vietnam is, in this respect as in many others, a useful lesson in how not to go about it. When American officials announced in the early stages that Vietnam was a crucial test of their credibility to contain Communism, they might have impressed the North Vietnamese (though not enough, it seems), but they also led the Ngos to conclude that American suggestions did not have to be taken seriously because the United States had too much at stake to abandon them. It should be noted, however, that some observers believe that even in these unfavourable circumstances there was still some chance that reform of the armed forces could have been achieved later if the CORDS system had been applied to ARVN. More recently, the Reagan administration showed the same tendency early on to inflate the importance of the struggle in El Salvador, but was still able to make significant progress after late 1983 in reducing abuses by the army and curbing the death squads. When US administrations have made a determined effort, it has often been possible to bring significant improvement in the performance of the armed forces, and in some cases, this has made all the difference.

Neither Jeane Kirkpatrick on the right nor the non-intervention advocates on the left offers a very appealing solution to the problem of instability in friendly countries. Dr Kirkpatrick would intervene in support of governments that can be defended only on the grounds that they are a lesser evil; Richard Barnet, Melvin Gurtov, Richard Feinberg and many others urge on us a restraint and that will not impress the Castros and Khomeinis of this world and the Soviets may not reciprocate. It would be comforting and convenient if the middle-range policies discussed in the pages above appeared unambiguously successful in the past and practicable in the future. Unfortunately, that is not what the record shows. US efforts to impose political solutions have weakened friendly dictators without convincing them to leave; human rights policies have helped undermine autocratic allies, who were replaced in Nicaragua, Cuba and Iran by regimes that are probably more autocratic and are certainly less well disposed to the United States; and reformist intervention has never enjoyed more than intermittent or partial success.

The effectiveness of the middle-range policies could probably be improved, but only by taking steps that would be controversial. If, for example, the manipulation of economic and military aid were not sufficient to persuade a ruler to abdicate on schedule, the US could intervene directly, as the Kennedy administration did in the Dominican Republic in 1961 and in Vietnam in 1963. Students of third world politics tell us that land reform stands the best chance of implementation in an undemocratic system. Venezuela was an exception, and El Salvador may turn out to be, but if that observation is correct as a general rule, the US may have to acquiesce in closing down parliaments in order to defeat the twin enemies of democracy, the reactionary right and the radical left. The success of reformist intervention may also hinge on the willingness of the United States to cut off support to regimes that prove to be incorrigible, thus running the risk of a victory for the far left. Finally, human rights policies do not appear to increase the stability of authoritarian governments, at least in the short run. If Americans feel that they must pursue them anyway, whether as a matter of moral obligation or to protect the US in public opinion inside the country or elsewhere, it would be best if they bear in mind the difficulties that a liberalising autocrat faces.

Viewed in this light, the middle options may appear to be less of a panacea than yet another in a series of Hobson's choices in dealing with political turmoil in the third world. In their amended form, these policies are not likely to generate much more enthusiasm than the nostrums of Dr Kirkpatrick and the non-interventionists. But unfortunately, as an earlier student of these matters noted, all good things do not go together.[25] In this context, that means that the best way to promote democracy may be to postpone it, the best way to save an embattled regime may be to threaten to lose it, and the best way to protect a weak society from external intervention may be to interfere. Democratic publics, left and right, may have little appreciation and still less patience with these paradoxes. But if they and their leaders wish to sustain the West's position in the third world without adopting policies largely irreconcilable with democratic ideals, they will find that the flawed, paradoxical and often frustrating strategy of reformist intervention, supplemented by prudent efforts to promote human rights and political solutions, remains the least unsatisfactory alternative.

Notes

1. Richard Feinberg, *The Intemperate Zone* (New York: Norton, 1983).
2. This observation was made by Steven David, 'Realignment in the Horn', *International Security*, vol. no. 2 (Fall 1979).
3. Scott Thompson, *Ghana's Foreign Policy* (Princeton: Princeton University Press), pp. 272, 304, 423, 433.
4. Douglas Pike, 'Communist vs. Communist in Southeast Asia', *International Security*, vol. 4, no.1 (Summer 1979), pp. 27–8, 33, 36.
5. Richard Lowenthal, 'Beyond Totalitarianism' in Irving Howe, (ed.), *1984 Revisited* (New York: Harper & Row, 1983), pp. 218ff.
6. Charles Krauthammer, 'Bringing a Third Force to Bear', *Time*, 127 (10 March 1986), p. 84.
7. Richard Thornton, *China: The Struggle for Power* (Bloomington: Indiana University Press, 1973), pp. 200–1..
8. Edmund Clubb, *20th Century China* (New York: Columbia University Press, 1978), p. 279; Thornton, *China*, pp. 201–4, 210–11.
9. Tang Tsou, *America's Failure in China* (Chicago: University of Chicago Press), pp. 427–8.
10. Warren Cohen, *America's Response to China* (New York: Wiley, 1980), p. 196; Lucien Bianco, *The Origins of the Chinese Revolution* (Stanford: Stanford University Press), pp. 182–3; Clubb, *20th Century China*, pp. 285, 295.
11. *Draft White Paper on Cuba*, p. 55.
12. *Draft White Paper on Cuba*, pp. 54–5, 57, 113.
13. Hugh Thomas, *Cuba: Or the Pursuit of Freedom* (London: Eyre & Spottiswoode, 1971), p. 985.
14. This is the judgement of the US Ambassador, Earl E. T. Smith, *The Fourth Floor* (New York: Random House, 1962), pp. 90–1. His view is shared by Philip Bonsal, *Cuba, Castro, and the United States* (Pittsburgh: University of Pittsburgh Press, 1971), pp. 20–1; Herbert Dinerstein, *The Making of a Missile Crisis* (Baltimore: Johns Hopkins

University Press, 1976), p. 30; and Ramon Bonachea and Marta San Martin, *The Cuban Insurrection* (New Brunswick, New Jersey: Transaction Books, 1974), pp. 200–1.

15. 7000 in the first round and 14,000 before the second round, as compared to 48,000 in the Sandinista's army by 1983. Richard Fagen testimony, US Congress, Senate Foreign Relations Committee, *Latin America*, 4 October 1978, p. 32; figure on Sandinistas from *The Military Balance 1983–4*.

16. John Booth, *The End and the Beginning* (Boulder, Colorado: Westview Press, 1982), pp. 128–9.

17. Booth, *End and Beginning*, pp. 128–30.

18. Quoted in Bernard Diederich, *Somoza* (New York: E. P. Dutton, 1981), p. 243.

19. Quoted in William Bundy, 'Who Lost Patagonia', *Foreign Affairs*, 58 (Fall 1979), p. 7.

20. I am trying to choose my words carefully here. Kennedy and the CIA did not kill Trujillo, and it is not possible to say for certain whether Kennedy actually wished that he be killed. 'Association' seems the most accurate way of phrasing it.

21. Roy Prosterman and Jeffrey Riedinger, *Land Reform and Democratic Development* (Baltimore: Johns Hopkins University Press, 1987), p. 173; 'After Parades and Promises, Duarte Falters', *New York Times*, 16 February 1987, p. 1.

22. Aristotle's *Politics*, Book IV, chapters XI–XII remains the classic exposition of this theme.

23. This point is made by Allen Goodman, *Politics in War* (Cambridge, Massachusetts: Harvard University Press, 1973), pp. 104–6.

24. As offered, for example, by Raymond Bonner, *Weakness and Deceit* (New York: Times Books, 1984), pp. 231, 366–7.

25. Robert Packenham, *Liberal America and the Third World* (Princeton: Princeton University Press, 1974).

Index